Public Expenditure in India

Public Expenditure in India

Policies and Development Outcomes

GAYITHRI KARNAM

OXFORD
UNIVERSITY PRESS

OXFORD
UNIVERSITY PRESS

Great Clarendon Street, Oxford, OX2 6DP,
United Kingdom

Oxford University Press is a department of the University of Oxford.
It furthers the University's objective of excellence in research, scholarship,
and education by publishing worldwide. Oxford is a registered trade mark of
Oxford University Press in the UK and in certain other countries

First Edition published in 2022

Impression: 1

Published in the United States of America by Oxford University Press
198 Madison Avenue, New York, NY 10016, United States of America

British Library Cataloguing in Publication Data

Data available

Library of Congress Control Number: 2022932461

ISBN 978–0–19–285756–9

DOI: 10.1093/oso/9780192857569.001.0001

Printed in India by Rakmo Press Pvt. Ltd.

Dedicated to
My Guru
Bhagavan Sri Ramana Maharshi

and my loving parents
Late Sri. K.A.Nagaraja Rao and Smt Ramalakshmamma

Contents

List of Figures

List of Tables

Acknowledgements

This book is an outcome of insights obtained from a number of research assignments undertaken for high-level policy bodies, to name a few the first State Finance Commission, Expenditure reforms commission, fourth state finance commission (Government of Karnataka), Planning commission, Sixth Central pay commission, fourteenth and fifteenth finance commissions (Government of India) spanning over thirty long years. The Shastri Indo Canadian institute's fellowship support twice to study the spending control measures and performance assessment frameworks in Canada and the international training at the Duke centre for international development (USA) on public budgeting and Kennedy school of government at the Harvard University (USA) on public financial management in a changing world have broadened the horizon.

My long academic journey has been enabled by the Almighty's blessings and a number of my personal and professional well-wishers. My pranams to Sri Raman Maharishi and Sri Sathya Sai Baba for guiding this journey. My entry into the Institute for Social and Economic Change (ISEC), Bangalore, was the turning point in my academic journey opening the doors to professional research. This book is an outcome of the Sabbatical leave that ISEC sanctioned to me; I am deeply indebted to ISEC, in particular Dr Chandrakanth, former Director for facilitating my sabbatical leave and many faculty members who groomed me in Public Finance research. Late Prof Hemlata Rao taught me the basics of public finance research and am greatly indebted to her for the motherly care and nurturing. Late Prof L.S. Venkata Ramanan was always empathetic to young PhD scholars and fortunate to have public finance doyens like Dr Thimmaiah and Dr M Govinda Rao closely monitoring our research. I am deeply indebted to Late Sri. T.R Satish Chandran, former Chief Secretary, Government of Karnataka and former ISEC Director, who entrusted the responsibility of undertaking Karnataka state expenditure evaluation for the first ever State finance commission appointed by Government of Karnataka and his guidance. My heartfelt thanks to

Prof R.S Deshpande formerly Director of ISEC, who has a passion for public finance research, took great interest in my research work, for reading through earlier drafts of this book and also writing a foreword for this book. I am thankful to Dr Ravindra, IAS, (Retd) former Chairman, ISEC Board of Governors, Dr Abdul Aziz and Dr Devendra Babu for their valuable suggestions on the draft manuscript. My former colleagues, Dr Usha Devi and Dr Gayatri Devi have stood by me all along and am highly thankful to them for their moral support and encouragement. A special thanks to Prof Dadibhavi, formerly with the Karnataka University, the first one who suggested to me to write a book on public expenditure for the benefit of students.

My stint as an Advisor with the Bearing Point Global Operations Inc for the India State Fiscal Management Program (USAID funded REFORM Project) under the able leadership of Sri. B.K. Bhattacharya, IAS (Retd) former Chief Secretary, Government of Karnataka helped me gain a lot of insights into the applied aspects of public finance. The enlightening discussions with senior government officers and the participation in public financial capacity building guided by the international experts from Duke Center for International Development enriched my understanding of applied public finances. Interactions with the USAID team led by Ms Madhumita Gupta, expats from the REFORM project—Mr Ron Hackett, Mr Robert Voetsch, Mr Douglas Brown, faculty of Duke University—Dr G.P Shukla, Dr Graham Glenday have led to an understanding of the international best practices in the field of Public Finance. I am thankful to senior civil servants like Sri Srinivasa Murthy, Sri. ISN Prasad, Sri. Ajay Seth- interactive sessions with them from time to time have been a great learning experience. Sri B.K. Bhattacharya has meticulously read through the draft chapters and gave constructive suggestions which have immensely helped me in my revisions. My sincere thanks to Sri B.K. Bhattacharya for the sustained support and encouragement and also writing a foreword to this book.

On the personal front, I am forever grateful to my parents, Late Sri. K.A Nagaraja Rao and Smt Ramalakshmamma for their vision to initiate seven of their offspring to higher education daunting challenges like non-availability of local access to higher education institutions and uncertain income flows due to vagaries of monsoon. Their sustained support and encouragement are mainly the source of my accomplishments;

Appa and Amma, I owe all this to you. While my parents initiated me to higher education, I would have failed to sustain career progress if my husband, C. Vijay Kumar did not extend his helping hand in continuing with my professional life. My academic tour which began when my children Visakh and Apoorva were just 6 and 3 years old and many more after that was possible due to his encouragement and the additional responsibilities he assumed in their care. The care given by my parents-in-law Late C.V. Subrahmanyam and Smt Vatsala to my children helped me focus on my academic career, a rare support that a daughter-in-law can get, I am forever indebted to them. Vijay has borne the brunt of reading the first drafts of all my research works starting with my PhD dissertation and giving insightful comments given his good understanding of government financial operations gained in office of the Comptroller and Auditor General's office where he worked. The excellent cooperation and the love I received from my children Dr Visakh and Dr Apoorva have always kept my spirits high and going. I will be failing in my duty if I do not thank my brother-in-law Late Sri Seshadri and my sister Aruna; my brother K. Raghavendra Rao and sister-in-law Mani for being with me through my thick and thin and always rejoicing my academic accomplishments.

My heartfelt thanks to Mr Ramanjini, Dr Khalil for helping me with my data analysis and technical support. ISEC administration has always been very supportive of all academic activities and I place on record my sincere thanks to the entire staff.

Most importantly, I am thankful to Oxford University Press for publishing this book. I owe my sincere thanks in particular to Mr Dhiraj Pandey for enabling this process.

Foreword I

The three major pillars of the Fiscal Policy structure of a country are (i) Taxation or Revenue Collection, (ii) Public Expenditure, and (iii) Management of Public Debt. In a federal polity, fiscal decentralization or the fiscal relationship between different tiers of Government also assumes importance.

The study of the Taxation or Revenue Mobilization aspect of fiscal policy has attracted much interest from experts in the field of Public Finance. On the other hand, it would appear that Expenditure Management has received relatively limited attention.

Viewed from the point of view of macro-economic implications, the impact of Taxation on incentives for investment and on the growth of the economy is always in the forefront of any discussion relating to fiscal issues. Associations of industry and business regularly highlight the impact of taxation on factors that affect their functioning, such as input costs, demand, profitability, export prospects, and so on. Such assessments are taken serious note of by the media, the general public, political parties, and the Governments. Similarly, individual measures of taxation such as personal income tax, Corporate Tax, Dividend Distribution Tax, Wealth Tax or Estate Duty, and Indirect Taxes such as Sales Tax and VAT are the subject of detailed discussion by Tax Consultancy organizations, and Chambers of Commerce and Industry.

On the other hand, discussions relating to Government's Expenditure Policy and Programmes attract rather limited attention from either the Public Finance experts or the general public. No doubt, some discussions by experts do take place on issues such as the impact of the Government Expenditure Program on macro-economic stabilization; whether any ongoing recession is due to deficiencies in effective demand; the necessity of a government stimulus programme to boost total expenditure; the appropriate size of a stimulus programme and so on. Unfortunately, there is a dearth of detailed technical analysis as to the optimal way of selecting programmes from among different alternatives, how best to assess the efficacy of an Expenditure programme, how to determine the most efficient method for delivery of goods and services by the Government, and other such issues.

Discussion on Government expenditure often gets converted into a discussion on public debt, as in recent decades in most developed and developing countries resource mobilization by the Government has failed to keep pace with the growth of expenditure, resulting in increased Government borrowing to meet the gap. The discussion then turns towards sustainability of Public debt, the interest burden of debt servicing, appropriate measures to introduce ceiling on Government Debt, etc. Consequently, questions relating to efficiency of Government expenditure, minimizing of the cost of service delivery, and the possibility of cost recovery from beneficiaries take a back seat.

In view of the above, Dr Gayithri's book 'Public Expenditure in India: Policies and Development Outcomes' will be very welcome to all those who are interested in understanding important dimensions of this major area of Government's fiscal policy.

Dr Gayithri, Professor of Economics at ISEC, Bangalore earned her PhD over 30 years ago on the basis of her thesis 'Growth and Pattern of Public Expenditure: A case Study of Karnataka'. Since then, she has devoted over three decades on teaching and conducting research in the field of Public Expenditure Policy. She has acquired useful knowledge and experience at the International level by participating in training programmes, conferences and seminars at various Universities and Research Institutions in the US, Canada, China, South Korea, and Iran. She has been very closely involved in studies on Public Expenditure conducted by the Planning Commission, Finance Commissions. Expenditure Reforms Commissions, etc.

Dr Gayithri explains in the first chapter titled 'Introduction and Overview' that the book begins with explanations of the technical terms used in Government Budgets as for example Revenue Expenditure, Capital Expenditure, Development Expenditure, the now abolished distinction between Plan and non Plan Schemes, etc.

In the next three chapters, the author analyses the trends in public expenditure at the Central and State government levels, the impact of Government expenditure on important human development indicators, shifts in priority over time in items of expenditure, the political economy of Government expenditure decisions, and other connected matters.

This is followed by Chapter 7 which deals with financial accountability issues in India, including Constitutional provisions and actual practices in the exercise of Parliamentary control over Government expenditure. The two next chapters in the book deal with Public Expenditure Reform (Chapter 8) and Performance Assessment of Government Expenditure Programmes (Chapter 9).

The issues discussed in Chapter 8 include (i) The presentation of a Performance Budget by a few selected central Government Ministries as recommended by the Administrative Reforms Commission (ARC) and (ii) the recommendation of the Rangarajan Committee in 2011 for a shift in Budgeting approach from a one year to a multiyear time horizon, and from an input-based Budget to an outcome-based Budget.

In Chapter 8, there is reference to the Expenditure Management Commission under Dr Bimal Jalan. This Commission was required to give suggestions for reducing the three major Heads of Subsidies (Food, Fertilizer, and Petroleum). The Commission was also asked to give suggestions for reducing Government's administrative costs, improving delivery mechanisms, and introducing the use of technology and better Accounting methods. Interested readers will be benefitted by referring to the recommendations of the Commission on this behalf.

In Chapter 9, there is a discussion on different methods of performance assessment of Government expenditure programmes at State and National levels in India, and also at an international level.

Chapter 10 (The final chapter) discusses the impact of the Covid-19 pandemic on the growth of Indian GDP, and consequential effects on the revenue and expenditure of the State and Central Governments. The Author discusses several measures which have been undertaken to tide over the situation, and also suggests further steps to be taken as one goes forward. This includes, for instance, (a) mandatory provision for earmarking of a prescribed budgetary allocation in per capita terms for the Health Sector, (b) weeding out of duplicate programmes and outdated schemes in order to create more fiscal space, (c) Expenditure Rules to restrict the growth in Revenue expenditure, coupled with the stipulation that fiscal deficit should be attributed entirely to Capital expenditure,

(d) complete overhaul of Government's social safety net interventions to ensure netting out of ineligible beneficiaries.

The publication of this book on Public Expenditure Management is_very timely. In India, there is serious anxiety at the highest levels of Government regarding the slow pace of implementation of capital Projects. In the media, doubts are being expressed as to the efficacy of some of the Government's expenditure schemes, for instance, the scheme for providing productivity linked incentives to selected industries.

In the UK, questions are being raised as to the viability of certain programmes of the Government, such as (a) the scheme to provide subsidy to industries in order to protect employment, (b) extending assistance to the self employed, and (c) to simultaneously increase revenue by raising rates of corporate taxes.

In the US, Government's proposals for substantial expenditure on infrastructure, and on extension of assistance to persons affected by the pandemic, are facing difficulties in getting the approval of the Congress due to political reasons.

Both in India and in the US, public debates have started about the need for Government to take responsibility for pre-school care and training of children in the age group 3 to 5. This is on both financial and other grounds.

At such a time, availability of a comprehensive book on Public Expenditure Management will be of great help to the Policy planners, Formulators of Budgets, Economists and Policy Advisors. Students, researchers, and teachers of Public Finance will also find the book extremely useful. I congratulate the author for the meticulous and comprehensive work she has put in to produce this book. I am confident the book will receive good recognition and wide circulation both in the academic world and in the world of policymakers and financial administrators.

B.K. BHATTACHARYA, IAS (Retd.)
Former Chief Secretary, and
Chairman, Expenditure reforms Commission,
Government of Karnataka.

Foreword II

Efficiency in public expenditure is recognized as a prime determinant of the process of economic development. However, in the literature focused on the analyses of budgets in Indian Public Finance public expenditure almost eluded the attention of the mainstream researchers also in the broader domain of development economics, with only a few exceptions. It is a well-established fact that public expenditure matters intensively in maintaining overall fiscal discipline. During the late sixties, when I was a student, the only book authored by Premchand (1966) was the lone available source and after that a few sporadic attempts but none analysed the subject thoroughly. Down the timeline came the Government of India report on efficient management of public expenditure during 2011. Largely, researchers have sparsely focused on issues in public expenditure during the 80s and 90s and specifically after the liberalization took its roots in many countries. On this background it is a pleasure to see this book filling the gap in the literature dealing with Public Finance. Professor Gayithri has been working in this area staunchly for over the last three decades, writing consistently and lecturing across the country and abroad. Current research scenario in public expenditure is also quite hazy both due to the less number of researchers engaging in this important area and also the tricky issues involved that calls extended in-depth work. This book addresses this neglected area thoroughly and encompassing most of the important issues.

In this meticulous work, Professor Gayithri handled the entire canvass of public expenditure keeping in view the theory as well as empirical apparatus in the subject. She has investigated into the finer areas of the subject with nimble probing, extremely competently getting into all the smaller or bigger issues with equal ease and analytical acumen. The book is spread over ten chapters and each one of these chapter's stands independently as incremental knowledge stock to the existing knowhow in public expenditure. Interestingly, the book equally serves the students of public finance as well as mature researchers in policy domain. The authority with which Prof Gayithri takes the grip over the subject matters in each chapter is clearly visible. It is interesting and privileged to see that during the elaborations she ignites the curiosity of those who would like to undertake further research in this area under public finance.

This volume is very comprehensive in its coverage and the author traverses between the borders of a research study and a wide-ranging sourcebook for keen students. Beginning with clarifying all those tricky concepts, which have been used in public expenditure literature and largely not explained by the pundits in the field, she elaborates their proper use and the changes that have taken place over time. This is very useful to the students a public finance and beginners in research. In Indian fiscal system, the public expenditure was tied in the synthetic shackles of 'plan and non-plan grants' and their tricky cousin concepts, a dominant blockage for decades and none of the experts tried to come out of it. She lucidly explained the concepts and discussed their use. In order to cater to the curious researchers, she discusses the public expenditure trends and composition over time. Further she elaborates this important area in the context of Indian Constitution. The Annual Financial Statement distinguishes the expenditure on revenue account from the expenditure on other accounts, as is mandated in the Constitution of India. She elaborates on Articles 112, 266, and 267 and explains the importance of presenting these statements on the floor of the house. I have experienced that the casual students of public finance do not bother to touch the Indian Constitutional aspects in the context of public expenditure as also in Federal Finance. True that many experts have written on Federal Finance but sidelined the issue of effective public expenditure which is an important component to be considered by the finance commissions. Prof Gayithri analyses the trends and composition of public expenditure arriving at the development outcomes. One of the important topics she has elaborated on in greater detail falls in Chapter 5, wherein, she dealt with the current institutional mechanisms in the public expenditure system. Government of India through Planning Commission appointed High Level Expert Committee on Efficient Management of Public Expenditure (PEM) and the Committee submitted its report in 2011. This report provided some framework but Prof Arindam Dasgupta (in EPW) called it as disappointing. Professor Gayithri actually goes ahead of the theme that has been dealt with in the PEM report. She discussed all the steps taken by the government in modifying the expenditure system. Actually, Professor Gayithri has done substantial work parallel with the Public Expenditure Committee of Government of Karnataka. Her in-depth interactions with the policy bodies and advice to the policymakers from time to time have given her the in-depth knowledge of the functioning in the expenditure system.

The past experience analysed here has given significant policy indicators and therefore, there is a lot to learn from this analysis by the author and learn from the corrective measures suggested. Prof Gayithri undertook this analysis and followed that by the current institutional mechanism in India were two chapters. The chapters provide significant material for the policy leads in the fiscal scenario of the country. The indications are quite obvious like the relationship between development and non-development expenditure over time (Fig 3.11) as well as changing composition of public expenditure from 1990 onwards. In a separate chapter, she has discussed very elaborately the sub-national level experience of public expenditure and its behaviour in the federal fiscal system. It is difficult to find such elaborate exercise in the literature, even though quite a few authors have written in this area of research but did not touch the finer issues that have emerged in the Chapter 4 of this volume wherein, she has also given basic problems confronted by the state governments and way forward to resolve some of the critical issues. She further discusses the control and management of public expenditure by the parliament very elaborately and emphasizes an urgent need to review the adequacy of the existing rules and calls for strengthening of the institutions that enforce public expenditure control. She has analysed in an innovative framework the public spending across states bringing out the differentials and need for a diverse analytical approaches. Besides this one of the very sensitive and ticklish issues she has taken for analysis is about the public expenditure on elections across states. In this elaborate chapter very interesting issues are brought out very dexterously. Accountability in public expenditure is one such very ticklish issue and that requires a wide churning of literature and historical understanding. Utilizing these two important ingredients Professor Gayithri has put quite a few interesting issues in the 7th chapter. Here again she provides intricate policies which are followed in the next part of the book as well.

In an overall synoptic view I would be happy to highlight five very significant areas analyzed meticulously in this book. First, the author has very adeptly clarified our understanding of various concepts, current issues in economic brass tacks of public expenditure and fiscal scenario in the country, taking both empirical and positivist approaches. Second, all through the chapters of the book the policy hints could be seen out of the hidden windows, sometimes in clear terms or at times as strong hints. These need to be picked up further. Third, the book covers a huge span of time as also the regions of the country with lissome efforts. The chapter on sub-national analyses gives out clear indications to the states in tightening their fiscal discipline. Fourth, the book covers the most ticklish issue of accountability in public expenditure and brought some sensitive issues for discussion. Last, the authority of the author on the literature, facts and history in the subject peeps through the pages of this excellent volume. Tremendous efforts spanning over three decades stand behind this admirable work. I am sure this work will be useful to the inquisitive researchers, fervent policymakers and intense students of public finance.

Prof. R.S Deshpande,
Former Director,
Institute for Social and Economic Change,
Bengaluru
National Fellow,
Indian Council for Social Science Research.

1
Introduction and Overview

Government plays a major role in the growth of a country's economy. Its public financial operations involving mobilization of revenue and spending have considerable implications on the economic growth, distribution, and stabilization. A thorough study of its dynamic behaviour is essential to make informed mid-course policy corrections to public financial policies in order to remedy macroeconomic imbalance. A critical review of public expenditure is imperative in ensuring the optimal use of public resources for the maximization of welfare. There are myriad questions that crop up the process of understanding public spending. Such questions broadly include: What is the size of public expenditure? What are the items on which the government spends money, and how are the decisions framed on the size and composition? How the government spending has grown over time and in relation to the national economy as measured by the gross domestic product (GDP)? What are the determinants of public spending—do the political factors outweigh economic factors in expenditure decisions? Is government spending competing with private economic decisions or complementing them? How efficient and effective is the government spending? What are the results or the impact of public spending on the social and economic development of the country? These are just a few broad questions, there could be a lot more when one tries to understand the micro-level aspects of public spending. It is important to probe into these aspects as governments are important stakeholders and their interventions can have large-scale implications for the economies.

India has experienced a significant growth in public spending both at the central and sub-national levels of government caused by the extensive and increased use of fiscal instruments in the sectoral development strategies adopted by the government ever since India attained independence. There have also been significant changes in governmental priorities from

Public Expenditure in India. Gayithri Karnam, Oxford University Press. © Oxford University Press 2022.
DOI: 10.1093/oso/9780192857569.003.0001

time to time. The initial years of planning focused on physical resource development with a large-scale emphasis on agriculture and industry, the subsequent realization to promote human resource development, poverty alleviation, and the more recent emphasis on inclusive development have brought about considerable changes in the nature of public spending.

The country has also seen major fiscal policy changes with the introduction of structural adjustment programme and stabilization measures. The framing of legislation like 'Fiscal Responsibility and Budget Management'(FRBM) to effect rule-based fiscal corrections has led the governments both at the centre and state levels to ensure fiscal consolidation by imposing a ceiling on the fiscal and revenue deficits and the public debt in a time-bound manner. The fiscal map of the country is going through major changes with the scrapping of the 'plan' and 'non-plan' categorization of expenditure. These sharp changes in the quantum and quality of public spending have great implications for the development outcomes in the country. While there are issues of effective translation of outlays into outcomes, there are also issues of allocative efficiency, in terms of whether public spending in the country is reflecting the impending needs of the society, which are highly diverse given the country's differential levels of development.

There is no dearth of literature in analytical expositions on the macroeconomic implications and impacts of the growing public expenditure in the Indian context in the form of sporadic research contributions. However, studies providing a professional understanding of basic concepts and their likely implications, analysis of long-term trends and the changes therein due to major policy paradigm shifts in the country since India's independence, political economy dimensions of public spending, the effectiveness of expenditure in terms of generating outcomes/results, and an understanding of international best practices in reforming public expenditure have not been reached out to the students of public finance and the public who are interested in having a correct understanding in one source. Each of the aspects listed above can become an independent book by itself; it remains a Herculean task to have them all in one volume. Although there are no tall claims made that the present volume provides answers to all the research questions that relate to public spending, it certainly is a modest effort to put together lead issues in one volume and summarize the key debates, especially with a view to help the students of public finance and policymakers in having a correct understanding of the concepts and their implications.

1.1 Understanding Key Expenditure Concepts and Classification of Public Expenditure

A professional understanding of basic concepts of public expenditure and their likely implications for the economy is an important first step in the conduct of meaningful research that ensures proper perception of policy implications. Public expenditure is classified in numerous ways, e.g. accounting classification comprises categories such as 'revenue' and 'capital'; functional classification comprises breakouts by 'general', 'social and community', and 'economic' services; and economic classification comprises 'consumption', 'gross capital formation', 'current' and 'capital' transfers', and 'financial investments'. There are also other terms used popularly in the discussion of public expenditure, such as 'development' and 'non-development' expenditure. New deficit concepts have been used ever since India launched the structural adjustment programme, like 'fiscal', 'primary' deficits and extended ones like 'effective revenue deficit'. A meaningful interpretation of trends in these variables is possible only when one understands the likely impacts of each of the categories of expenditure on the economy.

The budget discussions hitherto (until plan and non-plan distinction existed) invariably ended up judging the usefulness of public expenditure based on the size of the increase in the plan and non-plan components. The former got considerable praise, completely bypassing the fact that the results of spending emanate from the total spending. Such discussions have had adverse impacts on the policymaking and the budget speeches made by governments from time to time, as they chose to specifically highlight the sectors that had sharp increase in plan spending trying to maximize the political mileage. Chapter2 presents a narrative description of the concepts as defined in the policy documents such as the budget documents and the additions that have been brought in from time to time since India's independence. It provides conceptual understanding of the core concepts, discusses the major categories of expenditure as under 'revenue' and 'capital' accounts, functional categories as under general, social and community and economic services, and also presents a historical account of the changes that have occurred in the classification since India's independence. This is largely in the form of narrative description and some charts are used to illustrate the classification.

1.2 Public Expenditure in India—Trends and Composition

A systematic study of the trends and patterns of public spending over time helps in understanding the role played by the respective governments and the changes therein. An empirical analysis of the broad trends in public expenditure incurred in India by the central government since India's independence by providing analytical insights for India's development is included in Chapter 3 of this book. Given the constitutional responsibilities assigned to the centre and the sub-national governments, two individual chapters, Chapters3 and 4, respectively, provide analytical insights into the trends and composition of the centre and sub-national governments. This analysis attains importance in view of the longstanding criticism that the central government has been making inroads into state subjects and vitiating their fiscal space and priorities. The analysis presented in these two chapters tracks the broad trends and composition of public spending by each of the important policy phases governing fiscal development in the country. The chapters also highlight the status of select development outcomes in the country. The basis for this discussion is the data sourced from authentic sources like the Indian Public Finance Statistics, Ministry of Finance, Government of India, publications of Comptroller and Auditor General (CAG), and available academic literature. Descriptive statistics are used, and the data are presented through tables and charts.

India adopted a five-year planning model to promote citizens' welfare and country's development immediately after India's independence with the first five-year plan rolled out during 1951–56, which continued until the twelfth five-year plan during 2012–17 subsequent to which the Planning Commission was replaced with NITI Aayog. The planning process in the country extensively has used fiscal instruments resorting to direct public expenditure programmes or by proving tax incentives involving 'tax expenditure'[1] and, at times, a combination of both to promote development in the country, having its ramifications on the state of public finances in the country. Planning is very essential in setting up a sustainable development path for the country, which ideally is based on the impending needs of the society. Planning is not an end by itself and fails to serve its purpose if resource allocation does not match the requirement and accurate financial estimates are not worked out, considering short, medium to long-run costs associated with delivery of a programme. Therefore, planning and budgeting processes need to synchronize well in the planned development pursuit, failing which growth tends to get haphazard. The book finds that the link between the plan priorities as set out in each of India's five-year plans commencing with the first five-year plan till the twelfth five-year plan and the annual budgets presented is weak. With the exception of a couple of budget speeches that too in the initial years of each plan, budgets rarely address the plan priorities.

1.3 Public Expenditure Control and Management

An important issue that has considerable importance in the context of public financial operations relates to the public expenditure control mechanism that is built into the system and is working to ensure an effective use of the public resources. This gains all the more significance due to the fact that the resources that are used by the government are collected from the economic agents, such as citizens, corporate entities, and financial institutions, using the tax, non-tax, and borrowings; hence, making them accountable to all the money raised by the government and the manner in which the funds are expended. To ensure a strong accountability presence, it is essential that effective control is put in place at all the stages of public expenditure management, i.e. planning, execution and monitoring, and evaluation. Public expenditure planning has to necessarily reflect societal needs and resource allocation has to be based on precise estimates. An excess allocation can lead to wasteful and inefficient

[1] Tax expenditure refers to the revenue foregone by the government on account of the tax incentives announced by the government.

use of resources, and inadequate allocations will result in under provisioning or poor service delivery. This process of expenditure planning guided by the planned objectives of development needs informed guidance and control. Effective execution of expenditure programmes is very essential in the delivery of public services and needs constant vigilance and control. Concurrent monitoring enables midcourse corrections and the end evaluation helps assess the extent of success or failure and helps in the formulation of informed expenditure decisions in the ensuing budgets. Given the importance of controls and regulatory measures in the use of public money, an attempt is made in Chapter 5 of the book to document the current institutional mechanism in place to exert control on public expenditure and critically examine its effectiveness based on evidence.

1.4 Political Economy of Public Spending

Public financial decisions can rarely be independent of political economic interests of the policymakers. Public finance, according to Dalton, is one of those subjects that lie on the border of economics and politics. This tendency has also grown over time. Even though a majority of policy pronouncements are made to seem like welfare enhancement motives, the underlying aspiration is to protect their political interests. The initial years of independent India reflected the thinking of the then finance ministers, who were very eager to ensure economy in expenditure and arrest rapid growth in expenditure. Over time, the tendencies have changed and there has been a growing clamor to announce new schemes and programmes, very often duplicative in nature. Given the resource constraints, the tendency is to thinly spread resources and give wide publicity to the new and growing number of schemes. Very often, they also see mere changes in the nomenclature. An interesting feature has been that the country has only seen the addition of new schemes, but very rarely withdrawal of old schemes. This is a very unwelcome measure for any politician for their political career.

The political business cycle is one of the most tested concepts in the political economy literature. At the time of elections, politicians try to manipulate public spending towards preferred areas. The preference may be based on ideology, interest groups, level of competition, and so on. Incumbents would try to increase the overall spending or composition of spending in the election years. Chapter 6 attempts to analyse how public expenditure varies in high-, middle-, and low-income states in India during elections.

1.5 Public Expenditure Reform: The Indian Experiments and Lessons From International Experience

The ever-expanding role of the government in a developing country like India and its diverse roles in the pursuit of development and redistribution are justifiable; however, the need to ensure expenditure efficiency needs no reiteration in the pursuit of sound fiscal management. In addition, there is a need to review the growth and composition of public spending vis-à-vis changing societal needs and preferences from time to time. Public expenditure adequacy, efficiency, and effectiveness also need to be reviewed periodically. It is often noted in policy debates that it is very rare to come across abolition of any scheme by the governments in India, both at the central and state levels. Some progressive sub-national governments like that of Karnataka have attempted merging of schemes to arrest duplication. A number of studies have highlighted issues of duplication of schemes and there is also a considerable amount of overlap between the central and state schemes, leading to issues of fungibility by the sub-national governments. The incremental growth in government expenditure on the ongoing schemes, coupled with the constant addition of new schemes, can lead to fiscal unsustainability sooner or later. India has time and again appointed a number of committees to examine issues of tax reforms to enhance tax revenue. The most recent major indirect tax reform being the introduction of the Goods and Services Tax (GST). On the contrary, the issue of expenditure reform is inadequately addressed, barring some political statements in budget speeches. It is time to recognize that no amount of growth in tax and non-tax revenue will be sufficient to meet the unbridled growth in expenditure. The government can create sustainable fiscal space only by an optimal use of revenue resources. This holds good for all countries. Expenditure reform should not be a one-off measure, it should be built into the budgeting process as a continuous process by undertaking periodical evaluation of the programmes and the insights should guide the informed decision-making process. The importance of assessing the effectiveness of the scheme is echoed by both the academic and policy circles time and again.

Government's presence is felt in all the sectors in the country owing to the ever-expanding role of the government and its diverse roles in the pursuit of development and redistribution. Although these roles are justifiable, the need to ensure expenditure efficiency needs no reiteration in the pursuit of sound fiscal management policy. There are issues of shrinking fiscal space caused by stagnant tax and non-tax resources and rapidly growing current expenditure leading to an uncontained fiscal deficit, especially at the central government level. Currently, the fiscal consolidation effort is targeting the fiscal deficit and public debt, which have not yielded good returns in attaining fiscal discipline. Alternatively, the focus has to be to tone up fiscal discipline by setting controls on the growth of certain forms of expenditure right at the source, which is a more effective way of achieving fiscal consolidation rather than allowing the expenditure to grow by leaps and bounds. Such growth in committed expenditure makes the fiscal deficit correction process difficult and unachievable. India has already witnessed a number of failed fiscal consolidation attempts. There are good lessons that can be drawn from other country's cases. Chapter 8 presents an analytical exposition of the expenditure reform measures initiated by the Government of India from time to time, their adequacies/inadequacies and the best expenditure reform international initiatives for drawing lessons to improve the effectiveness of the fiscal consolidation process.

1.6 Outlays to Outcomes—The Programme Performance Assessment—Theory and Practice

Accountability in the public sector has been conventionally judged based on compliance with rules and procedures relating to the financial outlays by the government. The focus of this kind of accountability is mainly on the inputs, with the performance judged largely in terms of spending no more and no less than appropriated in the budget. Performance emphasis thus was mainly on the outlays, and very rarely the results of such spending programmes received any attention. In addition, budget allocations are traditionally guided by line item incrementalism, wherein the previous expenditures determine the current budget allocations. The two key implicit assumptions of line item incremental budgeting that often result in misallocation of resources are:(a) that societal needs and priorities remain the same and(b) increased spending is tantamount to enhanced services. Incremental budgeting practices have resulted in serious problems such as bloating of public expenditure. In addition fiscal consolidation has largely remained a challenge due to the mushrooming of schemes. Given the hard budget constraints, incrementalism has posed a serious threat to the achievement of efficiency in resource allocation. Developing countries cannot afford this for long given their socio-economic infrastructure inadequacies. A number of countries, including India, have encountered severe fiscal distress on account of such practices. In the Indian context, even though the government has been attempting fiscal consolidation through FRBM measures, performance assessment is still in a nascent stage. Global recognition of the disadvantages of such budgeting practices has resulted in variant forms of budget reforms that help improve public expenditure decision-making. There has been a sea change in the recent thinking, attaching large-scale importance to the 'results'/'outcomes' of public expenditure rather than the 'outlays'. Many nations and regional governments across the globe have been adopting varied forms of budgeting that focus on performance of programmes. The Government of India has used frameworks such as 'Performance Budget', 'Zero-Based Budget', 'Outcome Budget', and 'Results Framework Document' (RFD). Discussion of these performance assessment frameworks adopted by the Government of India, their adequacy, usefulness, and effectiveness is presented in Chapter 9. In addition, a discussion of the best international practices and the frameworks that tend to help improve performance assessment is presented.

1.7 Covid-19: Public Spending

As I was finalizing this book, the Covid-19 pandemic broke out, causing havoc on mankind and the global economy, and it continues unabated till date. Currently, India reports the second-highest number of cases, next only to the United States of America. Initially, the World Health Organization (WHO) praised India for its swift efforts in adopting lockdown and social distancing, and the country revealed a very small number of cases. The disaster brought to light the huge health infrastructure inadequacies and the unpreparedness of the health sector. Stringent measures in the form of lockdown and social distancing adopted to arrest the spread of Covid-19 have seriously impacted the economic growth that was already sluggish. Fiscal policies have a critical role to play in reviving consumer demand and boosting investor confidence. Many sectors have been adversely affected. The central and state governments of India have announced a slew of fiscal policy measures in an attempt to address human misery and revive the economic activity. The last chapter tries to present an overview of the fiscal measures taken up in India and its implications for government finances, which were already reeling under pressure owing to slower economic growth and limited fiscal space. Covid-19 has brought to light many inadequacies and weaknesses in the current policy regime. Lessons learnt from this should help the government address these weaknesses and introduce the necessary structural reforms. Some key public financial issues that need structural policy reforms to lead the country to high and sustained inclusive growth path are also discussed.

The purpose of this volume is to provide a comprehensive and updated understanding of empirical issues in public expenditure and its management in India to the academic community of public finance and policymakers. I am grateful to Prof Dadibhavi, who taught public finance at Karnatak University, for his suggestion to publish a book on public expenditure in India for the benefit of students studying public finance. Although a considerable amount of time has elapsed since this suggestion came, I feel I am better equipped now with all the empirical research that was carried out for various high-level policy bodies such as the Sixth Central Pay Commission, the Fourteenth and Fifteenth Finance Commissions, the Government of India, and the Karnataka state-level policy forums such as the Expenditure Reforms Commission and the Fourth State Finance Commission, just to name a few. I hope, by putting together major empirical issues revolving around the theme and summarizing the academic debates, the students are expected not only to

have an understanding but also to get back to these references for a more detailed understanding of the subject. Although it has been quite challenging to capture all the current issues of public expenditure and their ramifications for the Indian economy in a single volume, a beginning has been made and could be strengthened by future research by diversifying into unexplored or underexplored topics in public expenditure. Each of the chapters included in this book are potential themes for independent volumes.

2
Understanding Key Expenditure Concepts and Classification of Public Expenditure

2.1 Background

There is no dearth of literature involving analytical expositions on the macroeconomic implications and impacts of the growing public expenditure in Indian context. However, studies providing a professional understanding of basic concepts and their likely implications have not been reached out to the students of public finance and the public who are interested in having a correct understanding. The lack of accurate understanding is reflected in the quality of discussions that take place in the pre- and post-budget discussions, both in print and electronic media. However, the interest has grown over time, I was once invited by a lead news agency based in Bangalore to educate the senior mediapersons about how to meaningfully interpret budget decisions, especially the spending proposals. I have also encountered situations where even some of the government officers handling budgets on a day-to-day basis facing difficulties in the technical understanding of budget concepts and the impacts. This is especially true for 'plan' and 'non-plan' expenditure components. This distinction has been dispensed with by the government from the financial year (FY)2017–18, until then the budget discussions invariably ended up judging based on the size of increase in the plan and non-plan components, the former got considerable praise, completely bypassing the fact that the results of spending emanate from the total spending. Such discussions have had a tremendous impact on the policymaking and the budget speeches made by governments from time to time, as they chose to specifically highlight the sectors that had sharp increase in plan spending, trying to maximize the political mileage.

Public Expenditure in India. Gayithri Karnam, Oxford University Press.
DOI: 10.1093/oso/9780192857569.003.0002

Incremental spending, without taking into account the broader societal needs and requirements, is not helpful in making any judgements about governmental participation in the developmental role and pursuits.

This chapter makes an attempt to discuss the key expenditure concepts as presented in the budget and their likely implications. Expenditure classification of the central and state budgets are presented in Charts 2.1 and 2.2.

2.2 Expenditure Classification

Expenditure responsibilities are assigned to all the three levels of government, i.e. union, state, and local, in India; however, the spending in the third tier is of a very small magnitude. The union and state government budgets typically present the expenditure incurred under the following categories:

- Accounting categories: Revenue and capital expenditure
- Functional categories: General, social and community, and economic services

2.2.1 Revenue and Capital Categories

Public expenditure classification[1] as presented in Indian budgets, both at the central and state government levels, typically includes 'accounting' classification wherein expenditure is divided into 'revenue' and 'capital' accounts. The revenue and capital classification has been incorporated since the inception of the budget. The following technical details on the structure and contents of budgets are largely sourced from the Government of India (2019) due to the technicalities involved.

The Annual Financial Statement (AFS) is a document presented to the Parliament under Article 112 of the Constitution of India. It presents the estimated receipts and expenditure of the Government of India for the ensuing FY, which, in India, is from April 1 to March31. The receipts and

[1] For more technical details on budget classification, see Jacobs et.al (2009)

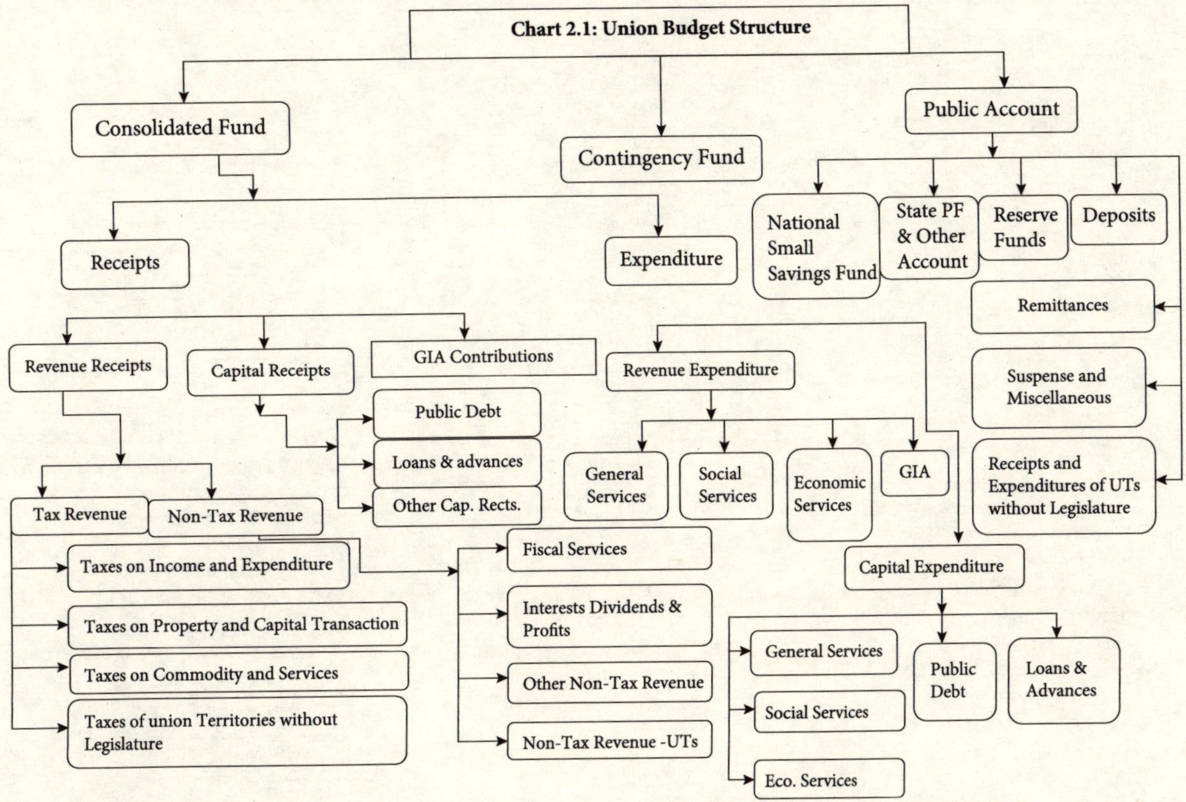

Chart 2.1 Union Budget Structure

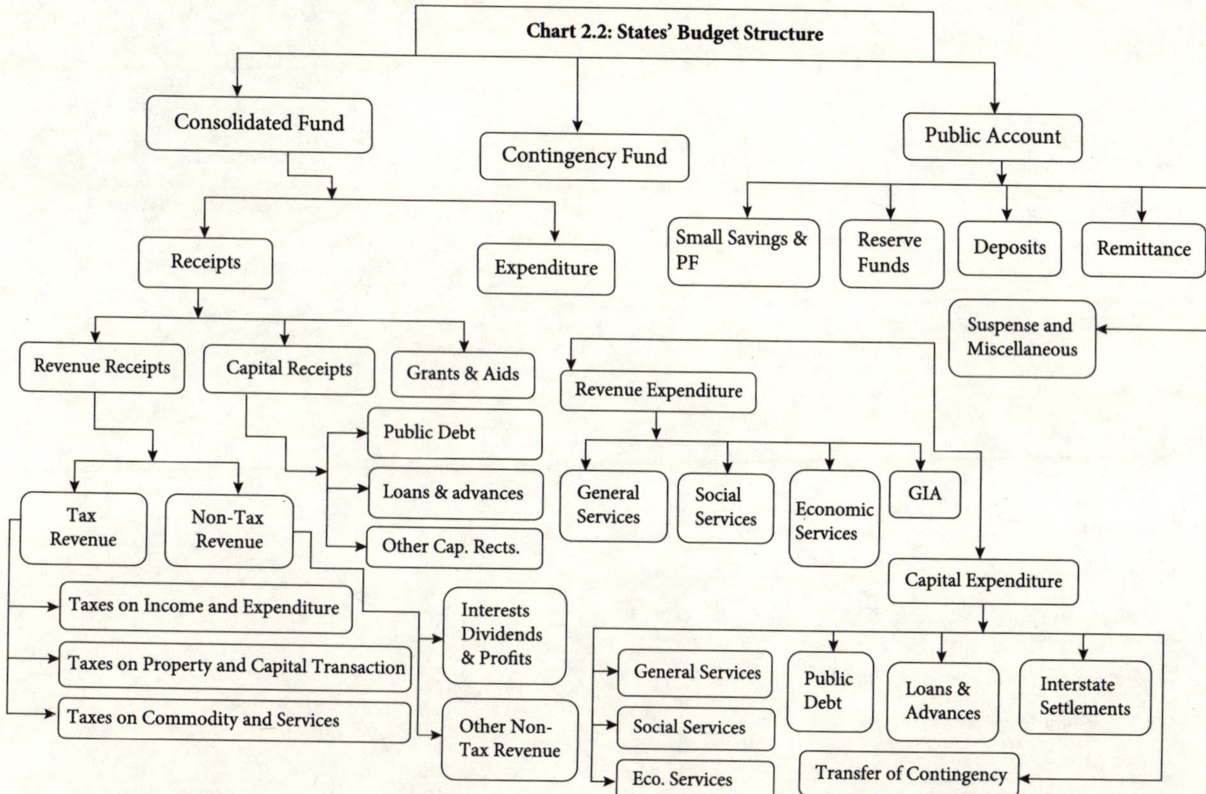

Chart 2.2 States' Budget Structure

disbursements are shown under the following three parts in which government accounts are kept:

The Consolidated Fund of India

The Consolidated Fund of India (CFI) was constituted under the Article 266 of the constitution. All revenues received by the government, loans raised by it, and also receipts from recoveries of loans granted by it, together form the CFI. All expenditures of the government are incurred from the CFI, and no amount can be drawn from the Consolidated Fund without due authorization from the Parliament.

The Contingency Fund of India

Article 267 of the constitution authorizes the existence of a Contingency Fund of India which is an imprest placed at the disposal of the President of India to facilitate meeting of urgent unforeseen expenditure by the government, pending authorization from the Parliament. Parliamentary approval for such unforeseen expenditure is obtained, *expostfacto*, and an equivalent amount is drawn from the Consolidated Fund to recoup the Contingency Fund after such *expostfacto* approval. The corpus of the Contingency Fund as authorized by the Parliament presently stands at Rs.500 crore. The budget 2021–22 has proposed to increase it to Rs. 30,000 crore.

The Public Account of India

Money held by the government in trust is kept in the Public Account. The Public Account is constituted under Article 266 (2) of the Constitution of India. Provident funds, small savings collections, and income of the government set apart for expenditure on specific objects, such as road development, primary education, and other reserve/special funds, are examples of money kept in the Public Account. Public Account funds that do not belong to the government and have to be finally paid back to the persons and authorities who deposited them do not require parliamentary authorization for withdrawals. The approval of the Parliament is obtained when amounts are withdrawn from the Consolidated Fund and kept in the Public Account for expenditure on specific objects. The actual expenditure on a specific object is again submitted for vote of the

Parliament for withdrawal from the Public Account for spending on the specific object.

AFS distinguishes the expenditure on revenue account from the expenditure on other accounts, as mandated by the Constitution of India. The revenue and the capital sections together, therefore, make the union budget.

The revenue budget consists of the revenue receipts of the government (tax revenues and other non-tax revenues) and the expenditure met from these revenues. Revenue expenditure is incurred towards the normal running of government departments and for rendering of services like general, social and community, and economic services, of which there are also commitments such as interest payments on debt, meeting subsidies, and grants-in-aid. Broadly, the expenditure that does not result in the creation of assets for the Government of India is treated as revenue expenditure. All grants given to the state governments/union territories and other parties are also treated as revenue expenditure even though some of the grants may be used for the creation of capital assets.

Capital receipts and capital payments together constitute the capital budget. Capital payments comprise of three heads of expenditure, the first one relates to capital outlay, which is in the nature of direct investments by the government in building infrastructure, acquisition of assets like land, buildings, machinery, equipment, as also investments in shares, etc. The second one pertains to public debt repayment or repayment of its borrowings and the third one relates to loans and advances sanctioned by the governments.

Public expenditure is an important fiscal instrument used by governments to discharge a number of its welfare and developmental goals. Capital expenditure, in particular, is used to enhance economic growth by creating economic and social infrastructure and generate employment. It has also been an important fiscal instrument that governments have used to revive the economies when in slump characterized by market failure to undertake any investments. Capital investments are usually financed through public borrowings. However, if the governments achieve a surplus in their revenue account, they can use that surplus for capital investments. On the contrary, when the governments run revenue deficits, they are bound to use borrowings to meet the consumption expenditure, which can adversely affect their finances in the long run. In India, most of the state governments that experienced revenue deficits since 1980s have become revenue surplus after they introduced the FRBM Act at varied points of time. The first Indian state that enacted the Fiscal Responsibility Legislation (FRL) was Karnataka, which, in 2002, even preceded the union government that came into effect from the FY 2003–04. The union government, however, continues to have a huge revenue deficit which is in the range of 60–70% of the fiscal deficit, implying that a major portion of the public borrowings are used for current consumption, which is not sound public financial management. This is in view of the fact that public investments in the normal course are expected to generate assets or income in future, and the borrowings are expected to be serviced through the returns of such capital investments. Borrowings tend to add to the current expenditure by way of interest payments. Capital spending is defined in Box 2.1.

Capital expenditures in the form of direct investment are generally welcome as they have a higher multiplier effect and thus add to a higher growth of GDP. Empirical evidence (Bose and Bhanumurthy, 2013) has revealed a stronger multiplier effect of the capital expenditure on the output, hence there is need to prioritize spending. However, deciding on a judicious combination of revenue and capital budgets has been a major challenge and very often the enthusiasm that is shown in starting new capital projects is absent when it comes to earmarking adequate funds for operation and maintenance of capital projects. In general, the annual budgeting process does not factor in the funding requirements of the capital projects that tend to stretch over many years. A large number of capital projects are initiated every year, sometimes by making a token allocation of Rs. 1, and many such projects starve of adequate funding and eventually end up with considerably higher time and cost overruns. Inadequate allocations to operation and maintenance of capital projects tend to defeat the very purpose of the capital projects and lead to poor results. Hence, there is every need to consider both revenue and capital budgets together for planning and budgeting and while appraising investment proposals there is need to factor in the operation and maintenance expenditure. Medium-term budgeting framework (MTBF) is helpful in factoring in the annual costs in a medium term.

A report on efficient management of public expenditure prepared by the committee instituted to examine issues of public expenditure headed

Box 2.1 Defining Capital

Governments around the world may define 'capital' in different ways. *Capital spending is generally about physical assets with a useful life of more than one year.* But it also includes capital improvements or the rehabilitation of physical assets that enhance or extend the useful life of the asset (as distinct from repair or maintenance, which assures that the asset is functional for its planned life).

Capital spending is sometimes equated with *investment* or *development spending*, where expenditures have benefits extending years into the future. Under this definition, governments may include physical assets for government use (e.g. office buildings), physical assets of a public good nature that also enhance private sector development (e.g. roads, water systems), and intangibles (e.g. research). It can be quite difficult to distinguish between investment and noninvestment expenditures, and if investment spending receives favoured treatment in the annual budgeting process, nearly all spending, whether recurrent or not, will end up being classified as investment.

Every government establishes some arbitrary cut-off point to distinguish capital from current expenditures. For budgeting purposes, the relevant distinction is between capital and current (or operating) expenditures. Current expenditures are purchases of assets to be consumed within one year, regardless of expenditure size. Small expenditures (e.g. less than $25,000) are recurrent, regardless of the fact that it could be consumed over a period longer than one year.

Source: As cited in Jacobs, 2008, p. 7, sourced from World Bank, 'Ukraine: Creating Fiscal Space for Growth: A Public Finance Review,' Report No. 36671-UA, 2006: p. 84.

by Rangarajan (Government of India, 2011a) discusses a number of issues relating to the revenue and capital distinction of the budgets. The report states that although the constitution distinguishes only between 'expenditure on revenue account' and 'other expenditure', in practice, 'expenditure on revenue account' has been taken to mean revenue expenditure. It is also felt that the 'revenue' and 'capital' classification may be dysfunctional from an economic management perspective. The committee observes that the maintenance expenditure has been neglected over the years due to the excessive preference for capital projects. Commenting on the rationale for 'revenue' and 'capital' separation, the report states that 'Separation provides greater control over public debt and its utilization. It facilitates implementation of the "Golden Rule" followed by many countries which requires that current account is balanced over an economic cycle and Governments borrow only to invest and not to pay for current spending. Debt financing of capital expenditures is justified to ensure intergenerational equity. The separation facilitates strategic allocation of borrowed funds for capital expenditure. It, thus, provides a framework for the best use of borrowed resources. It enables better determination of responsibility within Government' (Government of India, 2011a, xix).

Presenting the long-term trends in the ratio of revenue expenditure to capital expenditure and revenue receipts to capital receipts (see Figure 2.1) it is argued that ratio of revenue expenditure to capital expenditure has been increasing from 1956–57 with a large-scale volatility in the last decade. It has also been observed that ratio of revenue receipts to capital receipts which was by and large stable excepting the last decade reflecting increased borrowings (Singh, et.al (2017). A more detailed discussion of the trends in major categories of the central government expenditure is presented in the third chapter.

The Rangarajan committee further emphasizes on the need to exercise caution in the selection and execution of capital projects and recommends an economic analysis of budgets and disclosure of information on capital

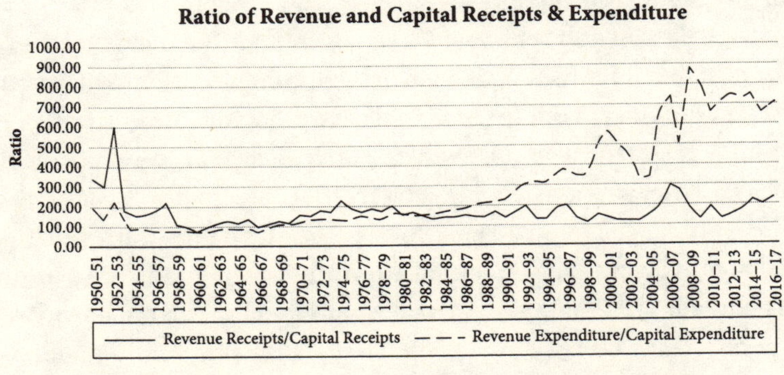

Figure 2.1 Ratio of Revenue and Capital Receipts and Expenditure

Source: CharanSingh et al., 2017.

formation. There are, however, counterarguments that revenue expenditure too should be subjected to such critical analysis. It is felt that there is undue emphasis given to the capital projects and new investments, leading to gross negligence of maintenance and operational costs and earmarking of inadequate allocations. Governments should desist from such practices as they tend to defeat the very purpose of capital projects.

There is every need to make sure that investment proposals include considerations of both capital and operating costs together for a holistic understanding of the costs involved and the benefits. The importance of capital budgeting reform is amply highlighted in literature. Discussing the historical evolution of capital budgeting, Jacobs structures it into six stages.[2]

The first stage is the great depression years during which efforts were mainly focused on designing ways to ensure economic recovery. Public borrowing for financing capital outlays was justified for emergencies but was not favoured otherwise. Gradually countries resorted to raise public borrowings to finance development projects. Jacobs (2008) cites Sweden as one such case that introduced a capital budget to be funded by public borrowing and used to finance the creation of durable and self-financing assets that would contribute to an expansion of net worth equivalent to the amount of borrowing. Subsequently, there was an extended application of the investment budget in other Nordic countries.

It is interesting to note that of the five stages of the historical evolution of a capital budget, the second stage had its origin in India, albeit, the purpose for which it was done was not for constructive reasons but only to justify larger borrowing. It is stated, 'The second stage took place during the late 1930s when the colonial Government in India introduced a capital budget to reduce the budget deficit by shifting some items of expenditure from the current budget. It was believed that the introduction of this dual budget system would provide a convenient way to reduce deficits while justifying a rationale for borrowing'(Jacobs, 2008, 8).

The third stage largely related to the low-income countries that prepared the five-year plans adopted from the Soviet model of planning. India too adopted the five-year planning model and completed twelve five-year plans, subsequent to which the Planning Commission was

[2] See Jacobs (2008) for a detailed account of capital budgeting practices.

replaced by NITI Aayog. The five-year plans conceived of many investment projects by the government to promote development; the Indian case was marked by changing sectoral emphasis from one five-year plan to another.

In the fourth stage, governments tended to apply quantitative appraisal techniques such as Programme Performance Budgeting Systems (PPBS) and Zero-Based Budgeting Systems to scientifically assess the capital projects in the 1960s and 1970s. Governments across the globe applied such frameworks with a great deal of fanfare for a few years and gave up only to be replaced with new frameworks. A more detailed discussion of such frameworks is provided in Chapter 9.

The fifth stage marked a revival of the debate and recognized the usefulness of capital budgets. However, this did not gain much support. Jacobs (2008, 9) states, 'A President's commission in 1999 investigating budget concepts in the United States concluded that a capital budget could lead to greater outlays on bricks and mortar, and as a result, current outlays could suffer. Having rejected the use of separate capital budgets, the commission advocated the introduction of accrual accounting in government accounts. The introduction of accrual accounting, which did not make any progress in the United States until the early 1990s, would have meant the division of expenditures into current and investment outlays.' Countries such as Sweden and other Nordic countries that had pioneered the capital budgeting effort in 1930s reviewed their thinking in the 1970s, seeking to reverse the excessive focus on capital budgets. The new approaches were thought of in the form of accrual budgets.

There are studies that have attempted to empirically verify the impacts of government expenditure and its composition on the GDP. A questionable finding of the study pertaining to some developing countries reveals that capital expenditure has tended to negatively impact the growth of GDP (Devarajan, et al., 1996).Although the authors attribute such results to the practices of developing countries (India is included in their study of developing countries) that incur excess expenditure on capital account due to their anxiety to promote growth, India's experience has been totally contrary wherein the governments have not only been spending smaller share on capital account but also slashing the capital expenditure in an adhoc manner to achieve fiscal consolidation goals.

The sixth stage was marked by a further push to accrual budgeting and accounting influenced by the experience of Australia and New Zealand from the late 1990s.

International Perspective

Empirical evidence suggests that the international practices[3] vary considerably with regard to budgeting for capital expenditures. 'Some countries have moved to accrual accounting and budgeting and they make distinction between operational and investment budgets. Others make a distinction between current and capital expenditure in accounts but not in budgets. There are others which have adopted modified accrual accounting without depreciation. In many countries, capital budgets are maintained through special accounts. Some have multi-year investment budgets. Most countries that distinguish between current and capital expenditures also show transfer payments of capital nature distinctly. In general, the shift to program budgets in developed countries in the 1960s and 70s led to some dilution of the need for separate capital budgets, as unified presentation of capital expenditures alongside related current expenditures and outputs became the norm in these countries. However, the need for distinguishing capital and current budgets seems to have been strengthened in the last decades or so with the introduction of accrual-based accounting and budgeting techniques, particularly in the OECD countries. While there is no unanimity of opinions on this issue and no uniformity in the country practices, there seems to be general agreement that planning and budget formulation needs to take an integrated holistic view of capital and current expenditure proposals and that a clear distinction between capital and current expenditures facilitates the budget execution and analysis' (Government of India, 2011a).

Rangarajan Committee too considers it important to have the distinction between the revenue and capital accounts going by the constitutional requirement to have government expenditure accounted under revenue and other expenditure. It is also observed that the FRBM Act too 'aims to ensure inter-generational equity in fiscal management and long-term macroeconomic stability by achieving sufficient revenue surplus. It also seems to conform to the classical view about use of borrowed funds and implicitly aims at balancing the current and capital sides of the budget in its application to the Union Government as a distinct budgeting and

[3] Government of India, 2011a.

accounting entity '(Government of India, 2011a, xx) The Committee is of the view that'. On balance, it can be said that the need for separation of revenue and capital budgets should be seen not merely as a rationalization of borrowing but in the wider context of the formulation of fiscal policy, in terms of overall expenditures and the appropriate mix of taxation and borrowing' (Government of India, 2011a, xix).

2.2.2 Plan and Non-Plan Categorization

Public expenditure under both the 'revenue' and 'capital' categories and that of functional categories was further depicted under the 'plan' and 'non-plan' categories until 2017–18. Plan expenditure represented the expenditure incurred on plan schemes included under the respective plan period, which became 'non-plan' upon completion of the plan period. This distinction has thenceforth been done away with. The Government of India committee on efficient management of public expenditure headed by Rangarajan has dealt with the need to do away with the plan and non-plan distinction in detail. The committee felt, 'Besides, a notion has widely gained ground among the policy makers and officials across all levels that plan expenditure is good and Non Plan is bad. This bias in favor of Plan expenditure and against Non-Plan expenditure has led to a situation in which essential Non Plan expenditure like maintenance of assets is neglected. This has also led to a motivation for showing higher plan expenditure and higher plan sizes both at Central and State levels. Further, several factors such as shift of plan focus from capital to revenue expenditure and the process of transferring expenditure of old schemes to Non-Plan at the end of each Five Year Plan mean that correspondence cannot be drawn between plan and development expenditure' (Government of India, 2011a, xiii).

The committee further opined that, 'The Plan/Non-Plan bifurcation of expenditure has contributed to a fragmented view of resource allocation to various programmes/schemes. With fragmented view, it is difficult not only to ascertain cost of delivering a service but also to link outlays to outcomes. Outcomes and outputs of programmes depend on total expenditure, Plan and Non-Plan put together and not merely on Plan expenditure which constitutes about 30% of the total expenditure only. To conclude, Plan and Non-Plan distinction in the budget is neither able to provide a satisfactory classification of developmental and non-developmental dimensions of Government expenditure nor an appropriate budgetary framework. It has, therefore, become dysfunctional. The Committee, therefore, recommends that Plan and Non-Plan distinction in the budget should be removed' (Government of India, 2011a, xiii).

2.3 Functional Classification of Budgets

The expenditure of the government is classified into functional heads. The functional classification broadly signifies the function of the government and the activity on which the expenditure has been incurred, examples include education, health, agriculture, etc. Functional classification helps in an understanding of the allocation of resources among sectors. Governments in India both at the centre and sub-national levels have played a vital role in the promotion of sectoral development as indicated by increased allocations over time. However, it needs to be understood that mere enhancement in the funding support is not tantamount to development. There is every need to plan the spending intervention to reflect the needs of the sector followed by an effective execution of the programmes. Given the dynamic nature of the needs, an analysis of the historical trends of public expenditure in each of the sectors vis-à-vis the sectoral development indicators help in understanding the progress made and also in providing insights into directional changes required in the public spending. Of course the presence of the private sector and their contribution to development cannot be ignored. The Classification of the Functions of Government (COFOG) established by the United Nations is a widely accepted international standard in this field.

The functional classification being followed as of now is a six-tier structure with a hierarchy of major, sub-major, minor, sub-head, detailed heads, and object head. The first tier of the functional classification, called the major head, denotes the functions of the government. The second tier of the functional classification provides the description of sub-functions. The third tier, denoted by the minor head, indicates the objective of the government being achieved through that particular expenditure. Below the minor head are the two tiers of sub-heads (fourth tier) and detailed heads (fifth tier). The sub-head indicates specific schemes or activities of the government under which the expenditure has been incurred and the detailed head indicates various components of the schemes or sub-schemes. The sixth tier of object head provides details about the object of expenditure. Thus, this forms a two-dimensional classification where the expenditure is classified into object heads for each functional head. The division provided by plan/non-plan classification is laid over the functional and object classification. This division cuts across the entire classification hierarchy into two columns (Government of India, 2011a, xiii).

The accounting categories of expenditure, i.e. the revenue and capital heads of expenditure, are further categorized under functional categories, which basically account for the functions performed by the government, and the broad budget heads are the same for both the central and state budgets. These include the following:

General services
Social and community services
Economic services

General Services

General services are general in nature and in government parlance, this item of expenditure is categorized as 'non-development' expenditure. Strictly speaking these expenditure items represent key support services without which development pursuits are difficult to be pursued. For instance without defence, the national security gets jeopardized and no development can occur. Similarly when the services of police, jails, and administration of justice fail there will be anarchy in the society, hence branding them as non-development expenditure is incorrect. General services include items of expenditure that relate to the following:

- Organs of state including items of expenditure pertaining to Parliament/State/Union Territory Legislature; President, Vice President/Governor, Administrator of Union Territories; Council of Ministers; Elections and Audit
- Tax collection and other fiscal services
- Interest payments and debt servicing
- Administrative services, including items such as Public Service Commission and Secretariat General services; police; jails; supplies

and disposals; stationery and printing; public works; external affairs; vigilance; and other administrative services
- Pensions and Miscellaneous General Services
- Defence services

Social and Community Services
The items included under the social and community services are given below:

- Education, sports, and culture
- Health and family welfare
- Water supply, sanitation, housing, and urban development
- Information and broadcasting
- Welfare of scheduled castes (SC), scheduled tribes (ST), other backward classes, and minorities
- Labour and labour welfare
- Social welfare and nutrition

Economic Services
The items included under the economic services include the following:

- Agriculture and allied services
- Rural development
- Special area programmes
- Irrigation and flood control
- Energy
- Industry and minerals
- Transport
- Science, technology, and environment
- General economic services

2.4 Economic Classification of Budgets

Although the classification discussed above relates to the manner in which budgets are presented in the AFS, there is a greater detailed analysis of budgets in the form of economic classification.

Economic-cum-functional classification of budgets are prepared by the governments both at the central and state levels.

2.4.1 Economic Classification

Economic classification of budgets analyses budget expenditure by the key economic categories, such as 'government consumption', which largely includes the wages and salaries and purchase of goods; 'transfers' comprising of both 'current' and 'capital' transfers; 'gross capital formation'; 'financial investment and loans to the rest of the economy'. The terms are self-explanatory and help in understanding the economic nature of government spending. A number of studies have observed that in India, government consumption comprising of wages and salaries and transfers are increasingly constituting a larger share in government spending and capital formation is declining over time. A more detailed discussion of the trends is presented in Chapter 3.

The economic-cum-functional classification of budgets presents the break outs of each functional heads of expenditure by the economic categories. For instance the wages and salaries, capital formation, and financial investments under the functional head 'education' get reflected under the education sector's economic-cum-functional classification. The broad increases in developmental heads of expenditure as under education, health, and agriculture may prove to be good for the economy, however, if the increases are largely on salaries, as has been observed in the case especially after the Fifth Pay Commission recommendations, then the real increase in the benefits under these heads become questionable.

2.5 Development and Non-Development Expenditure

Government publications such as 'economic survey', 'statistical abstract', and Reserve Bank of India (RBI)'s report on state finances, also publish data by 'development' and 'non-development' categories. Largely, the former is a summation of expenditure incurred on the 'social and community' and 'economic' services, and the latter represents 'general' services expenditure. Although such an analysis of public expenditure by development and non-development categories is useful in understanding the usefulness of public spending and the trends therein, the manner in which the development and non-development expenditures are defined is highly questionable. Assuming that the support services that are grouped under the 'general' services category, such as 'organs of state', 'administration of justice', 'police', 'jails', and 'defence', are all non-development in nature and branding all the expenditure incurred under the social and economic sectors as development is erratic and tends to bury the real nature of government expenditure in the nomenclature.

The discussion presented hitherto pertains to budget classification used in India and their likely implications; however, a mere analysis of government expenditure on these lines leaves many meaningful questions related to efficiency and effectiveness of public expenditure unanswered. Efficiency refers to an optimal provisioning of public services in terms of the cost of the public services, and effectiveness reflects the results or outcomes of public spending. Public expenditure, when analysed to examine the efficiency and effectiveness of major programmes, will help provide insights to undertake informed corrections in the public expenditure policies and allocations. Public finance literature addressing these issues has been increasingly contributing to the understanding of the usefulness of public expenditure, and it is important for the students of public finance to peruse the same.

3

Public Expenditure in India

Historical Trends and Composition

3.1 Introduction

Public expenditure has been an important fiscal instrument used by the governments to fulfil the professed goals and objectives that are dynamic in nature and undergo changes from time to time. The size and scope reflect the scale of operations and their nature. Historical evidence has revealed that state[1] was considered as a 'necessary evil' by the classical economists and was expected to perform limited tasks, and 'laissez fare', meaning leave the individual alone, was the principle governing the then thinking. This resulted in a situation wherein government expenditure as a percentage of GDP was quite small. An important measure used widely in the assessment of government's role in the national economy is to compute the percent share of government expenditure in the GDP. This is a standard tool used to make meaningful inter-temporal and inter-regional comparisons. The classical economists' premise that 'supply creates its own demand' miserably failed during the 'Great Depression' of 1930s, resulting in a major rethinking on the role of the government. J.M. Keynes advocated a very proactive role to government in pump priming the economy through compensatory finance, making the governments active economic agents. Governments also tended to assume more diverse roles with the passage of time, emerging from major events such as the World Wars, rendering welfare orientation to public spending. Varied roles assumed by the government from time to time such as the guardian, production agent, employer, and a driving force to optimize welfare depending on the contemporary economic requirements and

[1] State and government are used interchangeably.

Public Expenditure in India. Gayithri Karnam, Oxford University Press. © Oxford University Press 2022.
DOI: 10.1093/oso/9780192857569.003.0003

social compulsions have fostered the growth and composition of public spending across nations.

A systematic study of the trends and patterns of public spending over time helps in understanding the role played by the respective governments and the changes therein. Empirical literature pertaining to the study of growth and composition of public expenditure is abundant both in the international and Indian context. Many studies have empirically verified popular theories such as Adolf Wagner's 'Law of Increasing State Activity' and Peacock and Wiseman's theory of 'Displacement and Inspection effects'. The later extensions included a study of determinants of public expenditure following Solomon Fabricant's model. What these theories are all about and their empirical validation are briefly discussed later in this chapter. The overall purpose of this book is to provide a comprehensive insight into the public expenditure policies, its behaviour, and the likely implications, rather than getting into theoretical discourse.

3.2 Expenditure Theories and Empirical Evidences

The scope and focus of empirical literature on the study of public spending has undergone significant change from time to time and broadly grouped under three strands—positive theory, normative theory, and applied aspects.

3.2.1 Positive Theory of Public Spending

Positive aspects deal with the behavioural pattern of the public expenditure in the past and the present times. Positive theory pertains to 'that body of economic and political analysis which attempts to understand and explain the observed pattern and level of government expenditure and the changes in those expenditures over time' (Bird, 1970, 6). According to Bird (1970, 8), positive theory pertains to the following:

- Determinants of the volume of public expenditure
- Determinants of the composition of public expenditure—what goods and services are financed through the public sector and how the 'mix' of expenditure changes over time

- 'Behavioural' properties of public expenditure as centralization and stability

Contributions by Adolf Wagner,[2] the 'Law of Increasing State Activity', Peacock and Wiseman's 'Displacement Effect' hypothesis, and Fabricant and Lipsey's (1952) interstate variation of government expenditure opened the floodgates for empirical studies undertaken during sixties and seventies, which attempted to empirically test the prevalence of the public expenditure behaviour reported in each of the above seminal studies. Studies also attempted to use varied methodologies in the empirical verification. Wagner's theory and that of Peacock and Wiseman dealt with public expenditure behavioural aspects at the macro level, whereas Fabricant's study tried to identify the factors responsible for inter-state variation in public expenditure. Fabricant employed per capita income, degree of urbanization, and density of population to account for the inter-state variation of expenditure among the United States. A number of studies followed suit in the United States and many other country by either employing the same variables or by adding some others. Some studies also resorted to a different specification of the model in an attempt to better explain the inter-state variation in public expenditure. Subsequent studies have also tried to assess the impact of political factors by including variables like ideology of the political parties, government stability, elections, etc.

3.2.2 Normative Aspects

Normative theory of public expenditure deals with prescribing norms for the appropriate level of public expenditure. Norms are prescribed in order to attain the ideal conditions of allocation and distribution. Market failure to produce public goods characterized by 'non-excludability' and 'non-rival' has added to the importance of government.

[2] Wagner's contribution was in German, beginning 1863, but English translation of a portion of his work is available in Musgrave and Peacock (1967) (ed). Classics in the theory of Public Finance—Three extracts on Public Finance, translated by Nancy Cooke 1–15. A detailed English version of discussion of Wagner's theory is presented in Peacock and Wiseman (1961) and Bird (1970).

3.2.3 Applied Aspects

Applied aspects relate to the functional aspects of public expenditure and encompass the whole gamut of budgetary processes. Issues dealt with under the applied aspects are wide ranging and mainly address the public expenditure policies, implementation, and monitoring. Increasingly, the literature is examining aspects of efficiency and effectiveness of public spending; the former typically employs production frontier methodologies to assess the technical efficiency of public expenditure. A large number of studies have examined technical efficiency of education, health expenditure, etc.

3.2.4 Government Expenditure and Economic Growth

The two important theories that have attracted a lot of empirical testing relate to Adolf Wagner's 'Law of Increasing State Activity', which argues that as the economic activity grows, there is a tendency for the government activities to increase. Keynesian contribution, on the contrary, emphasizes on public expenditure's impact on the national income. The empirical literature, which has attempted validation of each of these theories, largely suggests that the causality between GDP and expenditure is not one sided, expenditure too tends to impact the GDP. A number of studies have attempted empirical testing of impact of public expenditure on economic growth. Varied methodologies have been used in terms of the model specifications and components of public expenditure[3]. Studies that have attempted to analyse the differential impacts of government consumption and capital investments (Ram, 1986;Aschauer, 1989; Rao and Sen, 1993;) have observed a positive impact of the latter on growth. Devarajan et al. (1996) argue by analysing the composition of public expenditure that excessive spending on capital spending by

[3] This discussion draws extensively from the author's research on Evaluation of Karnataka State finances conducted for the Fourteenth Finance Commission, 2014. For greater discussion on the methods of estimation see (Gayithri, 2014b).

the developing countries is tending to become unproductive. Tanzi and Zee (1997), providing a systematic discussion of the existing literature of the issues relating to fiscal policy and long-run growth, argue that the traditional approach of dividing the expenditure into public consumption and investment can be problematic in the assessment of growth implications of public expenditure. Instead they advocate classification of expenditure into productive (growth inducing which would include expenditures like education along with infrastructure investments) and non-productive (growth retarding) categories. Empirical estimations of growth implications of public expenditure have been attempted in the Indian context as well (Gayithri, 1988;Khunderakpam, 2003; and Pattnaik et al., 2005). Gayithri, using the Granger's bidirectional causality test, has analysed the relationship between the total government expenditure and the Gross State Domestic Product (GSDP) (for the time period 1957–58 to 1984–85) and observed that GSDP has a greater influence on expenditure compared to that of expenditure on GSDP. Khunderakpam (2003) has analysed the dynamic interaction between public expenditure and national income in India for the time period 1960–61 to 1996–97 and found that in the long run, causality strictly runs from public expenditure to national income and that of national income to public expenditure is weak. In the short run, the impact of public expenditure on income growth is negative, and it is argued that public expenditure turns negative when it is excessive; however, the paper does not provide any convincing argument to prove that the government expenditure is excessive in the Indian context. Pattnaik et al. (2005) have observed that gross capital formation in the public sector has a positive impact on the GDP; the paper also observes that the impact is even stronger in the post-reform phase, i.e. during 1992–2004 compared to the pre-reform phase of 1950–91. Another study covering a longer time period from 1950/51 to 2007/08 has examined the validity of Wagner's Law in India(Verma and Arora, 2010). The study has applied six versions of Wagner's hypothesis available in the literature and suggested the evidence of a long-run relationship between economic growth and growth of public expenditure and validated Wagner's theory.

3.3 Trends and Composition of Public Expenditure

India has experienced a significant growth in the public spending both at the central and sub-national levels of the government. Fiscal instruments are used extensively in the sectoral development strategies adopted by the government. There have also been significant changes in the governmental priorities from time to time. Although the initial years of planning focused on physical resource development, with a large-scale emphasis on agriculture and industry, the subsequent aim to promote human resource development, poverty alleviation, and the more recent focus on inclusive development have brought in considerable changes in the nature of public spending. The country has also seen major fiscal policy changes with the introduction of structural adjustment programme and stabilization measures in 1991. The framing of legislation like 'FRBM' to effect rule-based fiscal corrections has compelled governments, both at the centre and at the state levels, to attain fiscal consolidation by imposing ceiling on the fiscal and revenue deficits and public debt. The fiscal map of the country is also going through major changes with the scrapping of 'plan' and 'non-plan' categorization of expenditure. These sharp changes in the quantum and quality of public spending invariably have great implications for the development outcomes in the country. While there are issues of effective translation of outlays into outcomes, there are also issues of allocative efficiency,[4] in terms of whether public spending in the country is reflecting the impending needs of the society, which are highly diverse given the country's differential levels of development.

This chapter makes an attempt to analyse the trends in major public expenditure components such as 'revenue' and 'capital' accounts representing the 'accounting' classification and 'general', 'social and community', and 'economic' services representing the 'functional' classification of public expenditure. Ideally such long-time series data needs to be adjusted for inflation and population. In the present case, in addition to the

[4] A definition of technical and allocative efficiency was made by Farrell (1957). According to this definition, a firm is technically efficient if it uses the minimal possible combination of inputs for producing a certain output (input orientation). Allocative efficiency, or as Farrell called it, price efficiency, refers to the ability of a firm to choose the optimal combination of inputs given input prices. If a firm has realized both technical and allocative efficiency, it is then cost-efficient (overall efficient) (Badunenko, et.al, 2006).

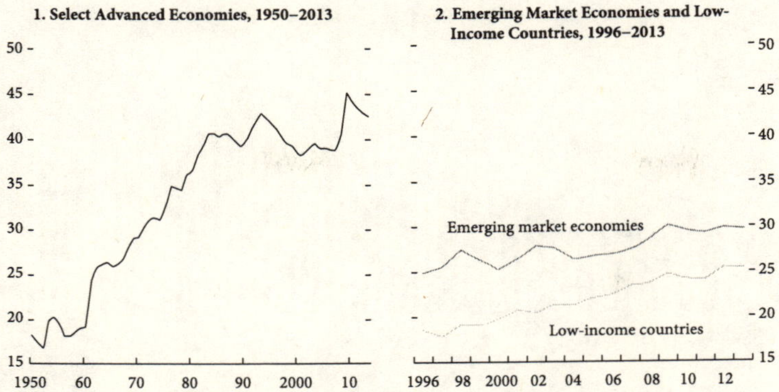

Figure 3.1 General Government Expenditure as Percent of GDP
Source: IMF, 2014, p. 22.

discussion of growth in nominal terms, their respective shares in the total and the GDP are undertaken to understand the relative importance.

This subject is vast, and to understand the policy implications of public spending, it is important to examine the quantum and quality of spending at a highly disaggregate level. This book does not aim at getting down to such highly disaggregate analysis owing to the long period included in the study, instead the attempt is to understand the macro changes in the growth and composition of public spending that the country has experienced over time.

Before we get down to a detailed disaggregate analysis of public spending, a quick glimpse of the temporal growth in central government spending and an international comparison is provided. A quick glimpse of general government expenditure as percent to GDP in an international comparison of covering select advanced economies, emerging markets, and low-income economies is presented in Figure 3.1.

A historical trend in the government final consumption expenditure as percent of GDP, which has more than doubled between 1960 and 2016 is presented in figure 3.2.

Despite being a very simplistic comparison, the sheer increase in the size of revenue expenditure from a meager, Rs.197.38 crore in 1947–48 to Rs.2,447,780 crore in the latest budget, i.e. 2019–20, reflects the sheer magnitude of increase in central government spending. The total government spending is estimated to be Rs.2,786,349 crore during 2019–20. Out

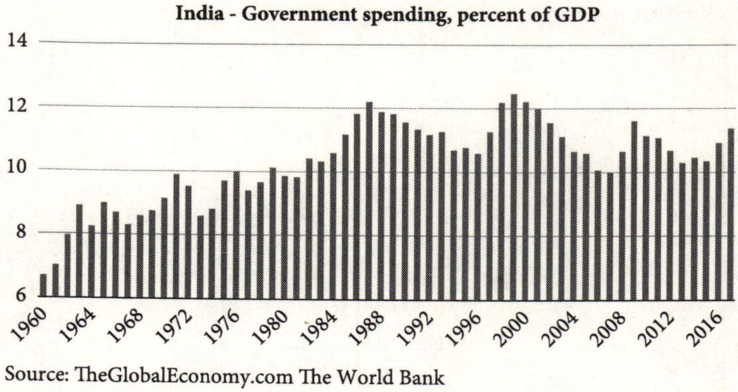

Figure 3.2 General Government Spending as Percent of GDP

Note: General government final consumption expenditure (formerly general government consumption) includes all government current expenditures for purchases of goods and services (including compensation of employees). It also includes most expenditure on national defense and security but excludes government military expenditures that are part of government capital formation (The World Bank) (https://www.theglobaleconomy.com/India/Government_size).

of the total expenditure, revenue expenditure constitutes a major chunk of the total expenditure with 87.85% share, and capital expenditure is estimated to be Rs.338,569 crore with a share of 12.15% in total. This is referred to as simplistic comparison because any long-term trend analysis needs to be invariably adjusted for price and population factors, the former indicates the real growth and the latter provides an understanding of the per head benefit from the public spending. Another important indicator applied to measure growth in government activity is to track the changes in the percentage share of government expenditure to GDP. Such an analysis not only indicates the extent of government activity in the national economy but also makes international and intranational (sub-national) comparisons meaningful.

A detailed discussion of central government spending in India is structured into four different phases and is guided by the policy regimes and major fiscal developments:

1. Initial years of independence: Largely, the effort was to define the path of development of independent India and overcome the huge deficit burden left behind by the British government.

2. The second phase pertains to fiscal expansionary phase starting from 1974–75 till 1990–91. This period also resulted in high fiscal and revenue deficits, and by 1991, the country had to announce major structural adjustment and stabilization measures.
3. Analysis pertaining to the period 1990–91 till the framing of the FRBM Act by the central government relates to the third phase. This period was marked by uncontained deficits despite conditionalities attached by the international agencies to gradually reduce the fiscal deficit to 3%.
4. The fourth phase pertains to post-FRBM till date. This period was marked by a number of fiscal reform initiatives, including rule-based governance of deficits.

The purpose is to provide a bird's-eye view of the public spending in India spanning a seven-decade period. The discussion is based on empirical policy studies that have provided some statistical analysis relating to the respective period and also the studies carried out by me from time to time.

3.3.1 Initial Years After Independence

Independent India's first budget for FY1947–48 was presented by Sri John Mathai.[5]The budgeted revenue was Rs.171.15 crores and the revenue expenditure was Rs.197.39 crores. The net deficit on revenue account[6] in the period covered by these estimates was Rs.26.24 crores. According to Premchand (1966, 125–6), government tried to shift expenditure from revenue account to capital account to show lesser deficit on revenue account during early years after India's independence. Giving an account of the pattern of financial control at the time of India's independence Premchand (1966) states, 'Most of the developmental activities were provided in the Revenue Budget. Though the Capital Budget was in existence, yet it was used mostly to divert a few items from the Revenue

[5] This discussion is largely based on the study of Premchand(1966)—For greater details, read Chapter 8: Aspects of Expenditure Policy. Discussion also uses budget speeches of the early years.

[6] Revenue deficit pertains to the difference between the revenue receipts and revenue expenditure.

Budget to the Capital Budget, so that the heavy deficit on the Revenue Budget could be reduced to tolerable limits'.

Counter Cyclical Fiscal Policy

Getting back to the discussion on public spending in the initial years of independence, one can clearly discern the awareness to apply countercyclical fiscal policy to ensure macroeconomic balance. The then budget speeches bear testimony to the same. Sri Shanmugam Chetty in his 1948–49 budget speech states, 'A view that has in recent years become almost unanimous among economists and financiers is that each year a Government's financial policy should be so planned as to rectify the economic maladjustments of the time, and to serve as a compensatory device to offset fluctuations in the private sector of economy. In a time of inflation, budgets should not only be balanced but there should be a comfortable surplus for mopping up the excess purchasing power and encourage economy in private spending. On the other hand, when a depression is on, Government should launch bold schemes of public expenditure if necessary' (Government of India, 1948, 3). Keynesian theories advocate a higher government spending, coupled with lower taxes, during a recession to help achieve economic recovery. The underlying reason is that higher government spending and lower tax rates help in boosting the aggregate demand upwards. The increase in public spending during recessions should be compensated by discretionary spending cuts during booms. Empirical literature has examined the effectiveness of countercyclical fiscal policy in the context of a number of countries. In the context of Asia, Jha et al. (2010)[7] examined the impact of tax cuts and government spending in stimulating the economic activity using historical data for ten Asian countries. Their results indicate that the impact of deficit spending is ambiguous, whereas that of the deficit financed tax cuts have stimulated economic activity leading to their conclusion that tax cuts may be a more effective countercyclical policy instrument than government spending.

In the Indian context, political statements apart, if one examines the fiscal policy in a historical perspective, although there have been

[7] See Jha et al.(2010) for detailed discussion on the effectiveness of countercyclical fiscal policy.

instances of significant increase in public spending and tax cuts during economic downturn of 2008 and the Covid-19-induced economic lockdown coupled with tax cuts, discretionary spending cuts during booms is not traced. If this countercyclical fiscal policy would have guided the country's public financial management all along, the country could have achieved a better fiscal space. The application or use of such policies should also be guided by an empirical verification of their practical utility rather than a blind replication used in other parts of the world. Jha et al. (2010) cite the work of Hemming et al. (2002) observing that industrialized countries have a longer tradition of using fiscal policy for countercyclical purposes than the developing Asian countries. Given the data deficiencies, it further states that there is no clear conclusion on the size and sign of fiscal multipliers in developing countries.

Economy/Prudence

The concern of the initial budgets was also more on achieving economy. The government appointed a committee under the Chairmanship of Sri Kasturbhai Lalbhai to suggest measures to ensure prudence and achieve economy in public spending. This thinking further gets reflected in the budget speeches. Sri Shanmugam Shetty, the then Finance Minister, in his 1948–49 budget speech stated, 'I feel it is the path of prudence to strengthen our revenue position and keep down our expenditure as much as possible' (Government of India, 1948, 25).

Perhaps in the only comprehensive study available on the aspects of public expenditure in the aftermath of the British rule, Premchand (1966, 248) identified the major factors that necessitated the adoption of economic measures by the Government of India. These included (i) the upsurge of national patriotism and opposition to the increasing debt incurred towards the payment of British forces maintained in the country to ensure 'law and order'; (ii) heavy expenditures and the continued post-war deficits; (iii) the existence of inflation in the economy and the persistent need to keep it under control through reduced public expenditures; (iv) the need to reduce expenditure on non-developmental purposes with a view to divert all the available resources for expenditure on development projects.

Public spending in the pre-independence era by the central government was largely on the non-development category (Table 3.1). The social

Table 3.1 Expenditure of Central Government on Revenue Account (Rs. Crores)

Years/Heads	1921–22	1936–37	1938–39	1950–51	1953–54 (RE)
Non-Development	104.03	74.94	76.02	295.02	331.78
Social Services	3.59	4.23	4.39	26.23	35.79
Economic Development	3.59	4.23	4.39	26.23	35.79
Total	109.93	80.91	82.03	335.87	388.78

Source: Premchand, 1966, p. 245.

Table 3.2 Developmental and Non-Developmental Expenditure of the Central and the State Governments

Heads/Years	1951–52	1955–56	1960–61	1961–62	1962–63 (RE)	1963–64 (BE)
Total Expenditure	998	1,470	2,563	2,808	3,440	4,157
Development Expenditure*	480 (48.1)	884 (60.1)	1,727 (67.3)	1,872 (66.6)	2,203 (64.1)	2,502 (60.1)
Non-Development Expenditure**	518 (51.9)	586 (39.9)	836 (32.7)	936 (33.4)	1,237 (35.9)	1,655 (39.9)

Source: Premchand, 1966, p. 246.

* Includes revenue and capital expenditure on development heads, loans and advances (net), and railways and P&T expenditure on expansion renewals and replacements, excludes working expenses of industrial and commercial undertakings.

** Excludes appropriation for reduction and avoidance of debt, transfers to special development fund and capital outlay on state trading.

Note: Figures in brackets indicate percentage to total expenditure.

services and economic development have revealed some signs of increase only after the independence. This got further strengthened by the closure of the second five-year plan, wherein the share of development spending (of the central and state governments) increased from 48.1% to 60.1% after reaching its peak at 67.3% in 1960–61, correspondingly the non-development expenditure has declined (Table 3.2).

3.3.2 Central Government Expenditure—Trends During 1974–75 to 1990–91

Central government expenditure has revealed major changes in the growth pattern characterized by a sharper growth in the revenue expenditure during the latter part of the period. The trends in nominal expenditure presented in Figure 3.3 clearly account for a sharper increase under both revenue and capital accounts after 1981–82; however, the gap between the revenue and capital expenditure was on a continuous rise marked by a continued and sharper increase in the revenue expenditure. Three distinct phases have been identified in the growth of public spending (Rao and Sen, 1993).Although the growth in expenditure was moderate until 1981–82, a more rapid growth was observed for both the revenue and capital expenditure till 1986–87, after which there was a sharp decline in the share of capital expenditure even when that of revenue expenditure remained stable.

The ratio of central government expenditure to GDP had increased from 12.52% in 1974–75 to 18.28%1990–91 (Figure 3.4). Although the share of revenue expenditure in GDP increased by 5.61% points, increasing from 7.15% to 12.76%, that of capital expenditure declined by 0.15% points, from 5.52% to 5.37%, during the above reference period. Further in terms of the composition of revenue and capital expenditure in the total expenditure, the sharper increase in the share of revenue

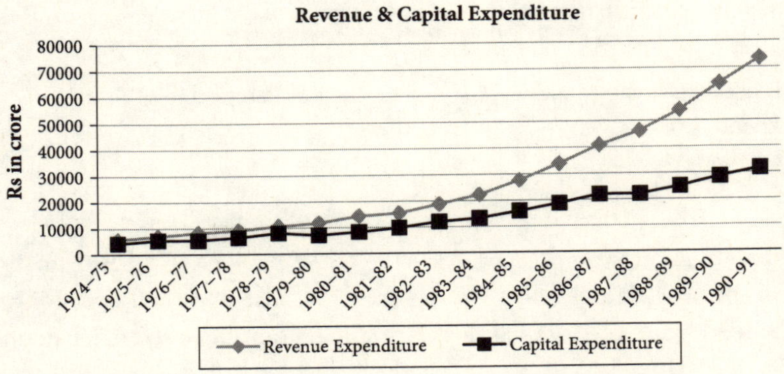

Figure 3.3 Nominal Growth in Revenue and Capital Expenditure
Source: RBI, 2004

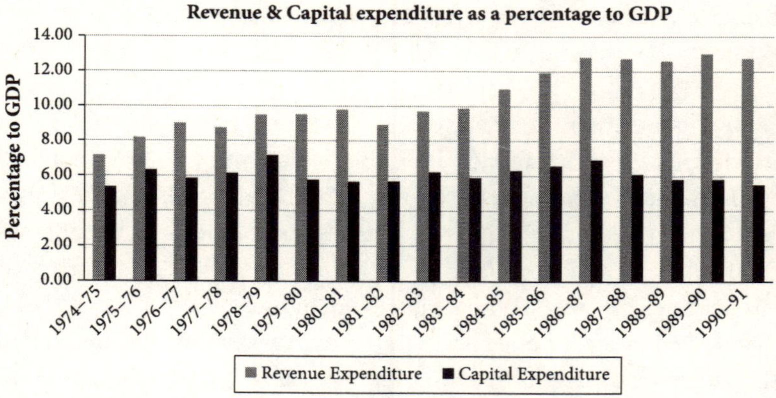

Figure 3.4 Revenue and Capital Expenditure as Percentage to GDP
Computed by the author.

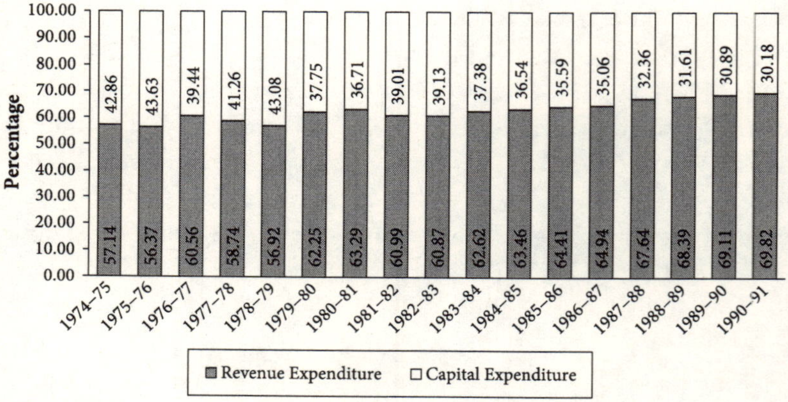

Figure 3.5 Revenue and Capital Expenditure as Percentage to Total Expenditure
Computed by the author.

expenditure from 57.14% in 1974–75 to 62% by 1979–80 and further to almost 70% in 1990–91.On the contrary, that of capital expenditure declined from 42.86% to almost 30% during the above reference period (Figure 3.5).

The increase in the share of interest payments in the total expenditure from about 11%in 1974–75 to 14% in 1981–82 and a further sharp increase to 21%in 1990–91 was a major factor responsible for the rapid growth in the share of revenue expenditure. Explaining this phenomenon Mundle and Rao (1992)stated, 'This must be attributed to both the increased volume of indebtedness to meet government consumption and investment requirements and increase in the effective rate of interest over the years. At the same time, even the past investments financed from borrowed funds did not yield adequate financial returns as the non-tax revenues, including interest receipts, were virtually stagnant during the 1980's.'

Functional Categories of Expenditure

Classification of government expenditure by functional categories indicates the functions for which the public money is expended, the broad categories being 'general', 'social and community', and 'economic' services. It was stated earlier, in Chapter 2, that in government parlance expenditure incurred on the social and community services and economic services is to be considered as development expenditure and that of general services is non-developmental expenditure. This inference is highly contentious as the final judgement of the usefulness of public spending pertaining to any category should be based on the effective achievement of the outcomes rather than on the nomenclature. Be that as it may, the actual distribution of expenditure by functional categories, i.e. 'general', 'social and community', and 'economic' services, revealed that the share of social and community services was very small and marginally increased from 3.6% in 1974–75 to 3.7% in 1990–91.The general services expenditure had a decline in share from 31.5% to 24.3% and that of economic services marginally declined from 25.5% to 24% during the above reference period (Table 3.3). The authors argued that the economic services expenditure increasingly was under the revenue account comprising of mainly subsidies and transfers. 'The share of subsidies increased from less than 10 per cent in 1974–75 to over 24 per cent in 1989–90 and that of transfers to individuals increased from 3.8 per cent to 7 per cent during this period'(Rao and Sen, 1993, 47).

Studies expressed concern over the then prevailing trends in public expenditure. Rapid growth in subsidies and transfers resulted in excess revenue expenditure over and above that of revenue receipts causing revenue deficits leading to reduced levels of capital investments. Interest

Table 3.3 Composition of Central Government Expenditure (Per Cent)

	Interest Payments	General Services	Social Services	Economic Services	Grants or Loans to States	Other Loans	Total Expenditure
(1)	(2)	(3)	(4)	(5)	(6)	(7)	(8)
Revenue Expenditure							
1974–75	17.2	44.4	5.0	15.1	18.3	—	100.0
1981–82	19.8	35.3	4.3	22.9	17.7	—	100.0
1986–87	22.1	33.4	4.5	21.5	18.5	—	100.0
1990–91	28.4	26.0	4.5	23.5	17.6	—	100.0
Capital Expenditure							
1974–75	—	6.9	0.9	45.0	18.7	28.5	100.0
1981–82	—	6.3	1.5	42.0	26.1	24.1	100.0
1986–87	—	13.2	2.7	37.2	24.3	22.6	100.0
1990–91	—	19.2	1.3	25.5	38.1	15.9	100.0
Total Expenditure							
1974–75	11.2	31.5	3.6	25.5	18.4	9.8	100.0
1981–82	13.2	25.6	3.4	29.3	20.5	8.0	100.0
1986–87	15.0	26.9	3.9	26.5	20.4	7.3	100.0
1990–91	21.2	24.3	3.7	24.0	22.8	4.0	100.0

Source: Rao and Sen, 1993, p. 45.

payments as percent to GDP increased from 1.37% in 1974–75 to 4% in 1990–91 (Table 3.4). Increased use of borrowed resources for consumption expenditure surfaced in 1979–80 at the central government level and in 1982–83; together for centre and states it reached 3% of GDP by 1990–91. (Rao and Sen, 1993). The authors emphasized the need to arrest the growth of revenue deficit and also lamented the fact that the government was not been able to effectively contain it.

Factors Determining the Trends and Pattern in Expenditure

Empirical research has addressed the issues guiding the trends and pattern and has also referred to the broad factors guiding the fiscal deterioration. Studies have mainly referred to the excessive spending resorted to by the government to gain political mileage. Fiscal decisions are best guided by the macroeconomic conditions prevailing in the country, but in practice, they are never devoid of political economy influences. Chatterjee (1997) stated, '[p]ublic finances were a shambles, after the "mindless spending spree in which Rajiv Gandhi and his men had indulged" (as cited in Corbridge and Harriss, 2000, 119–120). Inflation was high, foreign exchange reserves were low, and the fiscal deficit had doubled in the 1980s' (Dev and Mooij, 2002, 40).

Reflecting on the worsening situation of fiscal imbalances in the country, Rao and Sen account for the influence of special interest groups in the framing of fiscal decisions. They argue that fiscal corrective measures should have ideally addressed the reduction of the revenue deficit given its adverse macroeconomic impacts; on the contrary, the focus was on the reduction in the fiscal deficit owing to the International Monetary Fund (IMF) conditionality. It is stated that 'The manner of phasing out of fiscal imbalances while operating under the IMF conditionality provides ample testimony to the influence of special interest groups in determining fiscal decisions. At the outset, from the point of view of reducing inflationary potential in the economy, phasing out of governmental dissaving by cutting back unproductive spending and reducing revenue deficit should have received greater attention. Yet, emphasis was given to reducing fiscal deficit because it gave greater degree of freedom to the government to fulfil the conditionality. Thus, the government could fulfill the commitment to the IMF, not by reducing outlay on wages and salaries, subsidies and other transfer payments, but by cutting down capital

Table 3.4 Central Government Expenditure as a Percentage of GDP

(1)	Interest Payments	General Services	Social Services	Economic Services	Grants or Loans to States	Other Loans	Total Expenditure
	(2)	(3)	(4)	(5)	(6)	(7)	(8)
Revenue Expenditure							
1974–75	1.37	3.52	0.40	1.20	1.45	—	7.94
1981–82	2.00	3.57	0.44	2.32	1.79	—	10.12
1986–87	3.16	4.77	0.64	3.06	2.64	—	14.28
1990–91	4.00	3.70	0.65	3.35	2.50	—	14.25
Capital Expenditure							
1974–75	—	0.29	0.03	1.88	0.78	1.18	4.17
1981–82	—	0.32	0.08	2.13	1.33	1.22	5.07
1986–87	—	0.63	0.11	2.50	1.65	1.53	7.02
1990–91	—	0.94	0.06	1.24	1.85	0.78	4.87
Total Expenditure							
1974–75	1.37	3.81	0.43	3.08	2.23	1.18	12.10
1981–82	2.00	3.89	0.51	4.45	3.12	1.22	15.19
1986–87	3.16	5.66	0.82	5.58	4.29	1.53	21.04
1990–91	4.00	4.64	0.71	4.59	4.35	0.78	19.12

Source: Rao and Sen, 1993, p. 48.

Table 3.5 Central Government Revenues, Expenditures and Deficits as Percentages of GDP

	(Per Cent of GDP)						
		1990–91	1991–92	1991–92	1992–93	1992–93	1993–94
		(Actual)	(BE)	(Actual)	(BE)	(BE)	(BE)
	(1)	(2)	(3)	(4)	(5)	(6)	(7)
1	Revenue Expenditure	13.9	13.3	13.5	12.9	13.7	12.9
2	Capital Expenditure	6.0	5.3	4.8	4.2	4.3	3.7
3	Total Expenditure	19.9	18.6	18.3	17.1	18.0	16.6
4	Revenue Receipt	10.4	11.1	10.8	10.9	11.3	10.6
5	Capital Receipt	1.1	1.3	1.5	1.3	1.4	1.3
5.1	Of Which Disinvestment	—	0.4	0.5	0.4	0.5	0.4
6	Total Receipt	11.5	12.4	12.3	12.2	12.7	11.9
7	Revenue Deficit	3.5	2.3	2.7	2.0	2.4	2.2
8	Fiscal Deficit	8.4	6.2	6.0	5.0	5.3	4.7

Source: Rao and Sen, 1993, p. 59.

Notes: BE: budget estimates.

RE: revised estimates

expenditures on infrastructures, reducing transfers to State governments, selling public sector equity and transferring the surpluses of government enterprises, which could otherwise have been reinvested. Emphasising fiscal deficit reduction gave the Finance Ministry sufficient flexibility in fulfilling the stipulated targets without reducing the benefits going to dominant coalitions' (Rao and Sen, 1993, 59–60).

3.3.3 Post-Reform Scenario—Trends During 1991–92 Till 2003–04

India launched economic reforms in the year 1991 comprising of stabilization and structural adjustment measures in order to overcome the macroeconomic crisis the country faced in the 1990s. Fiscal deficit reduction was an important element of the fiscal stabilization programme. This was very essential in view of the huge fiscal deficit that the governments both at the centre and state levels had amassed over a period. It was as high as 10% of GDP and the rate of inflation, generally associated with high fiscal deficits, was 17% per annum. Rule-based fiscal deficit reduction was introduced by the framing of the FRBM Act in 2003–04, which came into force from the FY 2004–05. This section discusses the broad trends in deficits and the spending during the period 1990–91 till the framing of the FRBM Act. The gross fiscal deficit of the centre alone was as high as 7.85% of GDP in 1990–91, which has been brought down to 4.03% in 2004–05.Although the reduction in the fiscal deficit is laudable and in line with the overall fiscal objectives of the Government of India, the share of revenue deficit has been on the increase from 41.59% in 1990–91 to 79.71% in 2003–04 (Table 3.6), implying that the corrective measures have been increasingly sacrificing the capital investments made by the government. This trend, which had set in the previous phase itself, as discussed in the previous section, has got further accentuated during this phase.

In addition, the fiscal deficit reduction at the central government level is countered by an increased level of deficit at the state level, largely caused by a sharp decline in the net transfers to states as a proportion of the centre's receipts coupled with the states' own induced fiscal distress. Greater details of fiscal distress at the sub-national level are discussed in

Table 3.6 Trends in Central Government Deficits (Rs. Crores)

Years	Revenue Deficit	Fiscal Deficit	Revenue Deficit as a % of Fiscal Deficit
1991–92	16,261	36,325	44.77
1992–93	18,574	40,173	46.24
1993–94	32,716	60,257	54.29
1994–95	31,029	57,703	53.77
1995–96	29,731	60,243	49.35
1996–97	32,654	66,733	48.93
1997–98	46,449	88,937	52.23
1998–99	66,976	113,348	59.09
1999–00	67,596	104,716	64.55
2000–01	85,234	118,816	71.74
2001–02	100,162	140,955	71.06
2002–03	107,879	145,072	74.36
2003–04	98,261	123,273	79.71

Source: RBI (2005)

Chapter 4. A comparison of trends in revenue deficit at the centre and all states is presented in Figure 3.6. The growing fiscal burden at the level of state governments is revealed by the rapid growth in the revenue deficits at the level of state governments.

States have suffered a decline in the proportion of net transfers from the centre. Share of net transfers to states as a proportion of total receipts of the central government has declined (Table 3.7) from 33.3% in 1991–92 to 17.4% in 2003–04. States have also been increasingly contributing to the fiscal problems by way of their increased mismatch between resources and expenditure.

Broad Trends and Composition of Central Government Expenditure

The outpacing of the growth in government expenditure to that of government receipts continued to be a cause of considerable concern. This is more so on account of the fact that revenue expenditure has been growing faster than revenue receipts, thus causing revenue deficits. One cannot ascribe these developments entirely to the fiscal reform process in India as we had observed in the previous section that the growth in

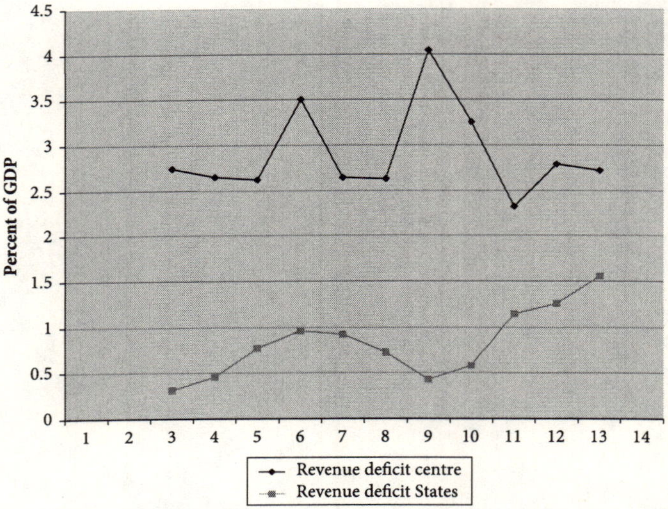

Figure 3.6 Revenue Deficits: Central and State Governments
Computed by the author.

Table 3.7 Net Transfer to the States

Years	Proportion to Centre's Receipts
1991–92	33.3
1992–93	32.4
1993–94	31.9
1994–95	32.6
1995–96	31.7
1996–97	32.7
1997–98	30.9
1998–99	23.6
1999–00	24.2
2000–01	26.1
2001–02	25.4
2002–03	22.1
2003–04	17.4

Source: Computed by the author using budget data.

revenue expenditure became sharper and also cut into the share of the capital expenditure. The trend analysis attempted in the present context for the period 1991–92 to 2003–04 reveals that the legacy of huge revenue deficits persisted and sharper decline is observed in the size of capital expenditure. Revenue expenditure has revealed a sharper increase (Figure 3.7) by 3.9 times, whereas that of capital expenditure has increased by 2.4 times. In addition, it has had a very sharp decline as a proportion of GDP from 5.59% to 3.95% during the above period (Table 3.8).

The percentage composition of total expenditure reveals that although the proportion of revenue expenditure has increased from 73.86% (1991–92) to 85.33% in 2000–01 but marginally decreased to 76.84% (2003–04), the share of capital expenditure has sharply declined from 26.14% to 14.67% in 2000–01, which subsequently increased to 23.16%during the above period (Figure 3.8).

However, the purpose of stating these facts is not to subscribe to the view that the entire revenue expenditure is wasteful and all capital expenditure is productive. These trends are disturbing due to the increased

Table 3.8 Trends in Central Government Expenditure (Rs. Crores)

Year	Revenue Expenditure	% to GDP	Capital Expenditure	% to GDP	Total Expenditure	% to GDP
1991–92	82,292	12.60	29,122	4.46	111,414	17.06
1992–93	92,702	12.39	29,916	4.00	122,618	16.38
1993–94	108,169	12.59	33,684	3.92	141,853	16.51
1994–95	122,112	12.06	38,627	3.81	160,739	15.87
1995–96	139,861	11.77	38,414	3.23	178,275	15.01
1996–97	153,933	11.25	42,074	3.08	201,007	14.69
1997–98	180,335	11.84	51,718	3.40	232,053	15.24
1998–99	216,461	12.43	62,879	3.61	279,340	16.04
1999–00	249,078	12.86	48,975	2.53	298,053	15.39
2000–01	277,839	13.30	47,753	2.29	325,592	15.58
2001–02	301,468	13.27	60,842	2.68	362,310	15.95
2002–03	338,713	13.75	74,535	3.03	413,248	16.78
2003–04	362,074	13.12	109,129	3.95	471,203	17.07

Source: RBI (2005) And author's computations.

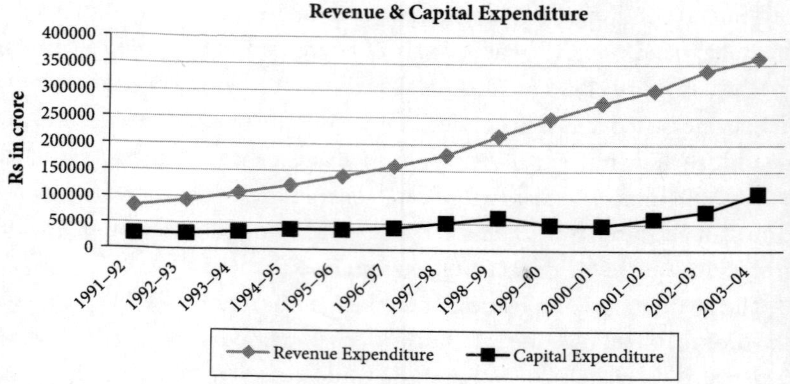

Figure 3.7 Growth in Revenue and Capital Expenditure
Plotted using RBI 2005.

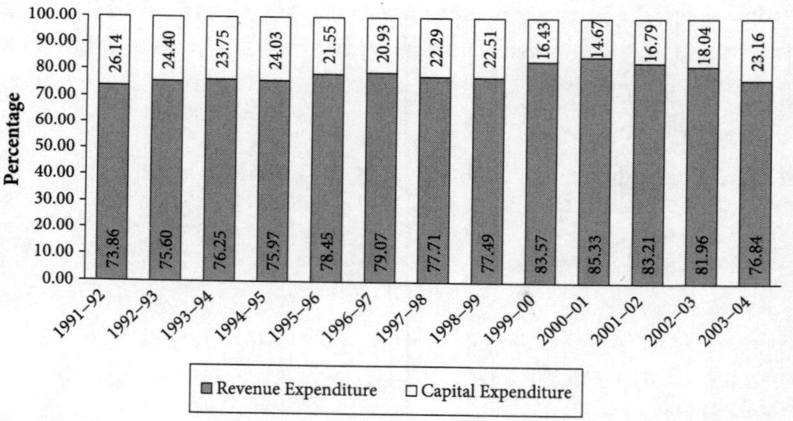

Figure 3.8 Composition of Expenditure by Revenue and Capital Expenditure
Computed by the author.

diversion of capital receipts to meet the growing revenue expenditure needs. A greater fiscal instability emerges from this on account of the mounting debt servicing liabilities caused by the diversion of capital investment funds. The governmental investment on infrastructure development got adversely affected due to the paucity of funds.

Economic Categories of Expenditure

The composition of expenditure by economic categories reveals that government expenditure is increasingly getting oriented towards transfer payments that too in the nature of current transfers. The data on economic categories presented in Table 3.9 reveals that the share of current transfers has increased from 43% in 1990–91 to 58.3% in 2003–04. Government consumption expenditure (comprising of compensation to employees and net government maintenance) and current transfers together have had a substantial increase from 64.3% in 1990–91 to 78.76%in 2003–04 (Table 3.9). The share of gross capital formation has declined from 8.19% to 5.63% and that of financial investment by the government has declined from 14.09% to 8.09% during the above reference period. A reference was made earlier to the study by Rao and Sen about the increasing nature of transfer payments characterized by subsidies even in the economic services.

Tanzi and Shome (1993) rightly observe that 'When on the one hand, a large part of the expenditures are explicitly or implicitly transfer payments to groups with high marginal propensity to consume and, on the other, infrastructural bottlenecks resulting from relative neglect by the government exist on the production side, low growth and inflation might be expected. If prices are attempted to be controlled either directly, or indirectly through administered prices, the inflationary tendencies crop up in the uncontrolled markets (e.g., rents, professional consultation fees etc.) or in the black economy (real estate prices, professional incomes, etc.), causing tax evasion and concomitant vicious circle of unfavorable effects' (as quoted in Shome et al., 1996).

These trends clearly account for the fact that fiscal deficit corrective measures have adversely affected productive investment, whereas wages and salaries and current transfers have continued to increase unabated. The Fifth Pay revision has enhanced the share of salaries and pensions from 17% of revenue receipts in 1995–96 to 21% in 1997–98.

Composition of expenditure by the development and non-development expenditure categories plotted in Figure 3.9 reveal that there has been a considerable increase in the share of non-development expenditure from 49.19% in 1991–92 to 55.46% in 2003–04, contrary to a decline in the share of the development expenditure.

Table 3.9 Economic Classification of Expenditure (Rs. Crores)

Year	Final Outlays			Transfer Payments to the Rest of the Economy			Financial Investments & Loans to Rest of the Economy (Gross)	Total Expenditure
	Govt. Consumption Expenditure	Gross capital Formation	Total	Current	Capital	Total		
1990–91	22,359	8,601	30,961	45,134	7,117	52,251	21,760	104,972
*	21.30	8.19	29.49	43.00	6.78	49.78	20.73	
1995–96	41,881	16,684	58,565	85,303	15,262	100,566	26,101	185,232
*	22.61	9.01	31.62	46.05	8.24	54.29	14.09	
1999–2000	68,831	26,074	94,906	161,548	20,481	182,030	30,572	307,509
*	22.38	8.48	30.86	52.53	6.66	59.20	9.94	
2003–04	87,169	23,996	111,166	248,436	32,038	280,474	34,490	426,131
*	20.46	5.63	26.09	58.30	7.52	65.82	8.09	

Note: * denotes percentage to total expenditure.

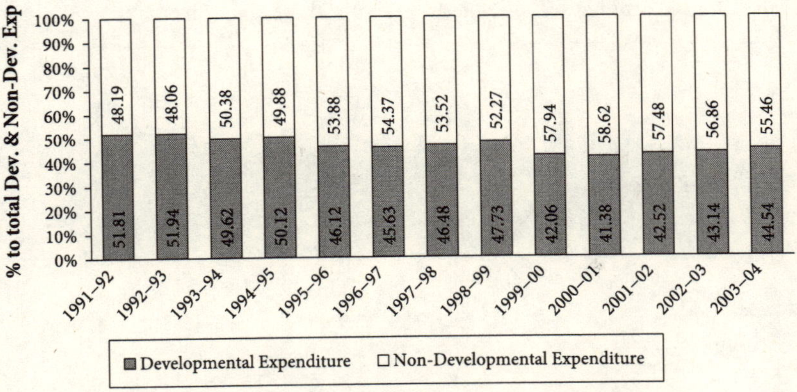

Figure 3.9 Composition of Expenditure by Development and Non-Development Categories
Computed by the author.

Trends in Non-Plan Expenditure

Composition of government expenditure by the plan and non-plan categories reveals that a major portion of the total expenditure is under non-plan category. Its share has also increased from 71.24% (1990–91) to 76.47% (2004–05). Main items under them are interest payments, defence, subsidies, etc. (Table 3.10). Non-plan expenditure is sticky downwards and thus cannot be compressed, unless the commitment itself is addressed.

The broad trends reveal that the central government expenditure during this phase is characterized by larger increases in the expenditure under categories such as revenue head, non-plan, non-developmental, and current transfer payments.

Corrective Measures

These trends discussed under the meaningful categories comprising of accounting, functional, economic, and development and non-development have revealed that government spending during this phase did raise many issues of concern. Dev and Mooij argue that, the Gandhian ideas did no longer appear in the budget speeches from 1993

Table 3.10 Composition of Non-Plan Expenditure (Rs. Crores)

	1990–91	1995–96	2000–01	2004–05
Interest Payments	21,498	50,045	99,314	126,934
*	27.94	37.94	40.88	34.74
Defence Expenditure	15,426	26,850	49,622	75,856
*	20.05	20.36	20.43	20.76
Subsidies	12,158	13,372	26,838	43,653
*	15.80	10.14	11.05	11.95
Grants to State and Union Territories	3,982	5,967	14,717	14,784
*	5.18	4.52	6.06	4.05
Loans and Advances to States and Union Territories	7,606	10,538	–140	612
*	9.89	7.99	–0.06	0.17
Others	16,263	25,123	47,083	64,799
*	21.14	19.05	19.38	17.73
A. Non-Plan Expenditure	76,933	131,901	242,923	365,406

*Indicates percentage share in total.

onwards but instead came a much larger emphasis on poverty alleviation schemes. Social sector expenditure became more important. There are extensive sections in the speeches explaining how additional budgetary support for the central plan makes it possible to increase the allocation for employment schemes, integrated rural development, health, and education. Referring to the populistic character in budget announcements, Dev and Mooij stated, 'One can hypothesise that from 1993 onwards; the Congress (I) government became aware that it had to face elections in a few years. The budget speeches became more populist' (Dev and Mooij, 2002, 45).

Discussing the fiscal correctives in the aftermath of economic reforms, Pattnaik et al. (2005) argue that 'the strategy of fiscal consolidation initiated in the early nineties was a mix of measures towards revenue augmentation through tax reforms and expenditure compression. Fiscal consolidation during the first half of the nineties was essentially achieved through expenditure containment due to a limited success in attaining larger revenue mobilisation. Notwithstanding the wide range of measures, the expenditure compression was mainly effected in the capital expenditure. Notably, the capital outlay of the centre declined from 3.0 per cent of GDP in 1986–87 to 2.1 per cent in 1990–91 and further to 1.0 per cent in 1996–97' (Pattnaik et al. 2005, 611).

There were some references made to these concerns by the government from time to time, the appointment of Expenditure Reforms Commission was an important measure taken.

While presenting the budget for 1999–2000, the Hon'ble Minister for Finance Mr Yashwant Sinha had observed that the high rate of growth of non-developmental expenditure by the government is a growing and critical source of concern.

Following initiatives were proposed in the budget speech:

> The most effective and lasting solution to this problem is to begin the process of downsizing Government. We are making an immediate beginning by abolishing four Secretary-level posts through a process of merger and rationalisation of Central Government departments. This will take effect on April 1, 1999.To carry this process forward in a systematic way towards reducing the role and the administrative structure of the Government, we will constitute an Expenditure Reforms Commission headed by an eminent and experienced person. In preparation for the next Budget, I propose to initiate a system of Zero Base Budgeting (Government of India, 1999).

Accordingly, the Government of India hereby set up an Expenditure Reforms Commission with Sri K.P. Geethakrishanan, as the Chairman.

The terms of reference of the Expenditure Reforms Commission included the following (Government of India, 2000):

- Keeping in view the evolving role of government, the need to foster convergence and avoiding overlap in the functions of different central government ministries, departments, and attached organisations and the role of the state governments, suggest a road map for reducing the functions, activities, and administrative structure of the central government;

- Review the framework of all subsidies, both explicit and implicit, examine the economic rationale for their continuance and make recommendations for making subsidies transparent and suggest measures for maximizing their impact on the target population at a minimum cost;
- Review the framework for determination of user charges of departmental and commercial entities and suggest an effective strategy for cost recovery through user charges;
- Review the adequacy of staffing under central government ministries, attached offices and institutions and suggest measures for rationalizing the staff and cadres of different services. In this context also review the existing arrangements for re-deployment and re-training of surplus staff to ensure that any additional manpower for new areas of government activities are met by re-deployment;
- Review the procedure for setting up of government funded autonomous institutions and their pattern of funding and suggest measures for effecting improvement and reducing budgetary support for their activities;
- Consider any other relevant issue concerning expenditure management in government and make suitable recommendations

Among the key measures Expenditure Reforms Commission examined were issues of rationalization of fertilizer subsidies through phased dismantling of controls, a ceiling on government staff strength through a two-year ban on new recruitment, introduction of voluntary retirement scheme, and redeployment of surplus staff. Endeavour was also made to promote transparency and curb growth in contingent liabilities by setting up the Guarantee Redemption Fund. As a part of these efforts, Administered Price Mechanism (APM) in the petroleum sector was dismantled from April 2002, restriction of fresh recruitment to 1% of total civilian staff strength over the four years was placed from 2002–03, and a new pension scheme of defined contribution for new recruits was introduced from 2003–04 (Pattnaik et al., 2005, 611).

3.3.4 Trends in Government Spending: FRBM and Beyond

The enactment of the FRBM Act in 2003–04 by the central government followed by many state governments[8] has played an important role in the fiscal operations of the Indian governments both at the central and subnational levels. The fiscal rules to rein in the fiscal and revenue deficit targets in a time-bound manner had great implications on the growth and composition of government spending. In addition to FRBM, the recommendations of various finance commissions too had considerable implications on the finances of the central and state governments; however, the focus in the following discussion will be mainly on the public spending.

Trends in Fiscal Deficit

Fiscal deficit reduction was an important element of the fiscal stabilization programme initiated in the year 1991 along with the structural reforms; however, we noticed in the previous section that fiscal deficit reduction could not be achieved in a sustained manner. The FRBM Act had mandated a gradual reduction in the same. The gross fiscal deficit of the centre alone which was as high as 7.8% of GDP in 1990–91 (noticed earlier) was brought down to 4.1% in 2005–06 (Table 3.11). This trend got reversed with the global recession in 2008, owing to the stimulatory fiscal measures announced by the government, such as enhanced public spending and lowering of tax rates causing a rise in the level of fiscal deficit. Although the then ruling government claimed that the rise in fiscal deficit was on account of the fiscal stimulus provided by the central government to revive the economy from recessionary trends, studies argued that the reversal was more on account of structural factors than the stimulus (Rao, 2015). Increase in expenditure after 2007–08 is argued to be on revenue account caused by election decisions to revise pay scales of government employees, farm loan waiver, and expansion of rural employment guarantee programme from 200 districts to the entire country.

[8] The Karnataka state had framed the Fiscal Responsibility Act prior to that of central government in 2002–03.

Table 3.11 Trends in Central Government Fiscal Deficit

Years	Fiscal Deficit (Crores)	Fiscal Deficit as % of GDP
2005–06	146,435	4.10
2010–11	373,591	4.79
2015–16	532,791	3.87
2016–17	535,618	3.48
2017–18	591,062	3.46
2018–19	649,418	3.42
2019–20 (RE)	766,846	3.77

Source: RBI (2020)

The fiscal consolidation debate has two strong points of view—one supporting enhanced fiscal deficit level in support of growth-augmenting investments and another strong point of view desisting such increase owing to its potential adverse macroeconomic impacts. The N.K. Singh committee has laid down a road map for fiscal consolidation by 2022. Trends in fiscal deficit are presented in Table 3.11. There has been a slippage from the target set for 2017–18 and 2018–19 caused by revenue shortfalls on account of GST. Even though the effort to reduce the fiscal deficit is laudable and in line with the overall fiscal objectives of the Government of India, the share of revenue deficit has been on the increase from 41.59% in 1990–91 to 75.05% in 2017–18, marginally declining to 65.14% (2019–20 RE) (Table 3.12), thereby implying that the corrective measures have been increasingly sacrificing the capital investments made by the government.

Broad Trends and Composition of Central Government Expenditure: Post-FRBM

The outpacing of the growth in government expenditure to that of government receipts has been causing considerable concern. This is more so on account of the fact that revenue expenditure has been growing faster than revenue receipts, thus causing revenue deficits. The trend analysis attempted in the present section during the post-FRBM period reveals that the legacy of huge revenue deficits persisted and sharper decline is

Table 3.12 Share of Revenue Deficit in Fiscal Deficit

Years	Revenue Deficit (Crores)	Fiscal Deficit (Crores)	Revenue Deficit as Percent of Fiscal Deficit
2005–06	92,299	146,435	63.03
2010–11	252,252	373,591	67.52
2015–16	342,736	532,791	64.33
2016–17	316,381	535,618	59.07
2017–18	443,600	591,062	75.05
2018–19	454,483	649,418	69.98
2019–20 (RE)	499,544	766,846	65.14

Source: RBI (2020).

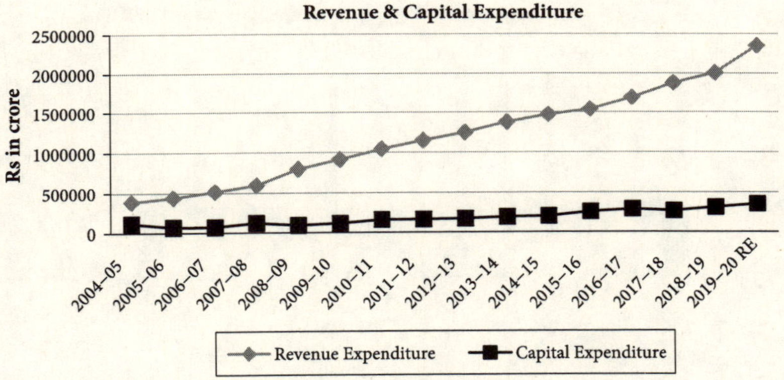

Figure 3.10 Trends in Revenue and Capital Expenditure

observed in the size of capital expenditure. The sharper nominal growth in the revenue expenditure from 2007–08 compared to that of capital expenditure is clear from Figure 3.10. Further its share in the total expenditure increased from 77.14% in 2004–05 to 87.07% in 2019–20 RE, whereas that of capital expenditure decreased from 22.76% to 12.93% during the above reference period (Figure 3.11). Revenue expenditure has had a decreased share in GDP from 12.06% (2004–05) to 11.55% (2019–20 R.E), whereas that of capital expenditure has recorded a shaper decrease from 3.56% (2004–05) to 1.72% (2019–20 R.E) (Figure 3.12).

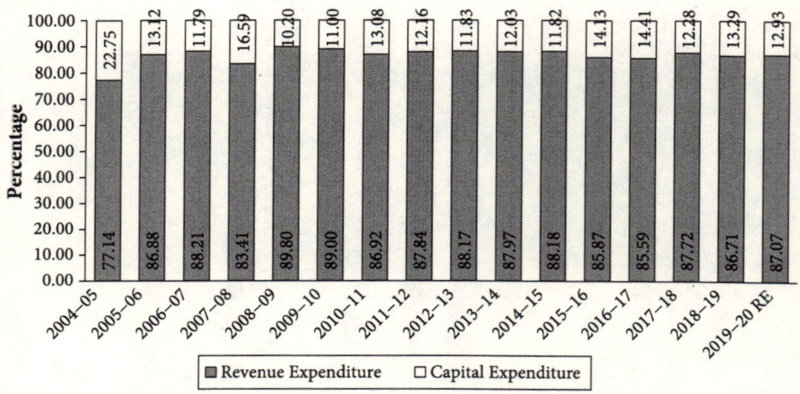

Figure 3.11 Composition of Revenue and Capital Expenditure
Computed by the author

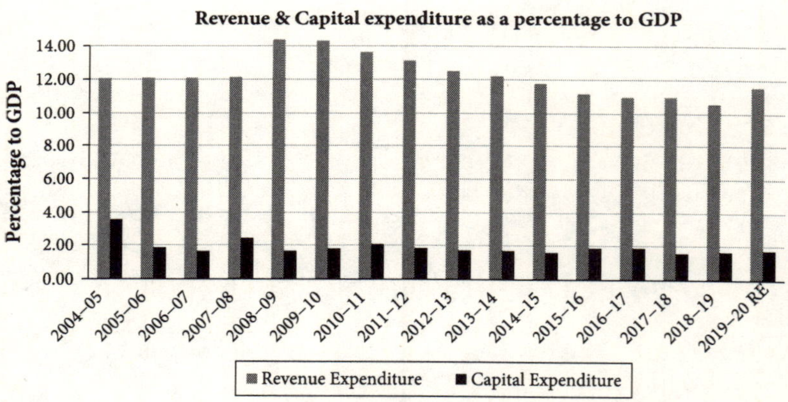

Figure 3.12 Revenue and Capital Expenditure as Percent to GDP
Computed by the author

The limited fiscal space available for capital expenditure due to a very large persisting share of the revenue expenditure is revealed in Figure 3.13.

The reduction in the relative growth and its share in the total expenditure is of concern given the larger multiplier effects of capital spending and its capacity to crowd in private investment as and when the government's capital investments occur in productive infrastructure areas, such as roads and bridges, irrigation, education, and health. These

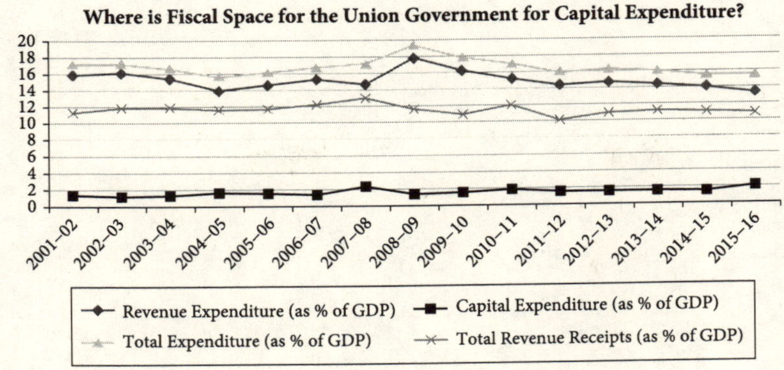

Figure 3.13 Fiscal Space for the Capital Expenditure
Source: Mukherjee (2019), p. 21.

investments enhance the productive capacity of the economy through the provision of infrastructure and capital goods. It is unfortunate that the impact of resource crunch and the need for fiscal correction have more often been in the form of compression of capital outlays (Pattnaik et al., 2005, 620).

Further tracing the historical changes in the profile of capital investments Pattnaik et al. (2005) observe that 'since the early years of independence, the investment profile has considerably changed. While in the earlier periods, direct capital formation from central budget used to be the norm, gradually the capital expenditure shifted to the states, Central Public Sector Enterprises, and other parastatals, changing the nature of government investment from direct creation of physical assets to financial assets in the form of equity and loans. Equity investments have also progressively declined as the Public Sector Enterprises gradually began to finance their capital expenditure by raising resources directly from the market. The process received a further boost when in 1993 the government switched over to the policy of "disintermediation" of external assistance to central PSEs under which central PSEs are now allowed to access external funding directly rather than through the central budget. These developments have contributed to a decline in capital expenditure/investment of the central government' (Government of India, 2005, as cited in Pattnaik et al., 2005,621).

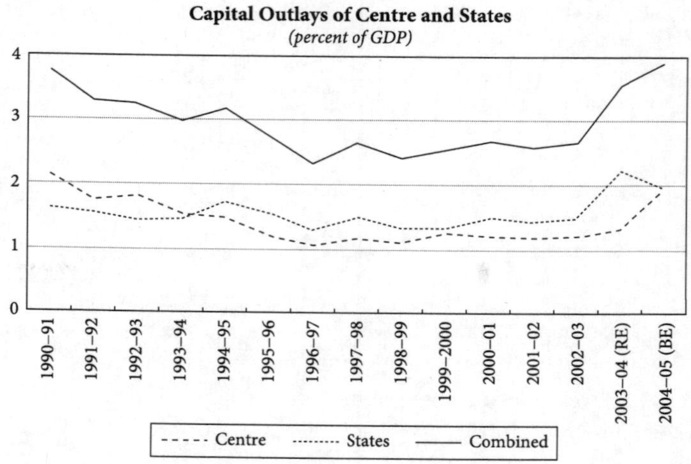

Figure 3.14 Capital Outlays of the Centre and States
Source: Pattnaik etal. (2005), p. 621.

Combined capital outlays of centre and states as percent of GDP is presented in Figure 3.14.

However, the purpose of stating these facts is not to subscribe to the view that the entire revenue expenditure is wasteful and all capital expenditure is productive. These trends are disturbing due to the increased diversion of capital receipts to meet the growing revenue expenditure needs. Greater fiscal instability emerges from this on account of the mounting debt servicing liabilities caused by the diversion of capital investment funds. The governmental investment on infrastructure development is getting adversely affected due to the paucity of funds. The deceleration in infrastructure investment during the reform phase will have serious setback to investment prospects. The problem has been further compounded, as the much-awaited private investment in infrastructure development has not come forth in adequate quantity, despite many concessions. It is also disturbing to note that whatever private investment has taken place is more in the areas that have commercial viability, which is quite obvious, and that private investments are guided by profit motive. A recent study (Anantharamu and Gayithri, 2017) has revealed that although there is excess investment in certain sectors like telecom, road, and power by the private sector, there is dearth of investment in rural

Table 3.13 Sector-Wise Projections and Actual Infrastructure Investments in the Eleventh Plan Period (INR billion, 2006–07 Prices)

Sector	Eleventh Plan	
	Projections	Investment (%)
Electricity (incl. NCE)	6,665.25	6,346.13 (95%)
Roads & Bridges	3,141.52	3,618.22 (115%)
Telecommunications	2,584.39	3,359.32 (130%)
Railways (incl. MRTS)	2,618.08	1,954.22 (75%)
Irrigation (incl. Watershed)	2,533.01	1,956.88 (77%)
Water Supply& Sanitation	1,437.30	962.49 (67%)
Ports (incl. Inland Waterways)	879.95	347.73 (40%)
Airports	309.68	292.82 (95%)
Oil & Gas Pipelines	168.55	468.51 (278%)
Storage	223.78	142.03 (63%)
Total	20,561.50	19,447.96 (95%)

Source: Anantha Ramu and Gayithri (2017).
NCE- Non-Conventional Energy
MRTS- Mass Rapid Transit System

infrastructure, sanitation, and rural water supply (Table 3.13). These are typically the areas that the government has to invest as the private sector shies away from such investments. Studies have also proved that public spending on social and physical infrastructures, besides being low, is beset with poor productivity (Rao, 2015). The declining capital investments by the government will have serious adverse implications for the development of sectors with infrastructure deficit.

N.K. Singh emphasizes the predominant role of government in the provisioning of infrastructure—'First we need to recognize that the State must accept the dominant responsibility on infrastructure. Private participation is not a substitute to the obligation of the state. Public–private partnership needs basic restructuring. Excessive reliance on such arrangements has limited value' (Singh, 2009, 252). However, it does make considerable sense to rely on private sector provisioning even if it so happens that private sector ventures only into areas that get them commercially viable, albeit stringently regulated, it enables the government to use its scarce resources for providing services such as rural infrastructure, where the responsibility largely lies with the government. IMF suggests that decline in public capital stock in advanced and emerging market economies has to be gradually arrested to avoid adverse effects on long-term growth and welfare. 'Slowing this decline would require more-productive public investment or increased private sector participation, including through public–private partnerships with appropriate safeguards and changes in the regulatory framework for private participation. In emerging market economies and low income countries, where infrastructure gaps remain large, in addition to raising investment, improving the efficiency of public investment is crucial to help'(IMF, 2014, 24).

A sector-by-sector review is needed to arrive at the distribution of responsibility between the public and private sectors in developing the sector-specific infrastructure. Commenting on the role of government vis-à-vis that of private sector in the context of higher education, Basu states, 'It is true that the private sector will typically come into areas which are commercially viable, such as business and finance education, engineering, medicine and some areas of economics. There is nothing wrong with this. In fact, this will allow government to allocate its precious money to disciplines that are important for society in the long run but may not be commercially viable, such as mathematics, physics, economic theory, philosophy and literature and also to support poor students with grants and fellowships. Freed of a large part of the burden it currently bears quite unnecessarily it will be able to do the other tasks more effectively' (Basu, 2016,180).

Economic Categories of Expenditure

The composition of expenditure by economic categories revealed that government expenditure is increasingly becoming transfer oriented, more so in the nature of current transfers. Although the gross capital formation has had a decline from 6.87% (2005–06) to 6.34% (2015–16) and capital transfers have had a substantial increase from 8.3% in 2005–06 to 12.9% in 2010–11 and declined to 7.78% in 2015–16 BE, the share of financial investments and loans to the rest of the economy increased from 2.27% to 5.39% and declined to 2.73%, respectively, during the above reference period (Gayithri, 2018). This growth in government expenditure, which is turning out to be largely in the nature of transfer payments, can have adverse macroeconomic implications. Rao (2015, 65) states '... over the years, there has been significant increase in transfers such as for employment guarantee and food security, national housing scheme, apart from periodic loan waivers and recapitalization of banks to meet capital adequacy norms.'

Tanzi and Shome (1993) rightly observe that 'When on the one hand, a large part of the expenditures are explicitly or implicitly transfer payments to groups with high marginal propensity to consume and, on the other, infrastructural bottlenecks resulting from relative neglect by the government exist on the production side, low growth and inflation might be expected. If prices are attempted to be controlled either directly, or indirectly through administered prices, the inflationary tendencies crop up in the uncontrolled markets (e.g., rents, professional consultation fees etc.) or in the black economy (real estate prices, professional incomes, etc.), causing tax evasion and concomitant vicious circle of unfavorable effects' (as quoted in Shome et al., 1996).

The composition of expenditure by the development and non-development expenditure categories plotted in Figure 3.15 reveals that there has been a considerable increase in the share of non-development expenditure contrary to a decline in the share of the development expenditure especially after 2014–15.

The period 2004–05 till 2019–20 (RE) was marked by a much sharper increase in the general services expenditure. The economic services expenditure also showed increasing trend, but that of social services was very negligible (Figure 3.16). In terms of percentage composition, the

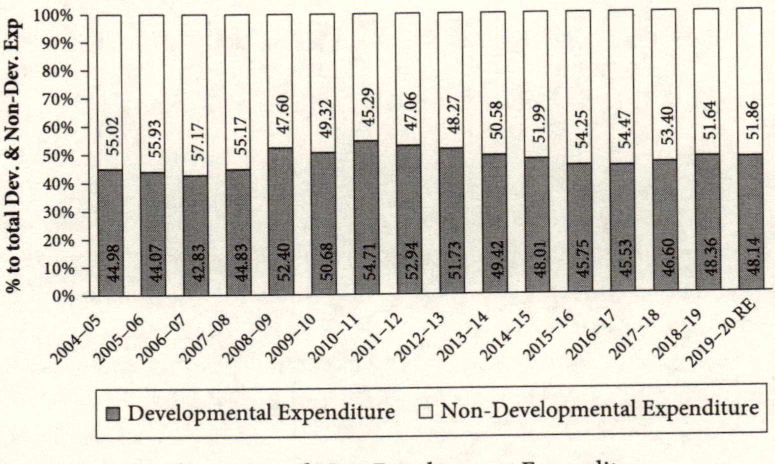

Figure 3.15 Development and Non-Development Expenditure

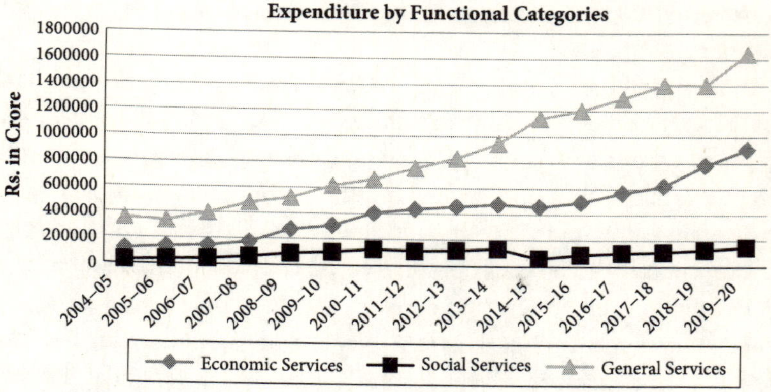

Figure 3.16 Expenditure by Functional Categories

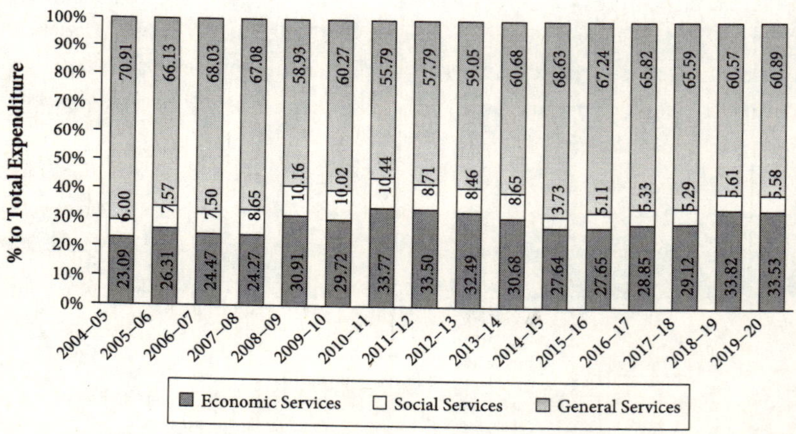

Figure 3.17 Composition of Functional Categories of Expenditure
Computed by the author

largest share is that of general services followed by the economic services and disappointingly the percentage share of social services has had a decline (Figure 3.17). Its share in GDP was less than 1% during most of the years (Figure 3.18).

The broad trends reveal that the central government expenditure during the last few years is characterized by a large increase in the expenditure under categories such as revenue head, non-plan,

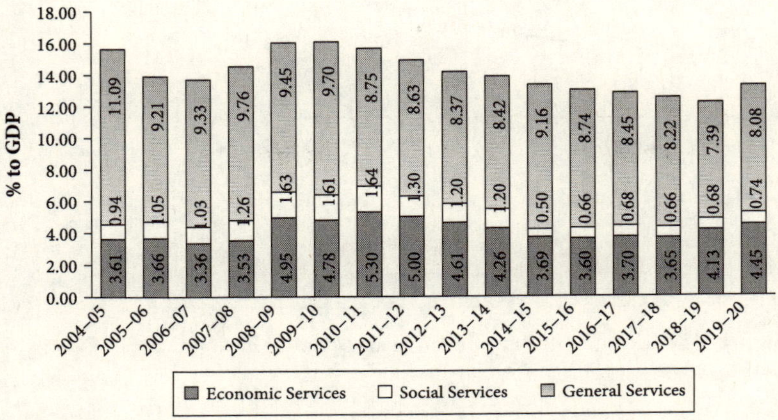

Figure 3.18 Functional Categories of Expenditure as Percent to GDP
Source: computed by the author

non-developmental, and current transfer payments. Inadequate and low levels of spending on social services and physical infrastructure are key concerns. There are concerns expressed about not merely the low allocations to social services and physical infrastructure but also the poor quality of spending leading to ineffectiveness of public expenditure (Rao, 2015).

3.3.5 Overall Trends: 1974–75 Till 2019–20 (RE)

Analysis of the trends in three phases together as presented in Figures 3.19–3.21 reveal that the declining trends in the share of capital expenditure, more or less stagnant share for the social sector have been observed all along. The much talked about corrective measures to the declining capital investments, social sector investments, and development expenditure as announced in various budget speeches or other policy forums have remained rhetoric. Dr Manmohan Singh outlined major fiscal reform initiatives in the 1991–92 budget speech and emphasised on the need to reduce fiscal, and revenue deficits. It is stated 'In the macromanagement of the economy, over the medium-term, it

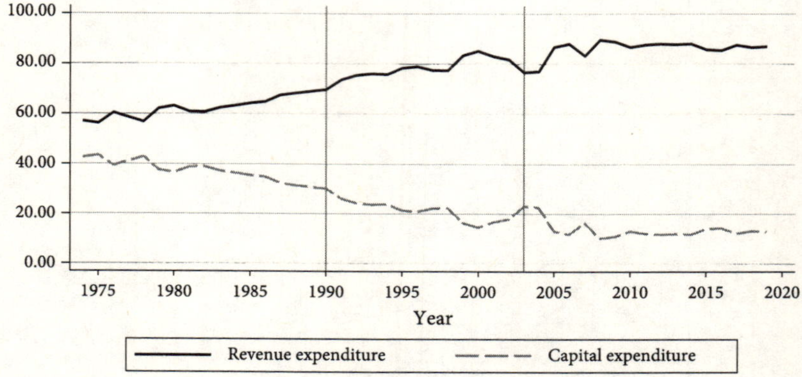

Figure 3.19 Composition of Revenue and Capital Expenditure
Computed by the author.

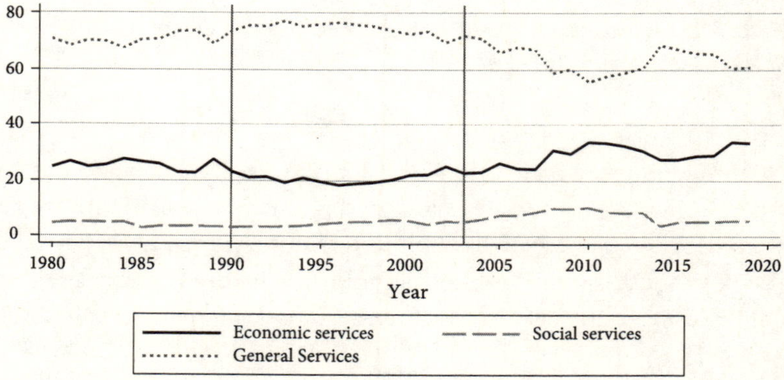

Figure 3.20 Composition of Functional Categories of Expenditure
Computed by the author.

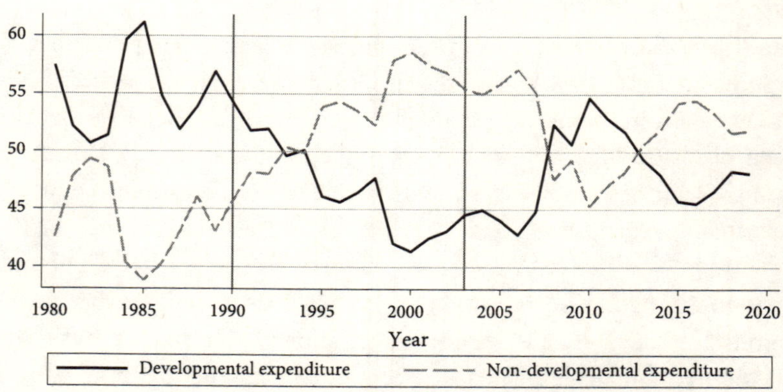

Figure 3.21 Composition of Development and Non-Development Expenditure
Computed by the author.

should be our objective to progressively reduce the fiscal deficit of the Central Government, to move towards a significant reduction of the revenue deficit, and to reduce the current account deficit in the balance of payments' (1991,8). There have been references to having the entire expenditure reviewed; Mr Chidambaram states in his 2005–06 budget speech 'We shall also ensure that programmes and schemes are not allowed to continue indefinitely from one Plan period to the next without an independent and in-depth evaluation ... We must use this opportunity to improve the fiscal health of the country. We must increase our revenues and reorient expenditure to pay for more outlays on education, health and infrastructure' (Government of India 2005, 22). In the current budget 2021–22, Mrs Nirmala Sitharaman too referred to review government programmes (Government of India, 2021a). Such statements are plenty; however, what is hard to find is any concrete and effective action plan put in place.

The discussion on the central government expenditure presented above has highlighted the deterioration in the quality of public spending from one phase to another. The concerns that guided the policy formulation in the initial years of independence to achieve economy and enhance effectiveness have withered away over time and increasingly the focus has shifted to spend more to gain public support. There has been growing eagerness to announce more and more new schemes with token allocations, oftentimes governments also have resorted to giving new names to old schemes. This tendency is more prominent during election times. The lack of seriousness gets reflected in the execution of schemes leading to poor translation of outlays to outcomes.

Inadequate control and monitoring of the government expenditure has resulted in practices like bunching of expenditure towards the last quarter of the FY. In order to ensure proper returns from government expenditure, there is need for proper monitoring of its growth. Quarterly monitoring of the departmental expense will put a stop to the present practices of rushing through the spending in the last quarter of the year. These practices exist in countries like the United Kingdom, (cash limits), Canada (envelope system), Japan (scrap and burn), and New Zealand (tit for tat), which are aimed at apportioning spending every quarter (Premchand, 1983, 281).

3.4 Corrective Measures

Given the increased public spending by the governments, both at the central and state government levels (discussed in Chapter 4), there is need to ensure allocative and technical efficiency to attain the desired results of public spending.

In doing so, the first important task is to take a fresh look at the governmental role and responsibilities. In the name of structural adjustment programme, there has been a considerable discussion about the role of state and the need to redefine the same. Basu aptly states, 'One mistake early Indian policy makers made was to try to micromanage the economy. While it is true that the government needs to attend to a range of policies, from shaping the quality of education in villages to managing the nation's international economic relations, it is imperative to realize that it is not feasible for the government to attend to all the varied and layered needs of society with equal diligence' (Basu, 2016, 68). Despite the fiscal reform process in India, the government has still not clearly defined its role, being fully aware of the fact that the past over-extension of government without an adequate backing of the resource growth has been mainly responsible for the present problems. The government has not effectively shed down some of its responsibilities that the private sector should be taking on. There is no justification whatsoever for direct participation of the government in areas such as hotel business, fertilizers, air lines, and textiles just to name a few. Government efforts to privatize some of these have not met with success.

About the programmes under various departments, there is a need for a comprehensive review of the role of government in the changing context. 'It is important to realize that no single entity, not even one as large as the state, should try to deliver it all. Instead its aim should be to create the right macroeconomic environment, where individuals with different talents, knowledge and enterprise can flourish. This is not to deny that the state must provide public goods for its citizens, help build infrastructure and also carry out redistributive functions in favor of the poor and the disadvantaged. But one of its central functions has to be to create a stable macroeconomic environment, where ordinary people's talent and enterprise can flourish' (Basu, 2016, 68). As a first step, the government should redefine its role and confine itself to some core activities. This however is easier said than done. Deciding as to what the core activities that help maximize the social welfare should be based on a comprehensive review of the existing programmes and ensure adequate private sector participation in the gaps left by the government. Core functions of a government vary from one country to another and even from one state to another and from time to time depending on the nature of societal needs. An illustrative list of activities by which governments can enhance the economic and social welfare by participating is given below, but strictly they should not be limited to these but should be guided by a periodical review of societal needs and priorities.

- An effective fiscal management that would prevent serious imbalances and ensure macroeconomic stabilization, an important fiscal function assigned to the governments by Musgrave
- Provision of internal and external security
- Regulation of private sector activity
- Ensure distributive justice by alleviating poverty and provision of basic minimum needs to the vulnerable sections of the society
- Provision of basic social and economic infrastructure

> Highlighting the importance of a proper diagnosis, Sachs has advocated a new method called 'clinical economics', to underscore the similarity between good development economics and good clinical medicine. It has been argued that the contemporary problems of poverty and human development call for 'clinical' solutions where the policy measures are taken on the basis of proper diagnosis (as cited in Pattnaik et al., 2005).

It is very important to decide on the appropriate size of public expenditure in the first instance. In India, it is generally assumed that compression of non-plan expenditure, which constitutes a very big share in the total expenditure, is difficult in view of its stickiness downwards. However, reforms in the budgeting practices from one of the current incremental budget to a suitable form of performance-based budgeting can certainly help in containing a routine increase in the size of public expenditure.

4

Trends in Sub-National Expenditure and Development Outcomes

State governments in India account for over 60% of total expenditure in the country (Rao, 2017). They also shoulder greater responsibility in providing social services. 'In the Indian federal polity the Constitution assigns the responsibility of providing important social and economic services to the State governments. In 1990–91, the States spent about 54 per cent of total expenditures incurred; their share in government expenditure on social services was close to 85 per cent and in the case of economic infrastructure about 55 per cent. Besides ensuring law and order and providing social and economic infrastructure, the States have an important role in ameliorating the condition of the poor as well' (Rao and Sen, 1993, 64).

There have been significant changes in the trends and composition of public spending at the sub-national level. Fiscal position of the states has also undergone changes from time to time, experiencing a rollercoaster ride. States moved from revenue surplus position to deficit and suffered severe fiscal distress during the eighties and nineties. The fiscal reforms introduced in the decade of 2000–09 aided in fiscal recovery and reduction of revenue deficit.

Broad trends in the state-level spending presented in this chapter largely pertain to 'all states' and the major issues relating to the trends and composition. The discussion is structured to reflect the major changes that have occurred. This discussion is based on studies that have attempted to analyse the state-level expenditures from time to time.

A detailed discussion of sub-national government spending in India is structured into three different phases guided by the policy regimes and major fiscal developments on the analysis presented for the central

Public Expenditure in India. Gayithri Karnam, Oxford University Press. © Oxford University Press 2022.
DOI: 10.1093/oso/9780192857569.003.0004

government in Chapter 3 to compare and contrast the finances at the two levels.

1. The first phase pertains to fiscal expansionary phase starting from 1974–75 till 1990–91. This period also resulted in high fiscal and revenue deficits, and by 1991, the country had to announce major structural adjustment and stabilization measures.
2. Analysis pertaining to the period 1990–91 till the framing of the FRBM Act by the central government relates to the second phase. This period was marked by uncontained deficits despite conditionalities attached by the international agencies to gradually reduce the fiscal deficit to 3%.
3. The third phase pertains to post-FRBM till date. This period was marked by a number of fiscal reform initiatives, including rule-based governance of deficits.

4.1 Broad Trends: 1974–75 to 1990–91

The 'all states' expenditure experienced a very sharp increase predominantly on the revenue account, whereas that of capital expenditure had a marginal increase in nominal terms between 1974–75 and 1990–91 (Figure 4.1).[1] However, in terms of their respective shares in the GDP

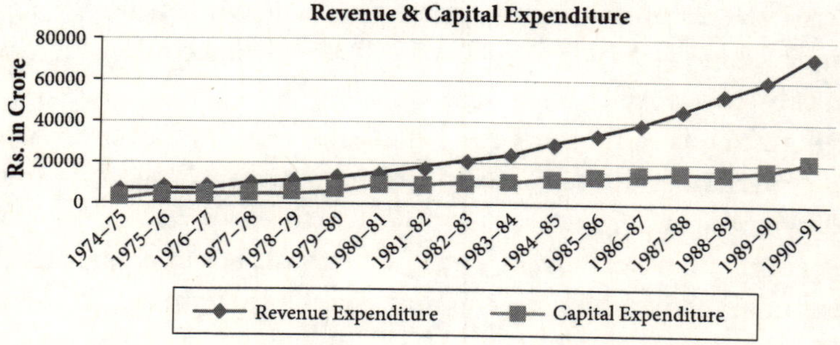

Figure 4.1 Growth of Government Expenditure (All States)
Source: RBI (2004).

[1] See the report by Rao and Sen (1993) for a detailed discussion on trends in state-level expenditure.

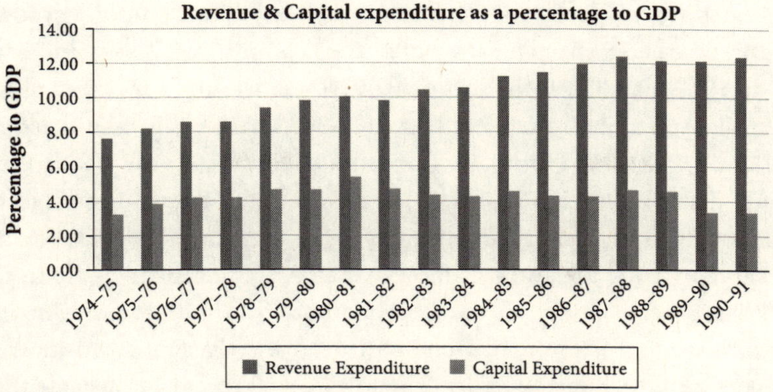

Figure 4.2 Revenue and Capital Expenditure as Percent of GDP (All States)
Source: Computed by the author using RBI (2004).

(Figure 4.2),although that of revenue expenditure had a continuous increase with the exception of a marginal dip after 1987–88, which quickly got back to the 1987–88 level, that of capital expenditure declined to 4.35%in 1990–91 after reaching its peak of 5.34% in 1980–81.

A detailed analysis of trends in expenditure for fourteen major states was presented in the study of state finances by Rao and Sen(1993). The study points out a number of issues such as a sharper increase in the revenue expenditure as compared to that of capital expenditure, owing to the rapid increase in items of expenditure pertaining to wages and salaries, subsidies, etc. The rates of growth computed by the study reveal that the per capita total expenditure of the states grew steadily throughout the seventeen-year period, despite the capital expenditure remaining stagnant during the eighties, which implies that the steady growth was largely guided by the growth in the revenue expenditure.

State-level expenditure did not follow the time pattern observed in the case of aggregate as well as central government expenditures (the details of central government spending were discussed in Chapter 3). Public expenditure in the states increased at a faster pace in the latter half of the seventies, but there was a deceleration in the decade of eighties whereas, in the case of the central and aggregate government expenditures, there was a significant fiscal expansion during 1981–82 to 1986–87.

The ratio of government expenditures to state domestic product (SDP) revealed a sharp increase of over 6% points from 12.8% in 1974–75 to 19% in 1980–81, the subsequent growth was not very rapid as the increase was only by 2.5% points in 1990–91 with the ratio reaching 21.5% in 1990–91 (Table 4.1). The authors, based on these trends, conclude that with reference to the states, the entire decade of the eighties was a period of fiscal restraint. Stating the factors responsible for the observed trends the authors observe that 'A significant increase in tax devolution consequent to the implementation of the Seventh Finance Commission's recommendations improved their resource position in the early Eighties, enabling the expenditures to grow at a faster rate than that was seen in previous years. The pressure to increase expenditures on quasi-public goods, subsidies and transfers continued to persist following the high expenditure growth at the central level. This was also aided by the proliferation of Centrally Sponsored Schemes in the early Eighties. But the growth in the revenue receipts of the States was not really adequate to support the spurt in expenditures, and by 1984–85 a deficit appeared in the revenue account of all the 14 States taken together' (Rao and Sen, 1993, 68–9).

Table 4.1 Government Expenditure as a Ratio of SDP for Selected States (Combined)

Year	Percentage of Expenditure of SDP			Share of Capital Expenditure in Total (%)
	Revenue	Capital	Total	
1974–75	10.0	2.8	12.8	21.8
1980–81	14.1	4.9	19.0	26.0
1985–86	16.9	4.2	21.2	20.1
1986–87	17.9	4.4	22.3	19.5
1987–88	18.5	3.9	22.4	17.5
1988–89	17.6	3.2	20.8	15.4
1989–90	17.6	3.4	20.9	16.0
1990–91*	18.2	3.3	21.5	15.2

Source: Rao and Sen (1993)

*Excludes Bihar as detailed information is not available.

4.1.1 Genesis of Revenue Deficits

The deficit concepts are discussed in Chapter 2, and it was highlighted that revenue deficits have greater adverse implications on the finances as they cut into capital investments since the borrowed funds, which should have been otherwise used for capital investments that help in growth augmentation, are used up for consumption expenditure. Such diversion of borrowed funds for consumption restricts the fiscal space for capital investments (Table 4.2). An added fiscal burden arises on account of committed interest payments emanating from public borrowings.

The trends during 1974–75 to 1990–91 captured by Rao and Sen (1993) reveal that owing to the rapid growth in revenue expenditure, coupled with a slower and inadequate growth in revenue receipts, resulted in a revenue deficit situation by 1984–85, taking the fourteen major states together. The all states average (surplus) of Rs.218 crore for the period 1980–85 became Rs.2,601 crore revenue deficits for the period 1985–91. A rapid growth in the committed items of expenditure like wages and salaries, interest payments, and subsidies had to be compulsorily met by shredding the capital spending. It is argued that deceleration in capital spending started in the FY 1981–82 itself, resulting in a situation wherein per capita capital expenditure has had an absolute decline after 1986–87.The authors state, 'during the decade of the Eighties, while the revenue and aggregate expenditure of the States continued to grow at high rates of over 6 and 5 per cent respectively, capital expenditures actually declined ... As a result, the share of capital expenditures in total expenditures declined from 26 per cent in 1980–81 to 15 per cent in 1990–91. Surely, capital expenditures got a residuary treatment'(Rao and Sen, 1993, 71).

Functional categories of expenditure

The nominal growth of expenditure by the functional categories, i.e. general, social and community, and economic services, has more or less followed similar path, with the economic and social and community services expenditure gaining higher growth than the general services (Figure 4.3). The larger expenditure responsibility that the state governments have in the provision of social and economic services gets clearly reflected in the composition of total expenditure and their respective

Table 4.2 Revenue Surplus/Deficit of Selected States

Revenue Surplus (+)/Deficit (-) in the Selected States			
States	**Average**		
	Year		
	1974–80	**1980–85**	**1985–91**
High-Income States	**303**	**153**	**–762**
Gujarat	55	90	–326
Haryana	44	19	–10
Maharashtra	150	6	–215
Punjab	55	38	–211
Middle-Income States	**170**	**–118**	**–1,155**
Andhra Pradesh	68	–70	–318
Karnataka	58	51	–73
Kerala	23	3	–219
Tamil Nadu	27	94	–213
West Bengal	–6	–196	–332
Low-Income States#	**401**	**183**	**–684**
Bihar*	114	–10	54
Madhya Pradesh	121	128	10
Orissa	16	11	–20
Rajasthan	8	–19	–216
Uttar Pradesh	142	73	–503
All Major States#	**874**	**218**	**–2,601**

Source: Rao and Sen (1993)

*Due to the lack of reliable figures for 1990–91, the last column actually refers to average for the period 1985–90.

#Figures in the last column exclude the figure for Bihar for the year 1990–91.

shares in GDP (Figures 4.4 and 4.5). Together these two categories have experienced an increased share from 61.75% in 1974–75 to 63.32% in 1990–91, correspondingly; there is a decline in the share of expenditure on general services.

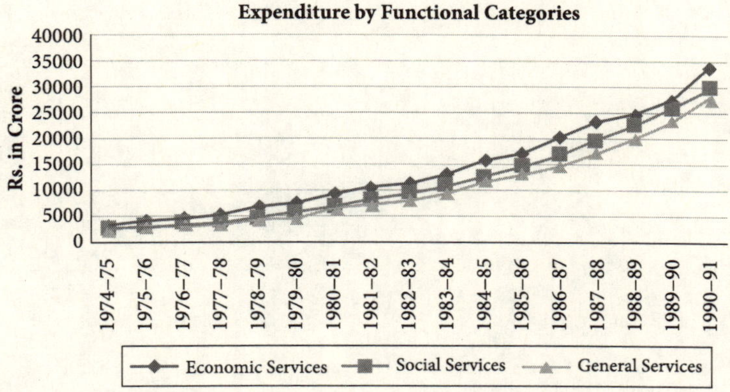

Figure 4.3 Expenditure by Functional Categories (All States)
Source: Computed by the author using RBI (2004).

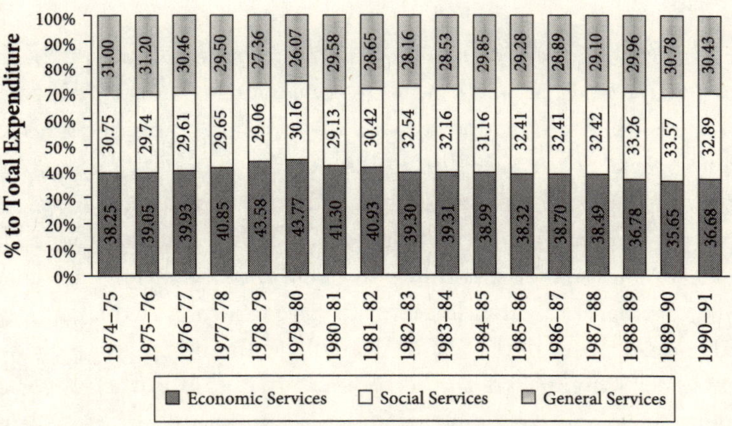

Figure 4.4 Composition of All States Expenditure by Functional Categories
Source: Computed by the author using RBI (2004).

Economic Categories of Expenditure

Some disturbing trends in economic categories of expenditure pertained to a sharp growth in wages and salaries and government subsidies. The authors argue that the government employees tended to

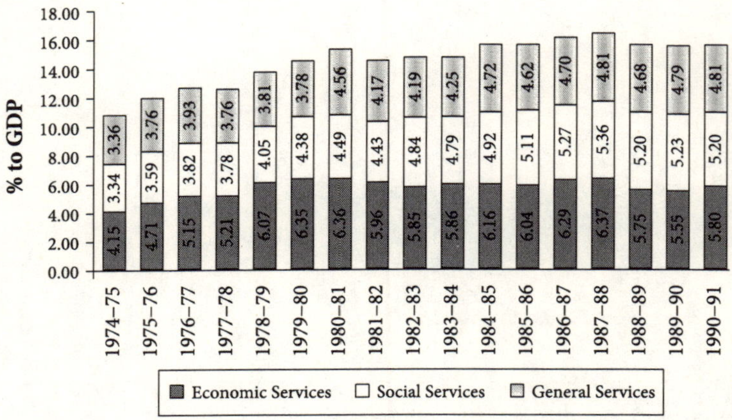

Figure 4.5 Expenditure on Functional Categories as Percent of GDP
Source: Computed by the author using RBI (2004).

have disproportionately larger gains in the community output, 'the total expenditure on wages and salaries in constant prices increased at about 10 per cent per year and given that the net employment increased at about 3 per cent per year during the decade, the salary per employee increased at about 7 per cent per year and this was about twice the rate of growth recorded in per capita income. It must also be mentioned that the wages and salary expenditure does not include various perquisites to the employees which also seems to have grown over the years. This clearly reflects the oligopolistic strength of the employees' organizations in securing a share of the community output in their favor disproportionate to their contribution to the community output' (Rao and Sen, 1993, 71).

The findings of Rao and Sen (1993) are quite revealing when it is observed that the wage and salary shares seem to be inversely related to per capita SDP. Among the high, middle, and low-income states, the share seems to be growing only in low-income States. The highest share during 1985–90 was observed in Madhya Pradesh (46%) and the lowest (18%) in Gujarat; Maharashtra too had a very small share. Kerala (41%) and Bihar (40%) also revealed a relatively large share.

Subsidies and Transfers

Academic literature has raised a number of issues on both explicit[2] and implicit[3] government subsidies in India, such as their proliferation, sharp growth, poor targeting resulting in 'inclusion'[4] and 'exclusion'[5] errors, and huge unrecovered costs. State governments tended to announce a number of poverty alleviation and social welfare measures during the sixth and seventh plan, which adversely impacted public finance in the country, especially at the sub-national level. Rao and Sen (1993) observed that the subsidy and transfer-related expenditure increased at a very high rate of 8% in per capita terms from 1974, which further accentuated to 8.4% in the eighties. The subsidy component doubled in its share in the total expenditure from 4% to 8%. Tamil Nadu reported a very sharp increase of 300% with its share rising from 3% to 13% in total expenditure. The sharp increase experienced in the committed expenditure not only resulted in a deceleration in the capital expenditure on infrastructure but also on the maintenance expenditure.

Subsidy programmes have not only restricted the fiscal space to fund other developmental activities but also resulted in a lot of inefficient use of scanty public resources caused by poor execution of the subsidy schemes (Srivastava et al (1997). Reflecting on subsidy issues in India, Shome (1998) states, 'Subsidies may be said to have suffered from three kinds of inefficiencies. First, there is global inefficiency because many subsidised inputs like water and electricity are wasted and sub-optimally utilised. Second, government, when acting as producer often turns out to be an inefficient economic agent. It is able to produce or provide goods at costs that are usually much higher than the corresponding cost for comparable private producer. Third, there is the inefficiency of administering subsidies itself. For example, food subsidies may be administered through better mechanism (e.g., coupon system) where inefficiencies in procurement, storage and distribution can be avoided.'

[2] Explicit subsidies are the direct subsidy schemes included in the budget.

[3] Implicit subsidy relates to the unrecovered cost of a public service. There are methodologies available to compute the implicit subsidies. For greater understanding of the estimation, read Mundle and Rao(1991)and Srivatsava et al.(2003).

[4] Inclusion errors refer to the inclusion of beneficiaries who are not entitled to a benefit.

[5] Exclusion errors refer to the exclusion of beneficiaries who are entitled to a benefit.

4.2 Public Expenditure Trends: 1991–92 to 2003–04

The decade of nineties was marked by severe fiscal distress featuring high fiscal deficit; growth in current expenditure dominating that of capital investments; expenditure on interest payments; and defense and subsidies experiencing a sharper growth. These trends were fuelled by the sharper growth in these categories of expenditure during 1985–86 to 1990–91 as compared to that of 1980–81 to 1984–85. Joshi and Little (1994) have analysed these trends and provided the averages for the above period (Table 4.3).

Discussing the rapid growth in India's combined (centre and states) current expenditure, Panagariya (2005) accounts for the rapid growth in defense spending, interest payments, subsidies, and the higher wages, following the implementation of the Fourth Pay Commission recommendations. Joshi and Little (1994) account for the growth in aggregate current government expenditures at the centre and state levels, which increased at 18.6% during the first half of the 1980s and rose to average 23%. As per their study, largely the increase was on account of defense, interest payments, and subsidies, whose average share increased from 7.9% to 11.2% of the GDP. Such a larger increase in the current expenditure was actually caused by a decline in the share of capital expenditure from 7.5% to 7.1%. The average fiscal deficit increased from 8% during 1980–81 to 1984–85 to 10.1% during 1985–86 to 1990–91 (Table 4.3).

The decade of 1990s was marked by major structural changes in the Indian economy, including the introduction of structural adjustment and stabilization programme in 1991. The reduction in the size of fiscal deficit was the major objective of the stabilization programme. The broad expenditure trends as revealed by the averages during 1990–95, 1995–2000, and 2000–04 for major categories presented in Table 4.4 reflect a considerable growth in total spending. However, growth continues to be more infavour of items like revenue and non-development categories. The sharper growth in the quantum of revenue expenditure and its share in the total, which has remained high at almost 80% of the total, are presented in Figures 4.6 and 4.7. Capital expenditure includes the repayment of debt and loans and advances given by the states, whereas capital outlay refers to the investment made by the government in creation of assets. We

Table 4.3 Fiscal Indicators: 1980–81 to 1989–90 (As Per Cent of GDP)

	Average 1980–81 to1984–85	1985–86	1986–87	1987–88	1988–89	1989–90	1990–91	Average 1985–86 to1989–90
Revenue	18.1	19.5	20	20.1	19.6	20.9	19.5	20
Current Expenditure	18.6	21.4	22.6	23.1	22.7	24.8	23.9	23
Defense	2.7	3.3	3.8	4	3.8	3.6		3.7
Interest	2.6	3.3	3.6	4	4.2	4.6	4.8	3.9
Subsidies*	2.6	3.3	3.4	3.5	3.6	4.2		3.6
Capital Expenditure	7.5	7.4	8.3	7	6.3	6.5	6	7.1
Total Expenditure	26.1	28.8	30.9	30.1	29	31.3	29.9	30.1
Fiscal Deficit	8	9.3	10.9	10	9.4	10.4	10.4	10.1

Source: Panagariya (2005).

*CSO estimates.

Table 4.4 Expenditure Pattern of State Governments (Rs. Crores)

Items	1990–95 (Avg.)	1995–00 (Avg.)	2000–04 (Avg.)
1	2	3	4
Aggregate Expenditure (1+2=3+4+5)	(16.0)	(15.2)	(17.3)
1. Revenue Expenditure of which	(12.8)	(12.6)	(13.8)
Interest Payments	(1.7)	(2.0)	(2.8)
2. Capital Expenditure of which	(3.2)	(2.7)	(3.6)
Capital Outlay	(1.6)	(1.4)	(1.6)
3. Developmental Expenditure	(10.8)	(9.6)	(9.7)
4. Non-Developmental Expenditure	(4.3)	(4.9)	(6.0)
5. Others*	(0.9)	(0.7)	(1.6)

Source: RBI State Finances (2006) p 21.

Avg.: average

RE: revised estimates

BE: budget estimates

*Includes repayments of loans to centre, discharge of internal debt, grants-in-aid, and contribution (compensation and assignments to local bodies).

Notes: 1.The4/5 year averages of ratio to GDP have been provided for a more meaningful comparison across periods.2.Figures in bracket are percent to GDP.3.Capital expenditure excludes public accounts.

have observed earlier that the states had high fiscal deficits, with a large component of revenue deficit amounting to the large-scale use of borrowed funds for consumption purpose.

The share of non-development expenditure has increased from 4.3% to 6%, and that of development expenditure has declined from 10.8% to 9.7% (Table 4.4). The share of social services expenditure in the total

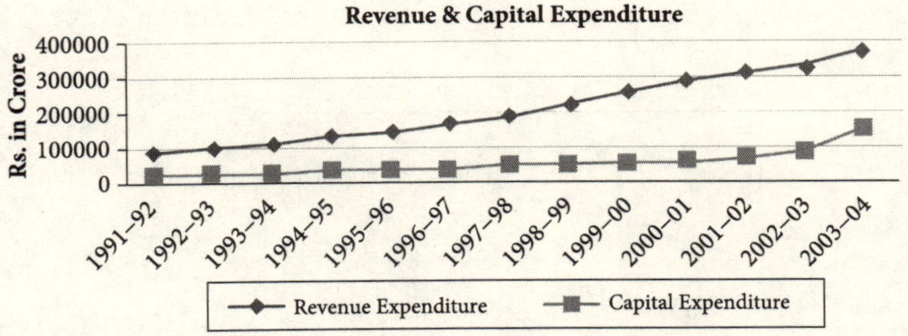

Figure 4.6 Trends in Revenue and Capital Expenditure (Nominal Terms)
Source: Computed by the author using RBI (2005).

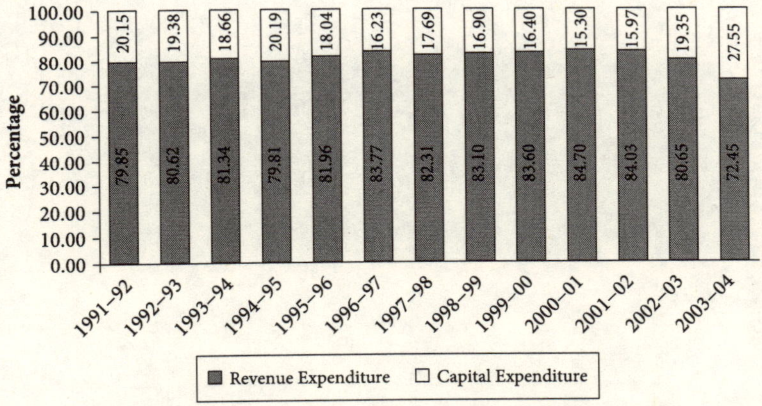

Figure 4.7 Composition of Revenue and Capital Expenditure (Percentage)
Source: Computed by the author using RBI (2005).

expenditure experienced a decline (Table 4.5) from 36.8% (average of 1990–95) to 32.5% (average of 2000–05). With reference to the share of social services expenditure in GDP, it has declined from 5.9% to 5.7% during the above reference period. Although these trends reflect the 'all states' picture, there are considerable interstate variations among states in terms of per capita real social services expenditure. The 'all states' trends in the general, social and community, and economic services expenditure and their respective shares in total and that of GDP are presented in Figures 4.8, 4.9 and 4.10, respectively.

Table 4.5 Trends in Aggregate Social Sector Expenditure of State Governments (Per Cent)

Items	1990–95 (Avg.)	1996–00 (Avg.)	2001–05 (Avg.)
1	2	3	4
TE/GDP	16.0	15.2	17.5
SSE/GDP	5.9	5.6	5.7
SSE/TE	36.8	36.9	32.5
PCSSE (Rupees)	420	-	1,244

Sources: RBI State finances (2006).

Note:PCSSE relates to two time points, i.e.1990–91 and 2000–01.

Avg.: average

SSE: social sector expenditure

TE: total expenditure

PCSSE: per capita social sector expenditure

'-': not available.

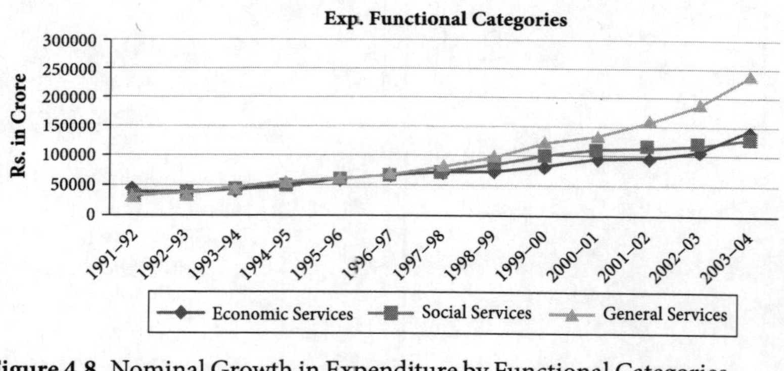

Figure 4.8 Nominal Growth in Expenditure by Functional Categories
Source: Computed by the author using RBI (2005).

Development Outcomes

Research evidence reveals a strong association between government spending and sectoral development, indicating the importance of government expenditure in the context of sectoral development. Theory and evidence of the links between government social sector expenditure, economic growth, and human development are presented in Box 4.1. Any understanding of public expenditure behaviour and its impacts

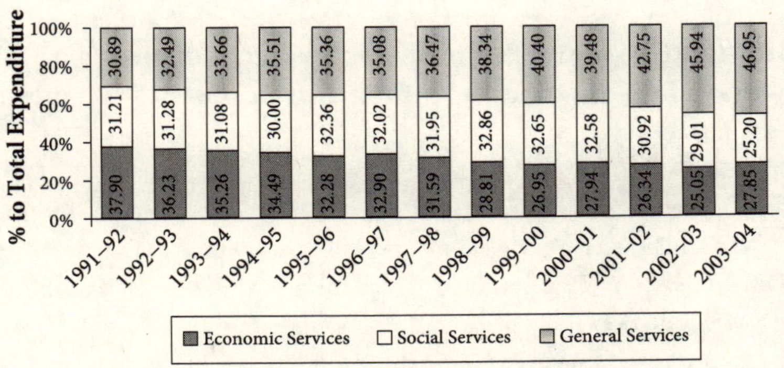

Figure 4.9 Composition of Expenditure by Functional Categories (Percentage to Total)
Source: Computed by the author using RBI (2005).

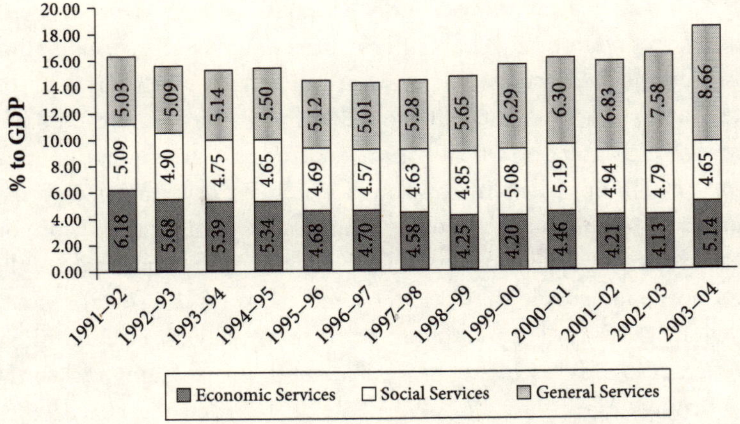

Figure 4.10 Functional Categories of Expenditure as Percent to GDP
Source: Computed by the author using RBI (2005).

is complete when one also examines the behaviour of the development indicators. However, an important caveat in this context is that there are other players also that contribute to development outcomes such as the private sector, non-governmental organisations (NGOs), and international aid agencies. Hence, it will be erroneous to attribute all the development to the public sector alone. There are difficulties isolating impacts

Box 4.1 Government Social Sector Expenditure, Economic Growth, and Human Development—Theory and Evidence

The theoretical underpinnings of the relationship between economic growth and human development are well documented in the literature (United Nations Development Programme (UNDP), 1990, Anand & Ravallion, 1993, Ghosh, 2006). Economic growth can have a positive impact on human development through three different channels: (i) through an increase in the general level of per capita income; (ii) through poverty reduction; and (iii) through higher public expenditure on education, health and related sectors. It is expected that an increase in the general level of per capita income is likely to increase the demand for education and health care, and may improve the human development of a country. Secondly, economic growth associated with poverty reduction may enable the poorer sections of the population to enjoy the fruits of growth and thus, may have a better impact on the human development indicators. In any economy it is the poorer sections of population who are more deprived of human development elements. The third channel through which the growth can improve human development is through the increased public expenditure on social sectors. Economic growth by increasing the revenue base of the economy may enable the State to spend more on the social sectors. Obviously, this is dependent both on the buoyancy of revenue collection resulting in a softening of the State budget constraint and on the political willingness to allocate proportionately for the social sectors. Thus, if the economic growth is to have a positive impact on human development, it would be required to have appropriate policies aimed at reducing income inequalities and higher public social sector expenditure and conversely, if the economic growth is to be sustainable in the long run it has to be supported by better human capital (UNDP, 1990).

In an economy, economic growth may be affecting the human development through all the three channels. However, there are studies which have reiterated the importance of public expenditure channel over and above the trickling down channel of economic growth in improving human development. A cross country study by looking into the relative importance of growth channel and public expenditure channel in improving life expectancy finds that public expenditure on health care contributed two-third of the improvement in life expectancy and economic growth through poverty reduction contributed only one-third (Anand &Ravallion, 1993). However, in the case of literacy, the study did not get any concrete evidence in favour of public expenditure on education. Moreover, there are countries like Sri Lanka, which achieved relatively higher human development despite being a developing country. The supported policies followed in Sri Lanka through higher public expenditure on social sectors are widely acknowledged in the literature (Dreze & Sen, 1989). An inter-State study on India also reveals that while the disparities in per capita income among the States are increasing, the disparities in social development are coming down, pointing to the importance of public social sector expenditure in achieving human development (Ghosh, 2006).

Source: RBI (2006), p. 56

of each of these players; however, a number of studies tend to associate the outcome indicators with the government programmes.

In a way, the broad performance indicators do serve well in providing a direction to future investments that are required in every sector. Hence, it is important to periodically review the performance considering appropriate performance indicators and development indices.

The status of the Human Development Index (HDI) in the international context (Table 4.6) corresponding to the period considered for expenditure analysis reveals that although India has been making progress, there is still a huge gap compared with the nations that have high human development. Indian states too have revealed huge interstate variations both in terms of per capita public financing of human development sectors and HDI. Bihar has remained in the last rank and Kerala in the first rank in the HDI through all the time points that the data has been presented (Table 4.7).

Discussing the state-level fiscal imbalances, Pattnaik et al. (2005) argue that state finances turned adverse, particularly in the second half of the nineties, thereby necessitating the initiation of reforms during this period

Table 4.6 HDI of India vis-à-vis Other Countries

	HDI Rank	HDI							
Countries	2004	1975	1980	1985	1990	1995	2000	2003	2004
1	2	3	4	5	6	7	8	9	10
India	126	0.412 (0.456)	0.438 (0.450)	0.476 (0.422)	0.513 (0.399)	0.546 (0.390)	0.577 (0.379)	0.602 (0.361)	0.611 (0.354)
Medium Human Development Countries									
China	81	0.525	0.558	0.594	0.627	0.683	—	0.755	0.768
Sri Lanka	93	0.607	0.649	0.681	0.705	0.727	—	0.751	0.755
Pakistan	134	0.363	0.386	0.419	0.462	0.492	—	0.527	0.539
Nepal	138	0.296	0.333	0.376	0.423	0.466	0.499	0.526	0.527
Bangladesh	137	0.345	0.364	0.389	0.419	0.452	0.506	0.52	0.53
Malaysia	61	0.615	0.659	0.695	0.721	0.76	0.79	0.796	0.805
High Human Development Countries									
Norway	1	0.868	0.888	0.898	0.912	0.936	0.956	0.963	0.965
Japan	7	0.857	0.882	0.895	0.911	0.925	0.936	0.943	0.949
Singapore	25	0.725	0.761	0.784	0.822	0.861	—	0.907	0.916
Korea	26	0.707	0.741	0.78	0.818	0.855	0.884	0.901	0.912
Rep of Kuwait	33	0.763	0.777	0.78	—	0.813	0.837	0.844	0.871

Source: RBI (2006)
Note: Figures in brackets indicate the distance of India from Norway (best performer) in terms of HDI, i.e. the difference between the HDI of the two countries.

Table 4.7 HDI for States

Sl. No.	States	1981	Rank	1991	Rank	2001	Rank
	1	2	3	4	5	6	7
1.	Andhra Pradesh	0.298	9	0.377	9	0.416	10
2.	Assam	0.272	10	0.348	10	0.386	14
3.	Bihar	0.237	15	0.308	15	0.367	15
4.	Gujarat	0.360	4	0.431	6	0.479	6
5.	Haryana	0.360	5	0.443	5	0.509	5
6.	Karnataka	0.346	6	0.412	7	0.478	7
7.	Kerala	0.500	1	0.591	1	0.638	1
8.	Madhya Pradesh	0.245	14	0.328	13	0.394	12
9.	Maharashtra	0.363	3	0.452	4	0.523	4
10.	Orissa	0.267	11	0.345	12	0.404	11
11.	Punjab	0.411	2	0.475	2	0.537	2
12.	Rajasthan	0.256	12	0.347	11	0.424	9
13.	Tamil Nadu	0.343	7	0.466	3	0.531	3
14.	Uttar Pradesh	0.255	13	0.314	14	0.388	13
15.	West Bengal	0.305	8	0.404	8	0.472	8
	All-India	**0.302**		**0.381**		**0.472**	

Source: RBI (2006)

at the state level as well. Sluggish central transfers to the states were partly responsible. The state-level reforms included the introduction of reform-linked assistance as a part of Medium-Term Fiscal Reform Programme and adjustment programme of some of the states as linked to borrowings from multilateral agencies. The expenditure management programmes of the states included restrictions on the creation of new posts, review of manpower requirements, lowering of establishment expenses, and reduction of non-merit subsidies through better targeting (Pattnaik et al., 2005,610–11).

4.3 Expenditure Trends: FRBM Phase

The state-level expenditure continued to be under stress during the early part of this period, and state finances were characterized by huge revenue and fiscal deficits. However, this period witnessed a number of policy corrective measures. Fiscal reform initiatives during this period brought in considerable changes in the fiscal scenario at the sub-national level. To start with, the Twelfth Finance Commission recommended rule-based fiscal correction process for the states. This involved framing of FRL by the state governments to cap the fiscal deficit at 3% level and also achieve zero revenue deficit by 2008–09, which would entitle them for debt rescheduling and a part of the state's debt to the union government would get written off. This initiated the process of framing FRBM legislation by states at different points of time to enforce rule-based fiscal correction. This period also, at least partially, was marked by a subsequent tremendous improvement in state finances as reflected by the data presented in Table 4.8. The improvement

Table 4.8 Structure of State Finances for General Category States (% of GSDP)

Average of	2001–05	2005–10	2010–15	2015–16	2001–16
	(11th FC)	12th FC)	13th FC)	(1st Year of 14th FC)	
Total Revenue Receipts	12.5	13.6	13.7	14.8	13.4
Own Sources of Revenue	8.4	8.5	8.7	8.5	8.5
Own Tax Revenue	6.8	6.9	7.4	7.2	7.1
Own Non-Tax Revenue	1.6	1.6	1.3	1.3	1.5
Central Transfers	4.1	5.1	5	6.3	4.9
Share in Central Taxes	2.8	3.2	3.2	4	3.1
Grants-in-Aid	1.3	1.9	1.8	2.3	1.7
Total Expenditure	16.9	16	15.9	17.7	16.3
Revenue Expenditure	15.1	13.5	13.8	14.9	14.1
Capital Expenditure*	1.8	2.5	2.2	2.7	2.2
Revenue Deficit	2.6	-0.1	0.1	0.1	0.7
Fiscal Deficit	4.7	2.5	2.4	3.6	3.1

Source: Mukherjee (2019)
Note: *Excluding loans and advances.

in finances is seen on both the revenue and expenditure fronts. States' resource position has improved from 12.5% of GDP (average of 2001–05) to 13.7% (average of 2010–15), with the total expenditure declining from 16.9% to 15.9% during the above reference period. It is important to notice that this decline is caused by a reduction in the revenue expenditure from 15.1% to 13.8% and an increase in the capital expenditure from 1.8% to 2.2%. This marked a welcome reversal of the declining trend in the share of capital expenditure witnessed from the late seventies. This was the scenario for 'all states' as one can observe sharper growth and also an increased share in the total for the capital expenditure category (Figures 4.11 and 4.12), their respective shares in GDP are presented in Figure 4.13. Further the timelines of state-level institutional reform initiatives are presented in Table 4.9.

Among all Indian states, Karnataka was the first to enact the legislation way back in 2002, even before the central government enunciated as mentioned earlier. Box 4.2 provides the details of state-level FRL.

Trends in State Finances

This period, as observed earlier, was marked by many noticeable fiscal policy changes.[6] The period also witnessed a major global economic

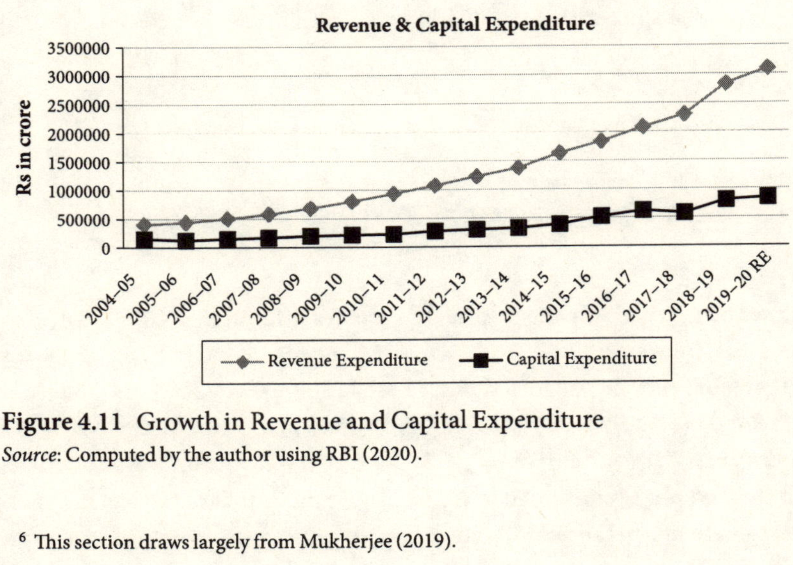

Figure 4.11 Growth in Revenue and Capital Expenditure
Source: Computed by the author using RBI (2020).

[6] This section draws largely from Mukherjee (2019).

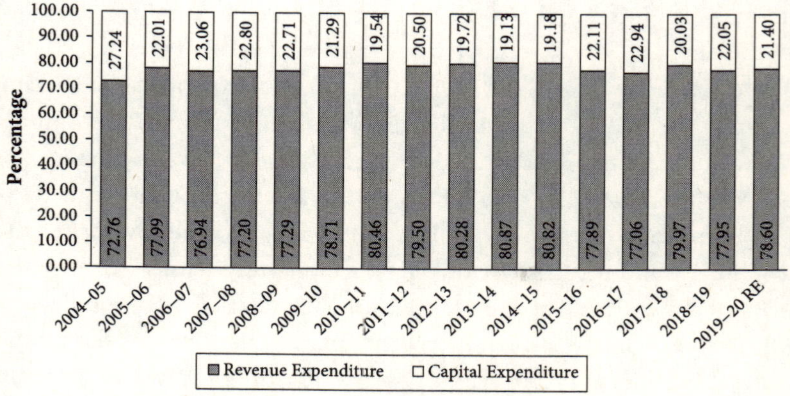

Figure 4.12 Composition of Revenue and Capital Expenditure
Source: Computed by the author using RBI (2020).

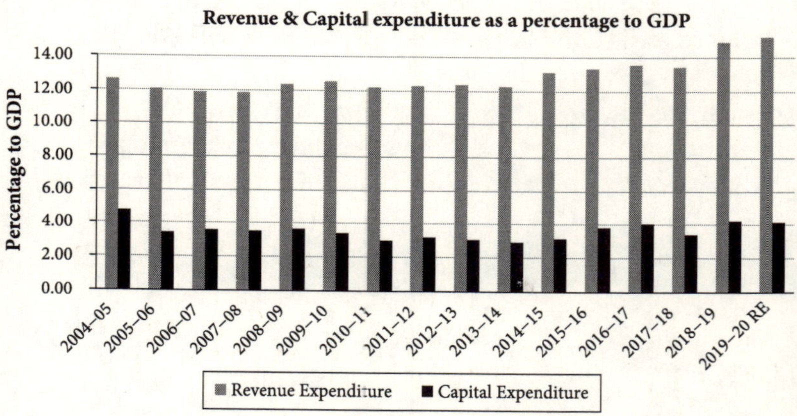

Figure 4.13 Percentage Share of Revenue and Capital Expenditure in GDP
Source: Computed by the author using RBI (2020).

slowdown, which affected the state finances. Mukherjee (2019) categorizes the time period 2001–02 to 2015–16 into five distinct phases for eighteen General Category states. Phase I (2001–02 to 2003–04), Phase II (2004–05 to 2007–08), Phase III (2008–09 to 2009–10), Phase IV (2010–11 to 2012–13), and Phase V (2013–14 to 2015–16). Trends in the deficits in the first phase continued to remain the same as that of the late nineties. Fiscal reforms in the form of rule-based fiscal correction helped in a quick

Table 4.9 Institutional Reforms by State Governments

Sl. No.	States	Value-Added Tax (VAT) Implemented	Fiscal Responsibility Legislation (FRL) Enacted	New Pension Scheme (NPS) Introduced	Ceilings on Guarantee Imposed	Consolidated Sinking Fund (CSF)	Guarantee Redemption Fund (GRF)
1	2	3	4	5	6	7	8
1	Andhra Pradesh	April 2005	June 2005	September 2004	S, September 2003	1999–00	January 2002
2	Arunachal Pradesh	April 2005	March 2006	No	No	June 1999	No
3	Assam	May 2005	September 2005	No	S, September 2005	1999–00	No
4	Bihar	April 2005	April 2006	September 2005	No	No	No
5	Chhattisgarh	April 2006	September 2005	November 2004	Yes	2001–02	No
6	Goa	April 2005	2006	August 2005	S, 1993 (Amended, 2005)	June 1999	October 2001
7	Gujarat	April 2006	March 2005	April 2005	A, 1963 (Amended, 2001)	December 2003	February 2002
8	Haryana	April 2003	July 2005	January 2006	Yes	Yes	July 2003
9	Himachal Pradesh	April 2005	2005	Yes	No	No	No

(continued)

Table 4.9 *Continued*

Sl. No.	States	Value-Added Tax (VAT) Implemented	Fiscal Responsibility Legislation (FRL) Enacted	New Pension Scheme (NPS) Introduced	Ceilings on Guarantee Imposed	Consolidated Sinking Fund (CSF)	Guarantee Redemption Fund (GRF)
10	Jammu and Kashmir	April 2005	No	No	No	No	2005–06
11	Jharkhand	April 2006	No	Yes	No	No	No
12	Karnataka	April 2005	April 2003	April 2006	S, April 1999	No	March 2000
13	Kerala	April 2005	August 2003	No	2003	June 2006	No
14	Madhya Pradesh	April 2006	May 2005	January 2005	A	No	January 2006
15	Maharashtra	April 2005	April 2005	November 2005	No	1999	No
16	Manipur	July 2005	August 2005	December 2004	S, January 2005	No	No
17	Meghalaya	April 2006	March 2006	No	No	November 1999	No
18	Mizoram	April 2005	No	No	No	1999–00	No
19	Nagaland	April 2005	August 2005	No	S, August 2005	No	No
20	Orissa	April 2005	June 2005	January 2005	A, November 2002	January 2003	2002–03
21	Punjab	April 2005	2003	No	A, Yes	Yes	No

22	Rajasthan	April 2006	May 2005	January 2004	May 2005	No	1999–00
23	Sikkim	April 2005	No	April 2006	December 2000	1999–00	2005–06
24	Tamil Nadu	No	2003	April 2003	S, May 2003	March 2006	March 2003
25	Tripura	October 2005	2005	NA	NA	NA	NA
26	Uttaranchal	October 2005	October 2005	October 2005	No	January 2001	No
27	Uttar Pradesh	No	February 2004	April 2005	No	No	No
28	West Bengal	April 2005	No	No	S, August 2001	April 1999	No
29	NCT Delhi	April 2005	No	No	No	No	No
	Sum-up	27	23	18	17	17	11

Source: RBI (2006)

NA: not available

A:administrative ceiling

S:statutory ceiling

Box 4.2 Adoption of Rule-Based Fiscal Policy by State Governments

Enactment of Fiscal Responsibility Legislation (FRL) in India at both the Centre as well as State level (23 States so far) has provided impetus to the process of attaining fiscal sustainability in the Central and State Government finances. The realization of underlying benefits of this institutional development would, however, depend on strict adherence to the targets set in FRLs of the respective Governments. Reduction in the key deficit indicators is critical for fiscal sustainability, particularly in view of the mounting level of debt which at its present level (more than 62% of GDP for the Centre and 32% of GDP for States) is higher than many countries.

Apart from fiscal sustainability, meeting the targets set in FRLs is crucial for maintaining credibility for potential investors at home as well as from abroad. As noted by Kopits (2001), 'all these rules share at least one feature in common: they seek to confer credibility on the conduct of macroeconomic policies by removing discretionary intervention'. It is established in the literature that rules are necessary to restrain politically rational policymakers who conduct discretionary policies with a deficit bias when facing electorate that fails to understand, or is indifferent to, the intertemporal budget constraints. In a federal system, fiscal rules can be usefully applied at the sub-national level of Government. Application of such rules at sub-national level is the key to economic performance particularly in those economies where the revenue/ expenditure of sub-national Governments constitutes a major portion of overall Government revenue/expenditure. Smaller the share of central Government, greater is the need for applying subnational rules to counter the moral hazard that may arise among sub-national Governments to incur fiscal imbalances with repercussions on the borrowing costs of the rest of federal system.

There can be two basic approaches to design fiscal rules at subnational level: first, bottom-up approach where sub-national Governments voluntarily make rules for themselves and secondly, top-bottom approach where rules are imposed by the central Government. The second approach is mainly relevant in the countries where the central Government frequently undertakes bail out of sub-national Governments. This approach also reflects the need to bring about a lasting fiscal adjustment encompassing the entire general Government or consolidated public sector, in the face of a possible sustainability problem with likely repercussions on the countrywide premium. The examples of the first approach are U.S., Switzerland, and Canada where sub-national Governments chose to adopt fiscal rules largely because of the need to build good reputation in financial markets in the absence of a potential bailout. In contrast, in Brazil (or in EU member countries under EMU), sub-national Governments are subject to centrally imposed rules to prevent moral hazard, particularly given a relatively small portion of fiscal activity under central (supranational) control. In this case, adherence to rules generally helps lower the individual Government's default risk premium, as well as the country risk premium faced by the entire federal (or supranational) Government. The degree of fiscal decentralization in India is comparable to countries having high degree of decentralization such as Sweden and Denmark (Kannan et. al., 2004). The State Governments collect about 40% of combined revenue receipts and incur around 50% of combined expenditure. In view of the relatively greater role played by the State Governments in Indian public finances, it is crucial for overall macroeconomic management that the State Governments follow rule based fiscal policy.

Twelfth Finance Commission (TFC) recommended that each State should enact FRL. This has been stipulated as a pre-condition for availing the debt relief recommended by the TFC. According to TFC, this legislation should, at a minimum, provide for: (a) eliminating revenue deficit by 2008–09; (b) reducing fiscal deficit to 3% of GSDP or its equivalent defined as ratio of interest payment to revenue receipts; (c) bringing out annual reduction targets of revenue and fiscal deficits; (d) bringing out annual statement giving prospects for the State economy and related fiscal strategy; (e) bringing out special statements along with the budget giving in detail number of employees in government, public sector, and aided institutions and related salaries.

Karnataka was the first among the States to enact the FRL in September 2002 followed by Kerala (2003), Tamil Nadu (2003), and Punjab (2004). Following the recommendations of the TFC, 19 more

States have enacted the FRL so far. The FRLs of the States have almost similar characteristics (Annex 2). The targets set in the FRLs of State Governments are similar to those set by the Central Government for itself, i.e., elimination of revenue deficit by 2008–09 and reducing GFD–GDP ratio to 3% by 2009–10 (GFD–GSDP for State Governments). It may be mentioned that the enactment of FRL by State Governments in India reflects a mix of the two approaches discussed above. While some State Governments have voluntarily enacted FRLs others were encouraged to adopt such legislations to avail benefits under incentive scheme recommended by the TFC.

The persistence of large fiscal deficits has resulted in accumulation of outstanding debts of the State Governments. Furthermore, use of borrowed resources for meeting the current expenditure requirements by the States resulted in widening of asset-liability mismatches over the period. This underscores the imperatives of eliminating the revenue deficit and generating sufficient revenue surplus which may be utilized for creation of assets without creating liabilities. Any deviation from the targets set under their FRLs by the State Governments may generate a chain effect among other State Governments to follow the suit thereby having deleterious effects in terms of undermining credibility of policy stance and adverse impact on macroeconomic, financial, external sector, and budgetary sustainability. Moreover, the States deviating from their FRL targets would have difficulties in raising the required resources due to market perceptions. It may be noted that fiscal discipline remains the major factor in determining the investment grade rating of the Indian economy by various international rating agencies. Hence, it would be desirable that the State Governments, which have enacted FRLs, adhere to the rules, while remaining States make efforts in the direction of adopting the rule-based framework.

Source: RBI (2006), p. 67

reduction in the fiscal stress in the form of a reduced fiscal deficit and the attainment of revenue surplus. The period was also marked by high economic growth and the introduction of state value-added tax (VAT)in 2005–06 by the majority of Indian states. Phase III experienced the global economic slowdown, causing a rise in deficits, which is attributable more to higher growth in expenditures than revenue mobilization. There was some relaxation of the fiscal deficit norm during the global economic slowdown that happened during 2007–08 both at the central and state government levels. Fiscal stimulation was the strategy adopted to create demand to counter the recessionary trends. Owing to these measures, revenue deficit increased from 1.4% of the GDP in FY 2007–08 to 4.3% in FY 2008–09. At the same time, the fiscal deficit of the central government increased from 2.7% in FY 2007–08 to 6.1% in FY 2008–09 (Kumar and Vashisht, 2009). It is stated, 'Electoral considerations made this into an expansionary exercise that included massive increases in public outlays in support of employment guarantee schemes, farm loan waivers, pay commission rewards, and increases in food and fertilizer subsidies. This fiscal expansion is expressed by the expansionary public outlays included some measures that implied a hefty transfer of purchasing power to farmers and to the rural sector in general. These included farm loan waivers, funds allocated to the National Rural Employment Guarantee Program (NREGP), Bharat Nirman (targeted for improving rural infrastructure) Prime Minister's Rural Road Program, and a large increase in subsidies for fertilizers and electricity supplied to the farmers.' They further add that 'All of these measures were taken because of political considerations and not in response to the global crisis' (Kumar and Vashisht, 2009, 20). Following these measures, the combined fiscal deficit, which had been on a course correction until 2007–08 at 5.4% mark, got unleashed further and reached 10% of GDP.

There was recovery in Indian state finances from the shocks in Phase IV, with more than 13% increase in the growth rate of revenue mobilization during 2009-–10 to 2010-–11. The fifth phase saw the return of revenue deficits (Mukherjee, 2019).

FRBM and State-Level Expenditure

Mukherjee (2019) presents an interesting analysis of expenditure pre-FRBM and post-FRBM by revenue and capital expenditure and also functional categories—general, social and community, and economic services. It is interesting to note that between the pre- and post-FRBM periods, the low-income states have not only managed to increase their share in capital expenditure in a significant manner (much higher than that of the middle and high-income states) but also managed to enhance their revenue expenditure share in their respective GSDP. Lower-middle-income states closely follow the same patterns of larger increase in capital expenditure, coupled with increased revenue expenditure. Bihar and Uttar Pradesh revealed the largest increase in their capital expenditure, the former by 166% points and the latter by 129% points, while Bihar also managed to bring its fiscal deficit within the 3% mark, reducing from 4.19% to 2.44%, that of Uttar Pradesh remained above the 3% mark at 3.79% however reduced from 4.68%. The middle-income and high-income have depicted similar trends wherein they have managed to reduce the revenue expenditure, as percent of their respective GSDP, and enhanced their share of capital expenditure in the GSDP (Table 4.10).

State level pre- and post-FRBM trends by functional categories of expenditure also account for positive developments. It has been stated in Chapter 2 that the functional categorization of expenditure classifies expenditure by the functions they perform. Although the expenditure incurred on social and community services and economic services is treated as 'development' expenditure and that of general services is treated as 'non-development' in government parlance, this categorization by mere nomenclature is highly contentious. What is important is to examine how effectively the expenditure programmes deliver the results. Albeit, the data reveals that all the General Category states (Table 4.11), except Jharkhand, have experienced a decline in the share of average general services expenditure in the post-FRBM period. With reference to the share of social and community services expenditure, all the low-income states, except Rajasthan, have revealed an increased share, with Bihar revealing the largest increase of 32% points among all the General Category states. On the contrary, all southern states, except Tamil Nadu, have a reduced share. Regarding the share of expenditure on economic services, Bihar leads again in terms of percent increase with a 74% point increase, with all other low-income states having an increased share, except Madhya Pradesh. All southern states have experienced a decline.[7]

The 'all states' trends in functional categories reveal a sharper increase in social and community services and general services, whereas that of

[7] For a more detailed discussion, read Mukherjee(2019).

Table 4.10 Impact of the FRBM Act in Expenditure Management of Indian States During 2001–16

States	Average Revenue Expenditure (% of GSDP)			Average Capital Expenditure (% of GSDP)		
	Pre-FRBM	Post-FRBM	% Change	Pre-FRBM	Post-FRBM	% Change
Andhra Pradesh	21.98	14.88	–32.30	3.15	2.52	–20.10
Bihar	18.94	20.27	7.00	1.79	4.75	165.80
Chhattisgarh	15.27	15.87	4.00	2.21	2.99	35.40
Goa	19.35	15.05	–22.20	3.00	3.19	6.40
Gujarat	14.45	10.39	–28.10	1.55	2.47	59.60
Haryana	12.33	11.37	–7.80	1.04	1.70	63.20
Jharkhand	12.39	15.03	21.40	2.19	2.89	31.90
Karnataka	15.45	14.45	–6.50	1.75	3.00	71.40
Kerala	14.77	14.54	–1.60	0.70	0.95	36.30
Madhya Pradesh	16.19	16.78	3.60	2.78	3.45	24.30
Maharashtra	12.42	10.59	–14.70	1.46	1.69	15.70
Odisha	17.60	15.78	–10.40	1.60	2.56	60.40
Punjab	16.97	14.80	–12.70	0.87	1.08	23.80
Rajasthan	16.17	14.71	–9.00	2.32	2.55	10.20
Tamil Nadu	14.20	12.88	–9.30	1.03	1.99	94.40
Telangana		14.02	—		2.43	—
Uttar Pradesh	15.57	17.85	14.70	1.77	4.04	128.90
West Bengal	13.89	13.39	–3.60	0.75	0.89	17.50
All General Category States	15.75	14.59	–7.40	1.81	2.52	39.20
Low-Income States (LIS)*	16.70	17.40	4.00	2.10	3.80	81.60
Low-Middle-Income States (LMIS)*	14.40	15.40	7.30	1.60	2.50	58.90
Upper-Middle-Income States (UMIS)*	15.00	14.10	–5.70	1.60	2.00	24.90
High-Income States (HIS)*	15.00	12.40	–17.10	1.70	2.10	21.40

Source: Mukherjee (2019).

Notes: *HIS implies High-Income States (Per Capita GSDP or PCGSDP is higher than or equal to the third quartile); UMIS implies Upper-Middle-Income States (PCGSDP lies between the second and third quartiles); LMIS implies Lower-Middle-Income States (PCGSDP lies between the first and second quartiles) and LIS implies Low-Income State (PCGSDP lies below the first quartile). ** Excluding loans and advances.

Table 4.11 Impact of FRBM Act in Structuring Expenditure of Indian States during 2001–16

States	Average Revenue Expenditure on General Services (% of GSDP)			Average Revenue Expenditure on Social Services (% of GSDP)			Average Revenue Expenditure on Economic Services (% of GSDP)			Average Revenue Expenditure on Interest Payments (% of GSDP)		
	Pre-FRBM	Post-FRBM	% Change	Pre-FRBM	Post-FRBM	% Change	Pre-FRBM	Post-FRBM	% Change	Pre-FRBM	Post-FRBM	% Change
Andhra Pradesh	8.78	4.80	−45.30	7.37	5.91	−19.8	5.62	4.13	−26.60	4.80	1.92	−60.10
Bihar	10.12	7.55	−25.40	6.35	8.42	32.50	2.47	4.29	73.80	4.48	2.25	−49.70
Chhattisgarh	5.20	4.11	−21.10	5.54	6.62	19.50	4.03	4.61	14.40	2.35	1.08	−53.90
Goa	7.94	4.66	−41.40	5.62	5.45	−3.00	5.78	4.94	−14.50	2.99	2.12	−29.20
Gujarat	5.32	3.88	−27.20	4.67	4.05	−13.50	4.39	2.43	−44.80	3.21	2.07	−35.60
Haryana	5.21	3.62	−30.60	3.68	4.07	10.50	3.39	3.59	6.10	2.47	1.50	−39.20
Jharkhand	5.42	5.75	6.10	4.50	5.67	25.80	2.46	3.61	46.60	2.27	1.80	−21.00
Karnataka	5.16	4.47	−13.30	5.34	5.25	−1.60	4.48	4.02	−10.20	2.23	1.72	−22.90
Kerala	6.88	6.61	−3.90	5.10	4.88	−4.20	2.72	2.16	−20.70	3.04	2.43	−20.10
Madhya Pradesh	6.02	5.35	−11.10	5.17	6.22	20.40	4.44	4.18	−5.90	2.84	2.01	−29.50
Maharashtra	5.67	3.88	−31.50	4.53	4.43	−2.20	1.99	2.11	5.80	2.23	1.66	−25.60
Odisha	8.69	5.55	−36.20	5.89	6.14	4.20	2.74	3.83	40.00	4.89	1.88	−61.60
Punjab	10.25	8.03	−21.60	3.91	3.52	−9.80	2.57	3.04	18.40	4.08	2.96	−27.40
Rajasthan	7.21	5.21	−27.70	6.18	5.79	−6.20	2.78	3.69	32.60	4.08	2.42	−40.80
Tamil Nadu	5.66	4.64	−18.00	4.71	4.86	3.10	3.15	2.42	−23.20	2.30	1.66	−28.00
Telangana		4.13			5.44			4.42			1.42	
Uttar Pradesh	7.65	7.44	−2.70	4.72	6.19	31.20	2.70	3.39	25.80	3.69	2.73	−26.00
West Bengal	6.98	5.71	−18.20	4.68	5.53	18.00	2.10	2.07	−1.60	4.13	2.84	−31.20
All General Category States	7.02	5.36	−23.60	5.22	5.41	3.60	3.33	3.44	3.50	3.42	2.04	−40.20

Source: **Mukherjee (2019).**

economic services trailed behind and had a reduced share in the total expenditure and GDP after 2009–10, becoming more prominent after 2017–18. The nominal growth, percentage share in total, and percentage share in GDP are presented in Figures 4.14, 4.15, and 4.16, respectively.

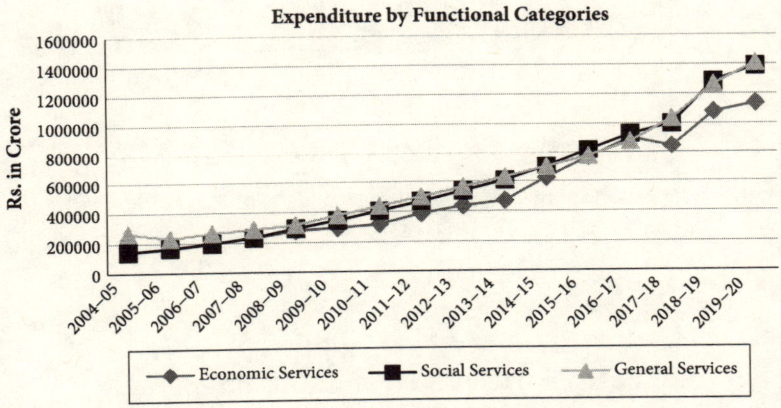

Figure 4.14 Nominal Growth in Expenditure by Functional Categories
Source: Computed by the author using RBI (2020).

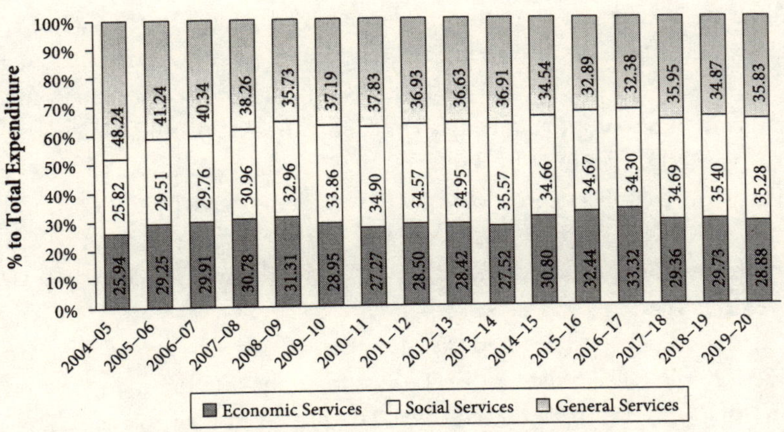

Figure 4.15 Percentage Composition of Expenditure by Functional Categories
Source: Computed by the author using RBI (2020).

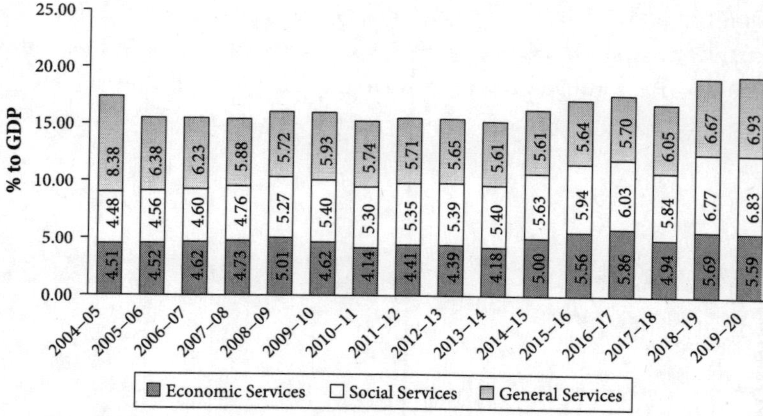

Figure 4.16 Functional Categories of Expenditure as Percent to GDP
Source: Computed by the author using RBI (2020).

4.4 State-Level Expenditure Trends: Post-Fourteenth Finance Commission

Recommendations of the Fourteenth Finance Commission marked a significant departure from the previous finance commissions, wherein the state share of shared taxes increased from 32% to 42%, amounting to an enhancement in the fiscal autonomy of states in the use of resource entitlements to their priorities. There have been debates suggesting that the real increase after considering the total transfers such as grants and support through the Centrally Sponsored Schemes, is not very significant. The Fourteenth Finance Commission also recommended relaxation of the 3% fiscal deficit cap by 0.25% points to GSDP if (1) debt to GSDP ratio is contained to 25%, and (2) the interest payment remained within 10% of the revenue receipts of the previous year.

There were yet other major fiscal reform initiatives, such as the introduction of GST, a major indirect tax reform, having large implications on the states' fiscal parameters. Ujwal Discom Assurance Yojana (UDAY) is yet another policy decision that has large-scale implications on states' debt positions. State governments also got into a spate of announcements, such as farm loan waivers, that have medium to long-term implications on states' expenditure liabilities.

Trends in Deficits

The sound fiscal health depicted by the states with the fiscal deficit maintained at a lower level than the targeted 3% mark, with an average of 2.2% (2006–11) and 2.4% (2011–16), was breached by 2015–16, with the fiscal deficit level reaching 3% of GDP in 2015–16 and 3.5% in 2016–17. There was a marginal decline as it reached 2.6% by 2019–20 budget estimates. In addition, the revenue surplus that the states enjoyed at 0.4% of GDP was on the decline and also turned into deficit in some years after 2015–16 (Table 4.12). The revenue surplus that most of the states had enjoyed enabled them to enhance their capital investments.

Composition of Expenditure

An analysis of expenditure during the period 2015–16 till 2019–20 budget estimates reveals that the states experienced a deterioration in the quality of spending, revealing a much sharper increase in their revenue spending as compared to the growth in capital spending. Although the share of revenue expenditure increased from 13.6% of GDP to 14.9% (81.27% to 83.49% as percent to total expenditure), that of capital spending, which was already low, declined from 3.1% to 2.9% (18.73% to 16.51% as percent to total expenditure) (Table 4.13).

States have accounted for a much larger share in the capital spending as compared to the centre (Tiwari and Surya (2019). In 2019–20, the states allocated Rs. 5.7 lakh crore (2.8% of GDP), while the centre allocated Rs. 3.8 lakh crore (1.8% of GDP) on capital outlays.

It is disheartening to note that states have been cutting back in capital outlay to a larger tune than other components of their budget. The deceleration in spending on capital can impinge the future economic growth of the nation. Capital outlay is the component of government's expenditure, which leads to the creation of assets such as roads and bridges, schools, and hospitals. In addition, capital investments have a larger multiplier effect that can enhance economic growth much faster. The analysis highlights the fact that capital outlays turned out to be less than the budgeted estimates by 14% during 2015–18. On the contrary, the reduction in the

Table 4.12 Major Deficit Indicators: All States and Union Territories with Legislature (Rs. Lakh Crores)

Item	2006–11 (Average)	2011–2016 (Average)	2015–16	2016–17	2017–18	2018–19 (BE)	2018–19 (RE)	2019–20 (BE)
1	2	3	4	5	6	7	8	9
Gross Fiscal Deficit	1.30	2.74	4.20	5.36	4.10	4.90	5.55	5.52
(Percent to GDP)	(2.2)	(2.4)	(3.0)	(3.5)	(2.4)	(2.6)	(2.9)	(2.6)
Revenue Deficit	-0.17	-0.02	-0.03	0.36	0.19	-0.34	0.13	-0.08
(Percent to GDP)	(-0.4)	(-0.0)	(-0.0)	(0.2)	(0.1)	(-0.2)	(0.1)	(-0.0)
Primary Deficit	0.20	0.98	2.02	2.81	1.17	1.71	2.36	1.98
(Percent to GDP)	(0.3)	(0.8)	(1.5)	(1.8)	(0.7)	(0.9)	(1.2)	(0.9)

Table 4.13 Expenditure Pattern of State Governments and Union Territories (Rs. Lakh Crores)

Item		2015–16	2016–17	2017–18	2018–19 (RE)	2019–20 (BE)
1		2	3	4	5	6
Aggregate Expenditure (1+2 = 3+4+5)		23.01	26.38	27.72	34.70	37.68
		(16.7)	(17.2)	(16.2)	(18.3)	(17.9)
1	Revenue Expenditure	18.70	21.22	23.40	28.75	31.46
	of which:	(13.6)	(13.8)	(13.7)	(15.1)	(14.9)
	Interest Payments	2.18	2.55	2.93	3.20	3.55
		(1.6)	(1.7)	(1.7)	(1.7)	(1.7)
2	Capital Expenditure	4.31	5.17	4.31	5.95	6.22
	of which:	(3.1)	(3.4)	(2.5)	(3.1)	(2.9)
	Capital Outlay	3.39	3.96	3.94	5.44	5.81
		(2.5)	(2.6)	(2.3)	(2.9)	(2.8)
3	Development Expenditure	16.14	18.62	18.77	24.04	25.75
		(11.7)	(12.1)	(11.0)	(12.6)	(12.2)
4	Non-Development Expenditure	6.38	7.20	8.26	9.84	10.98
		(4.6)	(4.7)	(4.8)	(5.2)	(5.2)
5	Others*	0.49	0.56	0.68	0.82	0.95
		(0.4)	(0.4)	(0.4)	(0.4)	(0.4)

Source: RBI (2019), p. 3

RE:revised estimates

BE: budget estimates

*Includes grants-in-aid and contributions (compensation and assignments to local bodies).

Notes:1.Figures in parentheses are percent to GDP.2.Capital expenditure includes capital outlay and loans and advances by state governments.

revenue expenditure, which tends to be largely committed in nature, was lesser than the budgeted estimates by 7% during the above reference period. These reductions were on account of lesser revenue realization and the states had to honour the FRBM norms in meeting the fiscal deficit targets. Committed expenditure items comprising of salaries, pensions, and interest payments constituted 53% of the revenue expenditure during the above reference period. However, in the case of four states, the capital outlay was more than the budgeted amount, and these states are Odisha (8%), Haryana (6%), Himachal Pradesh (5%), and Karnataka (2%). Among the states that spent less than the budgeted amounts were Jammu and Kashmir (51%), Assam (51%), and Goa (50%). It is also disheartening to note that certain key development sectors that experienced under-spending included rural development that witnessed the highest under-spending at 16%; sectors such as irrigation and welfare of SC, ST, and other backward classes each experienced underspending to the tune of 13%. Underspending was experienced by sectors like Health (10%), education (9%), and agriculture (9%). A report on state finances by RBI also accounts such a decline in capital investments in sectors like roads and bridges, irrigation, and energy for 2017–18 (RBI, 2019). This obviously is owing to a sharper increase at 68.24% points in revenue expenditure in comparison to 44% increase in the capital expenditure. Similar trends are observed for the development and non-development components of public spending, the former experiencing a smaller growth and shrinking in size as compared to the latter.

The PRS Legislative Research report highlights overspending in the energy sector (Dash, 2018). This could be due to the states' participation in the UDAY scheme. Of the nineteen states covered in the study, twelve states participated in the UDAY scheme and took over 75% of their Discoms' (electricity distribution companies) debt. The debt burden of these states swelled as their combined debt ran to Rs. 2.19 trillion. Rajasthan, for instance, took over its discoms' debt equal to 8.8% of its GSDP. It was 5.4% for Haryana, 4.8% for Madhya Pradesh, 3.8% for Punjab, and 3.5% for Uttar Pradesh (Dash, 2018).

Many states also announced schemes like loan waivers, which had considerable prolonged fiscal implications on the state budgets. A total sum of Rs. 231, 260 crores is involved in the loan waiver announced by ten states during the period 2014–15 to 2018–19. The details of the loan waivers by the states involved and the fiscal implications are presented in Table 4.14. Schemes like loan waivers tend to not only adversely affect the fiscal health of the states but also damage the credit culture of the society at large.

Table 4.14 Fiscal Impact of States' Farm Loan Waiver Programmes (Rs. Crores)

	State	Year of Announcement	Amount Announced	Amount Provided in the Budget					
				2014–15	2015–16	2016–17	2017–18	2018–19 RE	2019–20 BE
	1	2	3	4	5	6	7	8	9
1	Andhra Pradesh	2014–15	24,000	4,000	742	3,512	3,602	875	
				(0.9)	(0.1)	(0.6)	(0.6)	(0.1)	
2	Telangana	2014–15	17,000	4,250	4,250	2,957	4,016		6,000
				(1.0)	(0.9)	(0.6)	(0.7)		(0.9)
3	Tamil Nadu	2016–17	5,280			1,682	1,870	884	807
						(0.2)	(0.2)	(0.1)	(0.1)
4	Maharashtra	2017–18	34,020				15,020	6,500	405
							(0.8)	(0.3)	(0.0)
5	Uttar Pradesh	2017–18	36,360				21,102	5,500	600
							(2.0)	(0.5)	(0.1)
6	Punjab	2017–18	10,000				348	5,500	3,000
							(0.1)	(1.4)	(0.7)
7	Karnataka	2018–19	44,000				3,917	11,965	12,650
							(0.4)	(1.1)	(1.0)
8	Rajasthan	2018–19	18,000					3,000	3,240
								(0.4)	(0.4)

(continued)

Table 4.14 *Continued*

	State	Year of Announcement	Amount Announced	Amount Provided in the Budget					
				2014–15	2015–16	2016–17	2017–18	2018–19 RE	2019–20 BE
9	Madhya Pradesh	2018–19	36,500					5,000	8,000
								(0.9)	(1.4)
10	Chhattisgarh	2018–19	6,100					4,223	5,000
								(1.8)	(2.0)
Total			231,260	8,250	4,992	8,151	49,875	43,447	39,703
As percent of state governments' total expenditure				0.4	0.2	0.3	1.8	1.2	1.2
As percent to GDP				0.1	0.0	0.1	0.3	0.2	0.2

Source: RBI (2019)

Note: Figures in parentheses indicate loan waiver as a percent to respective states GSDP for the corresponding year.

4.5 The Overall Trends

The analysis presented this far under the three broad policy phases has given a lot of insights about the growth and composition of 'all states' expenditure. The three phases depicted together for revenue and capital expenditure reveals that (Figure 4.17) the sharpest increase in the revenue expenditure was between the time period 1991–92 and 2003–04; there has been a marginal recovery in the capital expenditure during the FRBM phase albeit it is still lower than the first phase, i.e. 1974–75 to 1990–91. The revenue surplus achieved by a number of states after the framing of the FRBM Act helped some states to enhance their capital investments. State fiscal problems have surmounted again in the recent past with Covid-19 aggravating the same.

A similar trend is observed for 'development' and 'non-development' categories of expenditure, with the period 1991–92 till 2003–04 witnessing a very sharp increase in the non-development expenditure (Figure 4.18). Distribution of functional categories of expenditure (Figure 4.19) accounts for an increase in the share of social and community and economic services after the FRBM has been framed. Here too the emphasis on social and community services is much higher than that of the economic services. These are good trends given the low HDI, however, the question remains whether the increase observed is adequate to take the states to achieve adequate level of HDI.

4.6 Development Outcomes

We have examined the drastic fiscal policy changes that have been unveiled, the major one being a rule-based fiscal correction process to rein in the rapidly growing deficits, both fiscal and revenue deficits, in the decade of nineties. State governments have been incentivized to follow the fiscal reform process. These changes, coupled with the macroeconomic changes like global economic recession, have had significant implications on state finances. The positive trends being an increase in the share of own revenue resources and enhancement of capital investments. We have also seen that there has been an improvement in the quality of spending especially in the poorer states marked by a larger increase

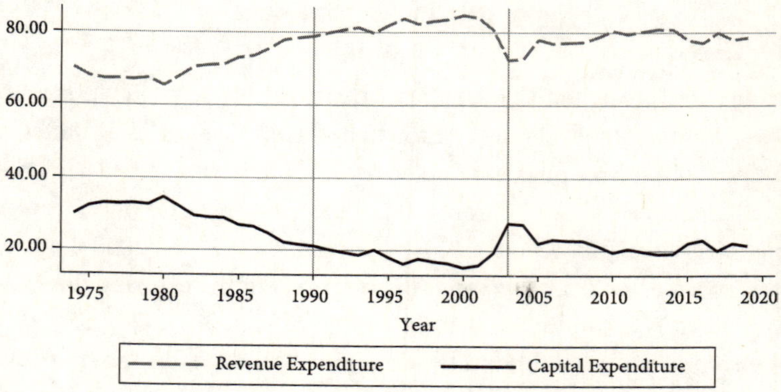

Figure 4.17 Revenue and Capital Expenditure as a Percentage to Total Expenditure
Source: Computed by the author using RBI (2005, 2010 & 2020).

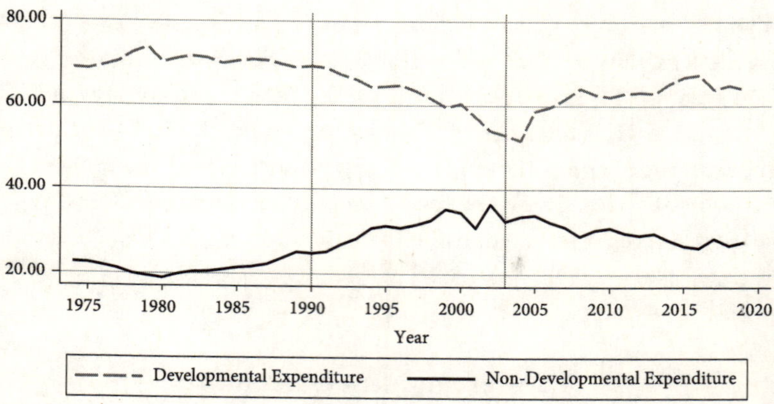

Figure 4.18 Development and Non-Development Expenditure as a Percentage to Total Expenditure
Source: Computed by the author using RBI (2005, 2010 & 2020).

in capital spending and social and economic categories of spending. However, there has been a marginal reversal after 2015–16, with the states slipping back into revenue deficit position. An important question that needs to be addressed in this context pertains to the development impacts in the states. Mundle et al. (2016) present a comparative analysis of the performance of eighteen major states in terms of change in ranks in

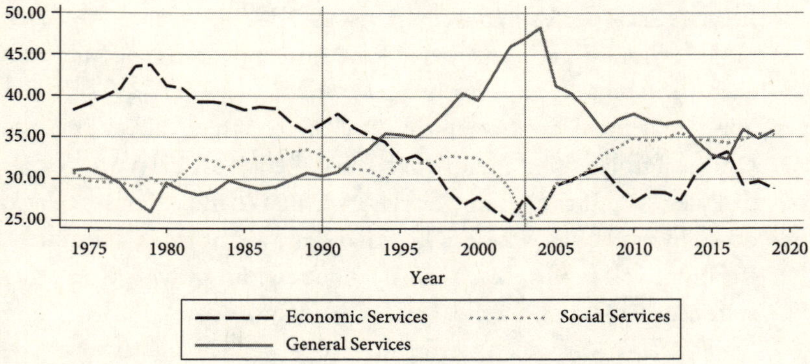

Figure 4.19 Expenditure on Functiona Heads as a Percentage of Total Expenditure

Source: Computed by the author using RBI (2005, 2010 & 2020).

2011 over that of 2001.The study's main focus is on governance performance of Indian states; this section summarizes the study's findings in the areas of fiscal, social sector, and infrastructure development.

4.6.1 Fiscal Performance

The study uses two important variables to assess the fiscal performance of states:

- The proportion of total state government expenditure allocated to development expenditure, i.e. economic and social services, and
- The states own tax effort, i.e. the ratio of the state's own tax revenue to GSDP.

Major findings of the study are given below:

- Six best fiscal performers in 2001 were Karnataka, Gujarat, Haryana, Andhra Pradesh, Tamil Nadu, and Chhattisgarh as measured by overall fiscal performance taking the spending behaviour of states with their tax effort.

- Relative fiscal performance improved in Odisha (improved by seven ranks), Chhattisgarh and Uttar Pradesh (improved by four ranks each), and Bihar (moved up by three ranks).
- The worst fiscal performers in 2001 were Assam, Uttar Pradesh, Odisha, Punjab, West Bengal, and Bihar. Relative fiscal performance declined significantly in Kerala and Jharkhand. Kerala moved down by five ranks, whereas Jharkhand moved down by four ranks. Relative fiscal performance also declined significantly in three other states, i.e. Gujarat, Haryana, and Uttarakhand.
- Gujarat and Karnataka performed very well on the expenditure front in 2001 and by 2011.On the expenditure side, Gujarat had the highest share of expenditure allocated to development services in 2001 at 70.4%, followed by 67% in Karnataka. By 2011, Karnataka, Andhra Pradesh, and Madhya Pradesh were spending more than 70% of total expenditure on development services compared to 69.8% in Gujarat.
- At the other end, Punjab, which was at the bottom with a development expenditure share of only 43.4% in 2001, was still at the bottom with 48.8% in 2011. In general, the development expenditure share increased in all the states, except Gujarat and Kerala.
- The maximum improvement over the decade was recorded in Bihar, with an increase of over 43% in the share of development expenditure, followed by an increase of about 34% in Odisha (Table 4.15) (Mundle et al., 2016).[8]

4.6.2 Infrastructure Delivery

Major findings of the study are mentioned below:

- Vast interstate differences existed in the level of infrastructure provided. The gap between the best performers and the worst performers remained in 2011, despite the gains made by the worst performers.

[8] See Mundle et al. (2016) for a more detailed discussion on states fiscal performance.

Table 4.15 Fiscal Performance

Rank	2001 States	Rank	2011 States		Rank	DAG ^{Fiscal} 2011 States	
1	Karnataka	1	Karnataka	(0)	1	Karnataka	(0)
2	Gujarat	2	Chhattisgarh	(+4)	2	Chhattisgarh	(0)
3	Haryana	3	Madhya Pradesh	(+6)	3	Madhya Pradesh	(0)
4	Andhra Pradesh	4	Andhra Pradesh	(0)	4	Andhra Pradesh	(0)
5	Tamil Nadu	5	Tamil Nadu	(0)	5	Tamil Nadu	(0)
6	Chhattisgarh	6	Gujarat	(-4)	6	Gujarat	(0)
7	Maharashtra	7	Haryana	(-4)	7	Haryana	(0)
8	Uttarkhand	8	Maharashtra	(-1)	8	Maharashtra	(0)
9	Madhya Pradesh	9	Odisha	(+7)	9	Odisha	(0)
10	Kerala	10	Rajasthan	(+1)	10	Rajasthan	(0)
11	Rajasthan	11	Uttar Pradesh	(+4)	11	Uttar Pradesh	(0)
12	Himachal Pradesh	12	Uttarkhand	(-4)	12	Uttarkhand	(0)
13	Jharkhand	13	Himachal Pradesh	(-1)	13	Himachal Pradesh	(0)
14	Assam	14	Assam	(0)	14	Assam	(0)
15	Uttar Pradesh	15	Kerala	(-5)	15	Kerala	(0)
16	Odisha	16	Bihar	(+3)	16	Bihar	(0)
17	Punjab	17	Jharkhand	(-4)	17	Jharkhand	(0)
18	West Bengal	18	Punjab	(-1)	18	Punjab	(0)
19	Bihar	19	West Bengal	(-1)	19	West Bengal	(0)

Source: Mundle, et. al. (2016).

Note: Figures in parenthesis indicate the change in ranks in 2011 with respect to 2001, and the change in ranks in DAG ^{Fiscal} 2011 with respect to 2011.

- Road density in Karnataka in 2011 at 10.8 km per 100 sq km was about five times that of road density in Odisha at only 1.95 km per sq km. Power availability in Bihar was only about one-fifteenth of the power available in Gujarat of 1,559 kWh per capita, despite a three-fold increase that happened in Bihar from 36 kWh per capita in 2001 to 117 kWh in 2011.

- The best performers in infrastructure delivery in 2001 were Gujarat, Maharashtra, Punjab, Kerala, Haryana, and Tamil Nadu in that order. Punjab's relative position declined to seventh while Karnataka's improved to third.
- Performance was the least in Chhattisgarh, Uttar Pradesh, West Bengal, Uttarakhand, Assam, and Bihar in 2001.
- The relative improvement during the period of the study 2001–11 was the highest in Uttarakhand, which moved up nine ranks.
- In a welcome development, Bihar and Uttar Pradesh, the two low-income states, recorded a drastic improvement by moving up fifteen and ten ranks, respectively, when infrastructure delivery was adjusted for the level of development. Earlier it was observed that the low-income states, especially Bihar and Orissa, improved their quality of spending.
- Two other states that significantly improved their DAG infra ranking after adjusting for their level of development are Madhya Pradesh, which moved up six ranks, and Jharkhand, which moved up five ranks.
- On the contrary, Uttarakhand and Himachal Pradesh dropped ten ranks each when the infrastructure output score was adjusted for development. Other states that slipped significantly in their DAG ranking for infrastructure (DAG infra) include (undivided) Andhra Pradesh, which slipped six ranks, and Kerala, Haryana, and West Bengal, which slipped four ranks each (Table 4.16) (Mundle et al., 2016).[9]

4.6.3 Social Service Delivery

Major findings of the study on social service delivery ranks included the following:

- Huge interstate variations in social services delivered prevailed similar to that of infrastructure delivery.

[9] See Mundle et al.(2016) for greater details.

Table 4.16 Infrastructure Delivery Ranks

Rank	2001 States	Rank	2011 States		Rank	DAG infra 2011 States	
1	Gujarat	1	Gujarat	(0)	1	Karnataka	(+2)
2	Maharashtra	2	Maharashtra	(0)	2	Gujarat	(-1)
3	Punjab	3	Karnataka	(+4)	3	Bihar	(+15)
4	Kerala	4	Tamil Nadu	(+2)	4	Maharashtra	(-2)
5	Haryana	5	Kerala	(-1)	5	Tamil Nadu	(-1)
6	Tamil Nadu	6	Haryana	(-1)	6	Punjab	(+1)
7	Karnataka	7	Punjab	(-4)	7	Uttar Pradesh	(+10)
8	Himachal Pradesh	8	Uttarkhand	(+9)	8	Madhya Pradesh	(+6)
9	Andhra Pradesh	9	Himachal Pradesh	(-1)	9	Kerala	(-4)
10	Jharkhand	10	Andhra Pradesh	(-1)	10	Haryana	(-4)
11	Odisha	11	West Bengal	(+5)	11	Jharkhand	(+5)
12	Rajasthan	12	Chhattisgarh	(+2)	12	Chhattisgarh	(0)
13	Madhya Pradesh	13	Rajasthan	(-1)	13	Odisha	(+2)
14	Chhattisgarh	14	Madhya Pradesh	(-1)	14	Rajasthan	(-1)
15	Uttar Pradesh	15	Odisha	(-4)	15	West Bengal	(-4)
16	West Bengal	16	Jharkhand	(-6)	16	Andhra Pradesh	(-6)
17	Uttarkhand	17	Uttar Pradesh	(-2)	17	Assam	(+2)
18	Assam	18	Bihar	(+1)	18	Uttarkhand	(-10)
19	Bihar	19	Assam	(-1)	19	Himachal Pradesh	(-10)

Source: Mundle, et. al. (2016).

Note: Figures in parenthesis indicate the change in ranks in 2011 with respect to 2001, and the change in ranks in DAG ^{infra} 2011 with respect to 2011.*

- Gross Enrolment Rate in Himachal Pradesh in 2011–12 had reached 100%, whereas it was only 63.7% in Assam. In health, the maternal mortality rate in 2010–12 was 66 in Kerala as compared to 328 in Assam, and the infant mortality rate in Kerala was 12 in 2011 compared to 59 in Madhya Pradesh.

- Five states, Kerala, Tamil Nadu, Maharashtra, Himachal, and Punjab remained in top ranks in social service delivery in both 2001 and 2011. Gujarat's rank moved down from the fifth place in 2001 to the ninth place in 2009, whereas West Bengal moved up from the ninth rank in 2001 to the sixth rank 2011.
- Six lowest performers in 2001 were Uttarakhand, Rajasthan, Madhya Pradesh, Jharkhand, Bihar, and Uttar Pradesh. By 2011, Madhya Pradesh and Rajasthan moved up from this category, while Odisha and Chhattisgarh slipped down to it.
- Uttarakhand revealed the largest relative improvement by moving up six ranks, whereas Madhya Pradesh improved by four ranks.
- On the contrary, relative decline in social service was the highest in Assam, which dropped nine ranks, whereas Gujarat dropped by four ranks.
- Bihar and Uttar Pradesh recorded a significant improvement in the DAG ranks for social service delivery (DAG social) moving up by sixteen ranks and eight ranks, respectively, similar to their performance in infrastructure delivery.
- On the contrary, Haryana dropped down nine ranks to the bottom and Gujarat dropped eight ranks to number seventeen out of nineteen states (Table 4.17) (Mundle et al., 2016).[10]

4.6.4 Performance Measurement

The discussion presented earlier provides an overall understanding of the status of state-wise development outcomes. It is important to identify development outcome indicators for all the sectors to track the performance in measurable terms over time. Needless to add is the importance of having authentic and accurate data to wet the progress as per the listed indicators. The most important step in this entire process is to use the performance data in the public expenditure decision-making process. On this front, India's performance is way off the mark. Performance measurement has been an area of serious

[10] See Mundle et al.(2016) for greater details.

Table 4.17 Social Service Delivery Ranks

Rank	2001 States	Rank	2011 States		Rank	DAG ^{Social} 2011 States	
1	Kerala	1	Kerala	(0)	1	Kerala	(0)
2	Himachal Pradesh	2	Tamil Nadu	(+2)	2	Bihar	(+16)
3	Maharashtra	3	Maharashtra	(0)	3	West Bengal	(+3)
4	Tamil Nadu	4	Himachal Pradesh	(−2)	4	Tamil Nadu	(−2)
5	Gujarat	5	Punjab	(+1)	5	Himachal Pradesh	(−1)
6	Punjab	6	West Bengal	(+3)	6	Maharashtra	(−3)
7	Karnataka	7	Karnataka	(0)	7	Punjab	(−2)
8	Haryana	8	Uttarkhand	(+6)	8	Karnataka	(−1)
9	West Bengal	9	Gujarat	(−4)	9	Uttar Pradesh	(+8)
10	Assam	10	Haryana	(−2)	10	Madhya Pradesh	(+2)
11	Andhra Pradesh	11	Andhra Pradesh	(0)	11	Jharkhand	(+5)
12	Chhattisgarh	12	Madhya Pradesh	(+4)	12	Andhra Pradesh	(−1)
13	Odisha	13	Rajasthan	(+2)	13	Rajasthan	(0)
14	Uttarkhand	14	Chhattisgarh	(−2)	14	Uttarkhand	(−6)
15	Rajasthan	15	Odisha	(−2)	15	Chhattisgarh	(−1)
16	Madhya Pradesh	16	Jharkhand	(+1)	16	Odisha	(−1)
17	Jharkhand	17	Uttar Pradesh	(+2)	17	Gujarat	(−8)
18	Bihar	18	Bihar	(0)	18	Assam	(+1)
19	Uttar Pradesh	19	Assam	(−9)	19	Haryana	(−9)

Source: Mundle, et. al. (2016).

Note: Figures in parenthesis indicate the change in ranks in 2011 with respect to 2001, and the change in ranks in DAG ^{Social} 2011 with respect to 2011.

concern as there is insufficient progress made even with a basic step of identifying appropriate performance indicators for many of the expenditure programmes. Data collection remains a farfetched dream. It is observed 'While there has been a recognition of the importance of M&E systems, a long felt need to put rigorous procedures as evident from various policy pronouncements, initial institutional arrangements to evaluate programs from major sectors, the initial enthusiasm did not last long. Although there were renewed sporadic statements, government wide evaluation capturing the major program performance at all the three layers of government remains a farfetched goal' (Gayithri, 2019,174). A number of countries have made a good progress in developing sound frameworks towards this end. India can study these and adopt a suitable model rather than reinvent the wheel. This book has discussed some frameworks in a subsequent chapter.

4.6.5 Quality of Public Expenditure

Quality of public spending is one aspect that has not drawn any serious attention of the policymakers until now. Although there are a couple of promises made in certain budget speeches and announcement of formulation of committees to look into the quality of government spending, none of these have been given a concrete shape.

Despite the recommendation of various bodies, right from the mid-eighties, about the containment and review of government expenditure, nothing much has been achieved until today. The government even today continues to have multiple schemes that are duplicative in nature. As a result, the resources are thinly spread on multiple schemes, which are not adequate at all for any of these programmes. There is also improper targeting under many programmes. A proper control of expenditure by examining each item of expenditure is needed as opposed to the present practice of automatic approvals. There is an urgent need to review the government expenditure by programmes rather than plan and non-plan categories, which thankfully the government has given up. Based on a review of programmes, there is a need to drop the programmes that have outgrown their utility and become redundant. This, however, cannot be achieved overnight. The process has to begin without further wasting any more time and resources.

4.7 Public Spending by the Local Bodies in India: Issues and Concerns

The study of local government expenditure incurred by the rural and urban local bodies has attracted considerable attention of the academic community. The literature raises a number of issues and concerns and emphasizes on the need to bring in effective policy correctives to enhance the fiscal autonomy of the local bodies. It has been argued that the local bodies can best prioritize public services given their proximity to the citizens and an understanding of their needs and preferences. The current situation wherein the share of local bodies' expenditure in the total expenditure is very small given their limited access to resources and a heavy dependence on the central and state transfers has put their fiscal autonomy to jeopardy. Several attempts made to reflect local priorities in the framing of expenditure policies through local planning initiatives have not been very successful. In the context of National Rural Health Mission (NRHM), it has been noticed that 'Bottom-up planning starting with village as a unit used as the main strategy of NRHM to meet the region-specific health needs would serve well to promote health sector development. The provision of effective and quality health services with a special focus on the backward districts with weak human development is also slated to be an important objective of NRHM. Analysing the district-level NRHM funds flow and expenditure in Karnataka, the present paper argues that the district-wise allocations are wrought with poor expenditure planning. Programme implementation plans and allocations significantly vary from one another. Such deviations in the earmarking of planned funds defy the very purpose of stringent bottom up planning involving colossal manpower and financial resources to track the grass-roots felt needs'(Gayithri, 2012,95).

Present book does not undertake a detailed analysis of the spending by the local bodies as it was attempted in the case of central government and all states due to non-availability of consistent and comparable data; instead, some key issues are taken up for discussion and limited data is presented as available in the existing literature. Many studies have referred to data inadequacies and the need to strengthen the same. The Thirteenth Finance Commission states 'There are significant discontinuities in data relating to revenue and expenditure of local bodies submitted by State Governments to FC-XI, FC-XII, and to this Commission. These discrepancies detract from the credibility of the data. Unfortunately, successive Finance Commissions, including our own, have been unable to independently verify the data provided on local bodies' (Government of India, 2009, 165).

4.7.1 Resource Constraints of the Local Bodies

The seventy-third and seventy-fourth amendments of the constitution are meant to strengthen the decentralization process of the rural and urban local bodies, respectively, in the country. Local planning, development, and administration in the rural areas are to be taken care of by the rural local bodies and that of urban areas local bodies are to be taken care of by the urban local bodies. Decentralization is expected to help in improving the quality of services being provided by the local bodies. The share of local government's public expenditure in the total expenditure is historically very small in the country and there have been suggestions from time to time to enhance it. FC-XIII had suggested that it should be increased to at least 15–16%. It also suggested that adhoc approaches in meting out transfers should be avoided.

4.7.2 Fiscal Autonomy

The lack of fiscal autonomy of the local bodies, be it of rural or urban, as indicated by their heavy dependence on fiscal transfers from the higher levels of government has been a major issue. Resource gap of panchayats for the period 2012–13 to 2017–18 analysed by Alok (2019) reveals that the majority of Indian states have a huge resource gap as indicated by the difference between the total expenditure and panchayat-own revenue, indicating the shrinking fiscal space(Table 4.18). Alok (2019) further presents the huge inter state per capita expenditure variations among Indian states by taking into account average expenditure incurred by the Gram Panchayats between 2012–13 to 2017–18. (Table 4.19).

Table 4.18 Resource Gap for Panchayats (Average of 2012–13 to 2017–18) (Rs. Crores)

Sl. No.	State	Expenditure by Panchayats	Own Resources of Panchayats	Resource Gap	Share of Own Revenue in Total Expenditure
General Category States					
1	Andhra Pradesh	5,976.9	406.0	5,570.9	6.8
2	Bihar	0.0	0.0	0.0	0.0
3	Chhattisgarh	7,477.0	47.5	7,429.5	0.6
4	Gujarat	16,438.2	1,089.6	15,348.5	6.6
5	Goa	134.4	0.0	134.4	0.0
6	Haryana	1,533.2	246.8	1,286.4	16.1
7	Jharkhand	769.5	42.4	727.1	5.5
8	Kerala	6,736.0	588.6	6,147.4	8.7
9	Karnataka	26,266.7	454.2	25,812.6	1.7
10	Madhya Pradesh	0.0	0.0	0.0	0.0
11	Maharashtra	36,595.8	7,546.1	29,049.7	20.6
12	Odisha	3,912.8	29.2	3,883.5	0.7
13	Punjab	604.1	409.4	194.7	67.8
14	Rajasthan	0.0	0.0	0.0	0.0
15	Tamil Nadu	5,116.6	827.6	4,289.0	16.2
16	Telangana	0.0	0.0	0.0	0.0
17	Uttar Pradesh	5,166.3	1,239.3	3,927.0	24.0
18	West Bengal	13,496.6	632.7	12,863.9	4.7
North Eastern/Hill States					
19	Arunachal Pradesh	0.0	0.0	0.0	0.0
20	Assam	3,045.7	46.2	2,999.5	1.5
21	Himachal Pradesh	118.8	11.7	107.1	9.8
22	Jammu & Kashmir	80.1	1.7	78.4	2.1
23	Manipur	39.2	0.0	39.2	0.0
24	Meghalaya	97.3	0.0	97.3	0.0
25	Mizoram	11.8	0.1	11.7	0.8
26	Nagaland	7.0	0.0	7.0	0.0
27	Sikkim	137.4	1.1	136.3	0.8
28	Tripura	123.2	6.9	116.3	5.6
29	Uttarakhand	445.1	142.2	303.0	31.9
	TOTAL	134,329.8	13,769.2	120,560.6	10.3

Source: Alok (2019), p 34

Table 4.19 Expenditure by Panchayats (Average of 2012–13 to 2017–18) (Rs. Crores)

Sl. No.	State	Expenditure by Panchayats				Rural Population 01/04/2018 (in Number)	Per Capita Expenditure
		District	Block	Village	Total		
General Category States							
1	Andhra Pradesh	300.8	5,210.7	465.4	5,976.9	36,829,377	1,622.9
2	Bihar	0.0	0.0	0.0	0.0	99,432,883	0.0
3	Chhattisgarh	5,256.2	1,433.5	787.4	7,477.1	19,799,214	3,776.4
4	Gujarat	6,532.3	8,601.1	1,304.7	16,438.1	36,989,065	4,444.1
5	Goa	0.0	0.0	134.4	134.4	730,923	1,839.3
6	Haryana	62.2	72.6	1,398.4	1,533.2	18,506,102	828.5
7	Jharkhand	234.6	151.8	383.1	769.5	27,332,753	281.5
8	Kerala	701.6	1,345.5	4,688.9	6,736.0	46,471,011	1,449.5
9	Karnataka	9,238.3	11,864.2	5,164.2	26,266.7	39,514,500	6,647.4
10	Madhya Pradesh	0.0	0.0	0.0	0.0	52,719,953	0.0
11	Maharashtra	32,550.0	272.7	3,773.1	36,595.8	63,317,990	5,779.7
12	Odisha	283.8	819.3	2,809.7	3,912.8	35,787,108	1,093.3
13	Punjab	21.3	114.5	468.3	604.1	17,715,979	341.0
14	Rajasthan	0.0	0.0	0.0	0.0	50,719,050	0.0
15	Tamil Nadu	232.8	1,384.2	3,499.6	5,116.6	39,555,747	1,293.5
16	Telangana	0.0	0.0	0.0	0.0	22,535,548	0.0

17	Uttar Pradesh	1,096.5	379.1	3,690.6	5,166.2	167,351,926	308.7
18	West Bengal	2,225.7	3,688.2	7,582.8	13,496.7	75,141,830	1,796.2
North Eastern/Hill States							
19	Arunachal Pradesh	0.0	0.0	0.0	0.0	1,241,248	0.0
20	Assam	808.3	360.1	1,877.4	3,045.8	29,625,377	1,028.1
21	Himachal Pradesh	19.0	43.2	56.7	118.9	6,773,988	175.4
22	Jammu & Kashmir	0.0	0.0	80.1	80.1	10,126,287	79.1
23	Manipur	3.5	0.0	35.7	39.2	2,361,566	166.0
24	Meghalaya	97.3	0.0	0.0	97.3	2,603,058	373.9
25	Mizoram	0.0	0.0	11.8	11.8	519,102	226.6
26	Nagaland	0.0	0.0	7.0	7.0	1,674,492	42.0
27	Sikkim	11.5	0.0	125.9	137.4	494,231	2,780.0
28	Tripura	29.6	23.5	70.0	123.1	4,491,866	274.2
29	Uttarakhand	142.0	55.3	247.8	445.1	7,193,225	618.8
	TOTAL	59,847.4	35,819.5	38,662.9	134,329.8		

Source: Alok (2019),p. 32.

4.7.3 Data Inadequacies

Data on physical and financial performance of the local bodies have been a matter of serious concern. FC-XIII observed that the quality of data provided varied across state governments, with some being of good quality, there were data inconsistencies in others. Gayithri et al. (2017) have observed that in a number of gram panchayat databases, a lot of expenditure items were posted under the 'others' category, posing difficulty in understanding the composition of expenditure. Center for Policy Research (CPR) (2014) study too reports the issue of about 30% gram panchayats reporting many items of expenditure under the 'others' category. Commenting on the serious data issues Gayithri et al. state 'While the efforts to create the Panchayat finances data are laudable, given the large-scale booking of data under "other items" there is an imminent need to build the capacity, especially of those in the backward districts in data entry and management as this data can help a great deal in corrective policy measures' (Gayithri et al., 2017, 65).

CPR (2014), citing the example of expenditure on the Mahatma Gandhi National Rural Employment Guarantee Act (MGNREGA) scheme, underlines discrepancies in the classification of expenditures under the scheme related head in different states. Some states have classified it as revenue expenditure, whereas others classified it as capital expenditure. There is also a variation in terms of presenting the data—in some village panchayats it is given under one head, whereas others have shown it under many heads. While citing the probable reasons, he states 'This misclassification might have also arisen because Panchayats maintain a plethora of bank accounts (particularly at the GP level) in which they deposit funds for various schemes. Since there is no standardisation in the number of Bank accounts and their nature, reporting PRIs particularly at village level maintain their accounts based on schemes for which they receive the money' (CPR, 2014, 65). The study further recommends the need to maintain up-to-date data online in an accurate manner.

4.8 Working of the State Finance Commissions

Gupta and Chakraborty (2019)[11] have reviewed the reports of the latest State Finance Commissions (SFCs) of twenty-five states in India. They

[11] For greater insights, read Gupta and Chakraborty (2019).

have examined the functioning and approach adopted by the SFCs. The study finds a large-scale variation per capita devolution recommended by the SFCs across states, the devolution itself is observed to be low and has no relation with per capita income. The study finds that (Table 4.20)

Table 4.20 Transfers Recommended by SFCs as PerCent of GSDP

Sl. No.	States	Devolution Average of		Total Transfers (Devolution + Grants) Average of	
		2010–11 to 2014–15	2010–11 to 2014–15	2010–11 to 2014–15	2010–11 to 2014–15
1	Andhra Pradesh (3rd)	0.36	—	0.36	—
2	Assam (3rd, 4th, 5th)	0.33	0.51	0.63	0.59
3	Bihar (3rd, 4th, 5th)	0.22	0.84	0.28	1.23
4	Chhattisgarh (1st, 2nd)	0.45	0.51	0.5	0.54
5	Gujarat (2nd)	0.49	—	0.59	—
6	Haryana (3rd, 4th, 5th)	0.19	0.33	0.19	0.34
7	Himachal Pradesh (3rd, 4th, 5th)	0.15	0.19	0.15	0.19
8	Karnataka (3rd, 4th)	2.9	3.09	2.99	3.17
9	Kerala (3rd, 4th)	1.17	1.5	1.17	1.5
10	Madhya Pradesh (4th)	—	0.47	—	0.47
11	Maharashtra (3rd)	0.98	—	1.47	—
12	Manipur (3rd)	1.48	1.51	2.35	2.44
13	Mizoram (1st)	—	0.25	—	0.26
14	Odisha (2nd, 3rd, 4th)	0.34	0.16	0.44	0.3
15	Punjab (3rd, 4th, 5th)	0.29	0.29	0.37	0.35
16	Rajasthan (3rd, 4th)	0.42	0.48	0.45	0.5
17	Sikkim (2nd, 3rd, 4th)	0.02	0.07	1.05	0.12
18	Tamil Nadu (3rd, 4th, 5th)	0.73	0.76	0.8	0.8
19	Tripura (2nd, 3rd)	0.25	—	0.25	—
20	Uttar Pradesh (3rd, 4th)	0.8	0.86	0.85	0.86
21	Uttarakhand (2nd, 3rd)	0.51	0.69	0.51	0.69
22	West Bengal (3rd, 4th)	0.17	0.14	0.17	0.14
	All State Average	0.82	0.96	0.93	1.02
	All State Average (without Karnataka)	0.58	0.58	0.69	0.63

Source: Gupta and Chakraborty (2019), p. 14.

all state average recommended devolution as percent of GSDP of states was less than 1%, albeit has had a marginal increase from 0.82% (average for the period 2010–11 and 2014–15) and 0.96% (average for the period 2015–16 and 2019–20. There are exceptions in the case of Kerala, Manipur, and Karnataka, where devolution to GSDP is observed to be greater than 1% of GSDP. Devolution in Karnataka stands at 3% of GSDP, the authors argue that this could be due to the salaries of deputed staff. CPR (2014) study too refers to this situation. He states 'In the case of some States, for example, Karnataka, Gujarat and Maharashtra, large amounts of expenditure are incurred towards the salaries of functionaries working under RLBs, who are typically deputed from the Government. This drives up the overall expenditure on establishment in these states, as compared to other States. It is quite likely that State-wide expenditure data omits the inclusion of such data' (CPR, 2014, 65). Excluding Karnataka, the all state average recommended devolution is 0.58% of GSDP (the average of both the time periods).

4.9 Issues in Urban Local Bodies

Urban local bodies too are facing financial constraints given the huge mismatch between their revenue and fiscal functions. Fiscal autonomy is poor due to their large-scale dependency on higher levels of the government. Trends in municipal revenue and expenditure as percent of GDP are presented in Figure 4.20.

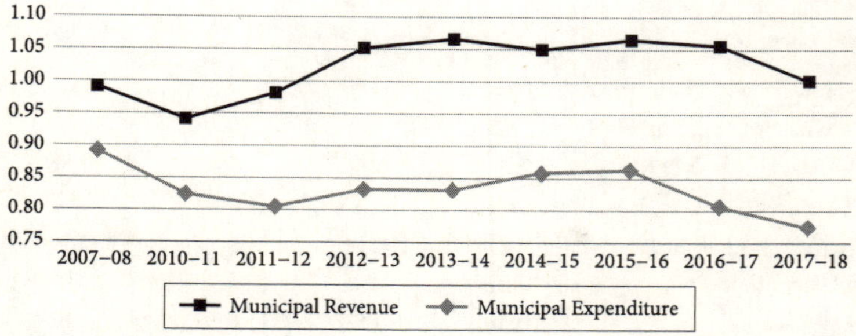

Figure 4.20 Municipal Revenue and Municipal Expenditure (Percent GDP)
Source: ICRIER, 2019, p. 7.

Municipal revenue accounts for a small share of GDP in India revolving around 1% of GDP. This ratio is much larger in other countries as stated in ICRIER (2019), the ratio being 4.5% for Poland, 6.0% for South Africa, 7.4% for Brazil, 13.9% for the United Kingdom, and 14.2% for Norway in 2010 (OECD 2012 as cited in ICRIER, 2019).

4.9.1 Municipal finance indicators

Municipal finance indicators taken as percent to GDP presented in Table 4.21 reveal the declining trend in own tax revenue; more or less stagnant and low non-tax revenue; larger and growing dependence on state government transfers; and although small but growing transfers from the central government. The growing dependence on the central transfers is revealed in Figure 4.21, depicting the shares of municipal own revenue and the transfers in the total municipal resources.

Regarding the composition of expenditure, a predominant share is that of revenue expenditure as observed by the available studies. Despite the huge infrastructure needs given the growing urbanization, the capital expenditure constituted a very small share in the total. The High-Powered Expert Committee (HPEC) for Estimating the Investment Requirements for Urban Infrastructure Services or Ahluwalia Committee (2011) estimated that India would need capital expenditure (not including the cost of land) of Rs.31 lakh crore at 2009–10 prices to meet the urban infrastructure deficit over 2012–31. The Operations & Maintenance (O&M) expenditure for the existing as well as new infrastructure was estimated at Rs. 18 lakh crore at 2009–10 prices (ICRIER, 2019). The study further states that despite an increase in per capita municipal expenditure in India, it still lags far behind the per capita spending of other countries. McKinsey (2010) estimates India's annual per capita spending on cities in 2010 at $50. This is much less compared to $362 in China, $508 in South Africa, and $1,772 in the United Kingdom. As for capital expenditures, India's per capita annual urban spending is $17 as against $116 in China, $127 in South Africa, and $391 in the United Kingdom. The report argues that India needs to increase the figure eightfold from $17 to $134 by 2030, raising it from 0.5% of GDP to 2% of GDP a year (Mohanty 2016, as cited in ICRIER, 2019).

Table 4.21 Municipal Finance Indicators (PerCent of GDP)

	2010–11	2011–12	2012–13	2013–14	2014–15	2015–16	2016–17	2017–18
Municipal Own Revenue	0.48	0.49	0.53	0.52	0.51	0.51	0.47	0.43
• Tax Revenue	0.30	0.31	0.32	0.30	0.30	0.30	0.28	0.25
• Non-Tax Revenue	0.18	0.18	0.20	0.21	0.21	0.21	0.19	0.18
Central Transfers	0.07	0.07	0.08	0.09	0.08	0.10	0.13	0.12
• CFC Grants	0.03	0.03	0.04	0.05	0.04	0.05	0.08	0.07
• Other Central Transfers	0.04	0.04	0.04	0.04	0.04	0.04	0.05	0.05
State Transfers	0.28	0.30	0.34	0 35	0.35	0.34	0.34	0.33
Borrowings	0.04	0.03	0.02	0.03	0.03	0.03	0.03	0.02
Other Sources of Revenue	0.07	0.09	0.08	0.08	0.09	0.08	0.08	0.10
Municipal Revenue Total	0.94	0.98	1.05	1.06	1.05	1.06	1.05	1.00
Municipal Expenditure	0.82	0.81	0.83	0.83	0.86	0.86	0.81	0.78

Source: ICRIER, 2019, p. 9.

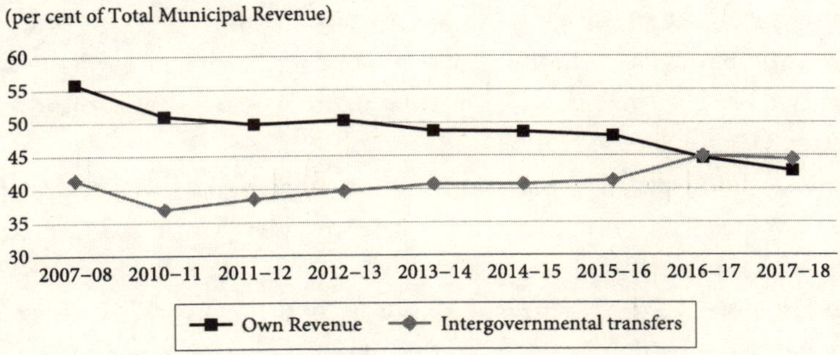

Figure 4.21 Municipal Own Revenue and Intergovernmental Transfers
Source: ICRIER, 2019, p. 11.

4.9.2 Budget making

The budgets prepared by the urban local bodies lack fiscal marksmanship as their budget estimates and the actuals vary significantly (Gayithri & Madheswaran 2015). ICRIER (2019), citing from the Comptroller and Auditor General (CAG) reports, indicates several lacunae in the preparation of municipal accounts. These problems include lack of budget preparation, absence of accurate and timely finalization of accounts in the prescribed formats, insignificant monitoring, and lackadaisical approach in the certification of accounts by urban local governments (ICRIER, 2019).

Many studies have referred to the issue of non-synchronicity of the period of recommendations of the SFCs and the union finance commissions as an issue, including the Thirteenth Finance Commission. ICRIER(2019) states the national finance commission and the state finance commissions should be constituted simultaneously to avoid the problem of 'gap' years in the transfers.

4.10 Way Forward

It is time to undertake a complete review of public expenditure at all the three levels of the government and weed out the schemes that have outlived their utility and have become redundant. This step requires political courage as no political party would ever be willing to roll back any ongoing programme fearing the loss of political mileage, coupled with that is the enthusiasm to announce new programmes in every budget. 'Coming back to power is more important than pursuing sound economics' (Singh, 2009, 121).

It is aptly observed, 'First and foremost, the need to withstand pressures for new, populist schemes. Those already committed constitute fiscal and implementational strains... District officials, the same agency who are already engaged in law and order and numerous development schemes, have neither the time nor capability to undertake added commitments' (Singh, 2009, 118). A forward-looking expenditure policy is the need of the hour. Commenting on the expenditure challenges Singh states, '... on expenditure outlays the reform of public expenditure policy is long overdue. There is a lot of money locked in the system. Implementation of public projects is running behind time. They have huge cost and time overruns. The procedures and processes and leakages involved detract from the advantages of large public investments. Merely increasing the expenditure in public outlays therefore is not the answer. Reviewing project implementation strategy must receive priority. This means revisiting the cumbersome rules, regulations and procedures for improving disbursement and actual money flow. How to get projects implemented efficiently with less delay and corruption remains a central challenge' (Singh,2009, 251).

The most important challenge is to shift the focus from merely enhancing the outlays to outcomes, the progress made in India towards the end is discussed in a subsequent chapter. Stating the steps involved in this direction, it is stated '... designing a system for monitoring outlay outcomes as well as fiscal and qualitative evaluation of public outlays is logical. Capacity building, particularly in states which would implement investment, would be important. To start with we need to:

- Move forward on statistical system upgrades to improve the monitoring of economy;
- Develop information management, paying attention to the decrepit statistical and management information system at all levels of government, but especially state and local; and
- Implement well throughout e-governance strategies' (Singh, 2009, 122).

5

Public Expenditure Control and Management

We have discussed the issues relating to the rapid growth that has taken place in government spending in India over time. An important issue that has considerable importance in the context of responsible public financial operations relates to the expenditure control mechanism that is built into the system and its function to ensure prudent use of the public resources. This gains all the more significance due to the fact that the public resources that are used by governments are collected from the economic agents, including citizens, corporate entities, and financial institutions, using tax, non-tax, and borrowings as instruments. The government is accountable to all the agents who are contributing to the exchequer. Hence, the prudency with which the funds are expended is of paramount importance in making governments accountable. To ensure a strong accountability presence, it is essential that effective control is put in place at both the stages of planning and execution. Public expenditure planning has to necessarily reflect the societal needs. Hence, resource allocation has to be based on precise cost estimates of meeting such expenditure needs. Excessive allocations can lead to wasteful and inefficient use of resources, and on the contrary, inadequate allocations result in under-provisioning, leading to poor quality service delivery. It is necessary to be informed that the needs of a society are not static and undergo changes from time to time. The process of expenditure planning has to be well informed to reflect the current needs and past achievements. Effective execution of the expenditure programmes is very essential in the delivery of public services and need constant vigilance and control. Concurrent monitoring enables midcourse corrections and the end evaluation helps assess the extent of success or failure, thereby helping in the formulation of informed expenditure decisions in the ensuing budgets.

Public Expenditure in India. Gayithri Karnam, Oxford University Press. © Oxford University Press 2022.
DOI: 10.1093/oso/9780192857569.003.0005

Given the importance of the controls and regulatory measures in the use of public money, an attempt is made in this chapter to document the current institutional mechanisms in place to exert control on public expenditure and critically examine its effectiveness using the existing evidence and discussions with the stakeholders.

5.1 *Exante and Expost* Control Mechanism

Expenditure control is necessary both before and after the spending takes place. The *exante* control on public spending is in the form of approval required for the proposed demands for grants by the Parliament/ Legislature even before the actual spending begins. *Expost* control is to examine if there is adherence to the spending proposals, this is taken up by CAG, a constitutional authority created for the purpose of scrutinizing fiscal operations. Public Accounts Committee (PAC) peruses these reports in ensuring accountability.

5.2 Constitutional Provisions and Procedures

Article 266 of the Indian Constitution renders the legal foundation of parliamentary control for the budget resources, which states that all revenues and receipts of the government should to go to a 'Consolidated Fund' and money can be withdrawn from the 'fund' only in accordance with the laws passed by the Parliament. Thus, the Parliament acts as the first point of control approving of the resources to be raised and the manner in which they will be expended during each FY. Hence, parliamentary control over public financial operations is an instrument of accountability at the highest level of the government. In view of the annual budget cycle that India follows, the principle of annuality acts as an important tool of parliamentary control over appropriations. In the process of seeking approval for grants, executive gets subjected to parliamentary control year-on-year.

As per the constitutional requirement, an AFS, in other words, the annual financial budget of the estimated receipts and expenditure of the government for the ensuing FY, is to be laid before both the houses of the Parliament by the President at the beginning of the FY. In India, each FY runs from April 1 to March 31. The central government presented its budget on the last day of February for a number of years, and this practice has now been changed to the first day of February. Finance minister Mr Arun Jaitley started the practice of presenting union budget on February1, 2017, departing from the colonial tradition of using the last working day of that month. The rail budget was merged with the union budget in 2017 after it was presented separately for ninety-two years.

The budget statement includes estimates of revenue, expenditure proposals for the ensuing budget, revised estimates for the current FY, and actuals for the preceding year. These estimates are categorized under the 'revenue' and 'capital' accounts. The nature of these categories and what comprises them were discussed in Chapter 2. The statement presents the receipts and payments of the government under three parts in which the government accounts are kept: (a) Consolidated Fund, (b) Contingency Fund, and (c) Public Account. The Consolidated Fund was constituted under Article 266 (1) of the Constitution of India. All revenues received by the government by way of direct and indirect taxes, government borrowings, and receipts from loans flow into the CFI.

Government expenditure in its entirety is met from this fund, barring the exceptional items that are met from the Contingency Fund or the Public Account. Most importantly, no money can be withdrawn from this fund without the Parliament's approval. However, as per the Constitution of India, there are certain expenditures that are 'charged' on the Consolidated Fund, which need not be submitted for the approval of the Parliament, albeit, they could be discussed if the Parliament wishes to discuss. The 'voted' expenditure invariably needs the approval of the Parliament. AFS presents these expenditure proposals as estimates to the Parliament in the form of Demand for Grants. The public expenditure control exerted by the Parliament rests with the power it has to scrutinize the demands for grants and either approve of them or approve subject to a reduction in the estimates submitted. After the grants are approved by the Lok Sabha, they are put in Appropriation Bill, and any expenditure out of the Consolidated Fund can be made only after it is passed by the Parliament. Once the Appropriation Bill is passed, it is called the Appropriation Act. According to Kalse (2013), 'Appropriation Act is an important means of parliamentary control on the public finance as it serves as an authorisation to the issuance of money from the Consolidated Fund of India to incur the sanctioned sum of expenditure. Further, it also restricts the amount of expenditure to the sums authorised and to be incurred only for the purpose for which authorized.'[1]

There could also be situations when the funds sanctioned by the Annual Appropriation Act for a particular service may prove to be inadequate or additional expenditure is needed for a new service that was not contemplated at the time of budget approval. Such additional expenditures can be met from the supplementary estimates. The Finance Minister has to seek Parliament's approval by placing the supplementary estimates before the closure of the FY. Supplementary Appropriation Act containing the demands sanctioned by the Lok Sabha as well as the expenditure charged on the Consolidated Fund is passed by the parliament.

5.3 Parliamentary Financial Committees

Parliamentary committees that are of relevance in the context of public expenditure control are the financial committees comprising of PAC, Estimates Committee, and Committee on Public Undertakings (CoPU).[2] An outline of their composition and functions is presented below.

5.3.1 PAC

Parliament as one of the key state institutions has a prime role to play in the framing of public policy and also ensure its effective implementation. The committee system assumes great importance in a parliamentary democracy. Owing to the wide gamut of responsibilities, Parliament as a single body cannot have an effective control over the government. In addition, the rapid growth in the gamut of government activities has made the task of effective control even more difficult. Certain committees have been constituted to take care of designated responsibilities. In this

[1] For greater details read Kalse (2013).

[2] This section which provides the technical details of the composition and functions of these committees is drawn extensively from Government of India (n.d.a) Retrieved from https://bit.ly/2OuRV9P,on April 08, 2020.

chapter, we discuss only the committees that deal with public financial aspects.

PAC is important in the context of public finances and is made responsible to ensure that public funds are used for the purpose for which they were allocated and probe into the reasons for any excess expenditure over and above the authorized level. PAC has a long history and was first set up in 1921 in the wake of the Montagu–Chelmsford Reforms.[3]

PAC is now constituted every year under Rule 308 of the Rules of Procedure and Conduct of Business in Lok Sabha. PAC consists of not more than twenty-two members, of which, fifteen members are elected by Lok Sabha every year from among its members according to the principle of proportional representation by means of single transferable vote and not more than seven members of Rajya Sabha are elected by that house in like manner. The term of office of members of the committee does not exceed one year at a time. A minister is not elected a member of the committee, and if a member, after his election to the committee is appointed as a minister, he ceases to be a member of the committee from the date of such appointment. The chairman of the committee is appointed by the Speaker from among the members of the committee from Lok Sabha.

The committee examines the accounts showing the appropriations of the sums granted by the Parliament for government's expenditure. The committee also examines the accounts of the government corporations as well as autonomous and semi-autonomous bodies. The committee has the power to hear officials or take evidence connected with the accounts under examination. The functioning of the committee is based on the reports prepared by the CAG. The reports prepared by the CAG serve the purpose only when the PAC effectively uses them to ensure that grants made to the various departments are used only for the purposes set out in the estimates. PAC reviews the transactions of the departments after the budget has been executed to ensure that money is spent as the Parliament intended, that due economy is exercised, and that no waste or extravagance or losses occur in expenditure. The committee is not an executive body and has no power to disallow any item or to issue an order. Its

[3] For a historical account of the Committee's constitution and its functions see Premchand (1966) and Government of India (n.d.a) Retrieved from https://bit.ly/2OuRV9P ,on April 08, 2020.

reports are technically made to the Parliament. The reports have no force in themselves but they carry great weight and influence. The government usually accepts its recommendations. A beneficial result of the activities of the committee is that it reminds the officials that their actions are subject to scrutiny on behalf of the Parliament and this is a great check on the slackness, negligence, or absolutism of the executive (Kalse, 2013).

Scope and Functions

The functions of the committee, as enshrined in Rule 308(1) of the Rules of Procedure and Conduct of Business in Lok Sabha, include examination of accounts showing the appropriation of sums granted by the Parliament for the expenditure of the Government of India, the annual finance accounts of the government, and such other accounts laid before the house as the committee may think fit. In scrutinizing the Appropriation Accounts of the Government of India and the Report of the CAG of India thereon, the committee has to satisfy—

- that the money shown in the accounts as having been disbursed were legally available for, and applicable to, the service or purpose to which they have been applied or charged;
- that the expenditure conforms to the authority which governs it; and
- that every re-appropriation has been made in accordance with the provisions made in this behalf under rules framed by competent authority.

It shall also be the duty of the committee—

- to examine the statement of accounts showing the income and expenditure of state corporations, trading and manufacturing schemes, concerns and projects together with the balance sheets and statements of profit and loss accounts which the President may have required to be prepared or are prepared under the provisions of the statutory rules regulating the financing of a particular corporation, trading or manufacturing scheme or concern or project and the report of CAG thereon.
- to examine the statement of accounts showing the income and expenditure of autonomous and semi-autonomous bodies, the audit of

which may be conducted by the CAG of India either under the directions of the President or by a statute of Parliament; and

- to consider the report of the CAG in cases where the President may have required him to conduct an audit of any receipts or to examine the accounts of stores and stocks. If any money has been spent on any service during a FY in excess of the amount granted by the house for that purpose, the committee shall examine with reference to the facts of each case the circumstances leading to such an excess and make such recommendation as it may deem fit.
- to ascertain whether financial allocations granted by the Parliament has been spent by the government 'within the scope of the demand.' The main objectives behind this is to ensure that a) money recorded as spent against the grant must not be more than the amount granted, b) the expenditure brought to account against a particular grant must be of such a nature as to warrant its record against the grant and against no other, and c) the grants should be spent on purposes which are set out in the detailed demand and they cannot be spent on 'any new service not contemplated in the demand'.

The functions of the committee extend 'beyond the formality of expenditure to its wisdom, faithfulness, and economy'. The committee thus examines cases involving losses, nugatory expenditure, and financial irregularities. When any case of proved negligence resulting in loss or extravagance is brought to the notice of the committee, it calls upon the ministry/department concerned to explain what action, disciplinary or otherwise, it had taken to prevent a recurrence. In such a case, it can also record its opinion in the form of disapproval or pass strictures against the extravagance or lack of proper control by the ministry or department concerned. Another important function of the committee is the discussion on points of financial discipline and principle. The detailed examination of questions involving principle and system is a leading and recognized function of the committee. The committee is not concerned with questions of policy in the broad sense. As a rule, it expresses no opinion on points of general policy, but it is within its jurisdiction to point out whether there has been extravagance or waste in carrying out that policy.

The committee also looks into regularization of excesses over Grants if any money has been spent by the government on a service in excess of the amount granted by the house for the purpose. The committee examines with reference to the facts of each case or the circumstances leading to such an excess and makes such recommendations as it may deem fit. Such excesses are thereafter required to be brought up before the house by the government for regularization in the manner envisaged in Article 115 of the Indian Constitution. To facilitate speedy regularization of such excess expenditure by the Parliament, the committee presents a consolidated report relating to all ministries/departments in advance of other reports. The committee looks upon savings arising from incorrect estimation or other defects of procedure no more leniently than it does upon excesses. It regards estimating on the safe side to be as faulty as estimating on the low side. In the words of the committee 'from one point of view, "safe" estimating might be regarded as even more objectionable, as it might easily lead to extravagance, waste or worse.'

The functions of Committee are also crucial as Lok Sabha, having voted large sums of the taxpayers' money, in the interest of the taxpayers, does expect in due course a detailed account of how the money has been spent. It must satisfy itself that the money so voted were directed to the intended purposes and were spent prudently and economically.

The CAG examines the yearly accounts of the government and after scrutiny certifies the accounts, subject to such reservations as he chooses to make, and submits his reports to the President who causes them to be laid before the Parliament. It is difficult, if not impossible, for Lok Sabha to examine in detail the accounts, which are complex and technical. Further it cannot spare the time required for such examination. It is for these reasons that Lok Sabha has constituted the PAC and entrusted it with the detailed examination of those accounts. Another important function of the committee is the discussion on points of financial discipline and principle. The detailed examination of questions involving principle and system is a leading and recognized function of the committee.

PAC at Work

The committee's work depends a great deal upon the results of audit and examination of the accounts of the Union Government carried out by the CAG. The audit by the CAG is comprehensive and manifold. It includes (a) accountancy audit, (b) regularity audit, (c) appropriation audit, (d) propriety audit or what is also known as discretionary audit, and (e) efficiency-cum-performance audit. In recent years, the technique of efficiency-cum-performance has been attempted in the audit of developmental schemes. The audit examines as how far the implementing agency is adequately discharging its financial responsibilities in regard to the various schemes undertaken by it and ascertains whether the schemes are being executed effectively and their operations conducted economically and whether they are producing the results expected of them. In fact, the institution of audit plays a crucial role in the functioning of the PAC, and the CAG is often termed as 'friend, philosopher, and guide' of the committee. At the beginning of its term every year, the committee makes a selection of audit paragraphs included in the various reports of CAG for in-depth examination. In addition to the above, the committee may also select one or more suo moto subjects for in-depth examination during the year (in consonance with Rule 276 of the Rules & Procedure) apart from those included in CAG reports/paras. After holding deliberations and taking note of the time available at the disposal of the committee, the committee selects the most important subjects/paragraphs on which oral examination is to be conducted.

Action Taken on Recommendations

The government is required to intimate the committee the action taken or proposed to be taken by it on the recommendations contained in the report normally within six months of the presentation. The action taken replies of the government are considered by the committee and after due classification of the replies, an Action Taken Report is presented to the Parliament. The government is further required to intimate the committee the action taken or proposed to be taken by it on the recommendations contained in Chapter I of the Action Taken Report and also to furnish final replies based on the earlier recommendations contained in the Original Report in respect of which either no replies had previously been received or only interim replies had been received. The action taken thus reported by the government is laid on the Table of the house in the form of a statement without any further comments by the committee. This system not only ensures accountability of the executive to the Parliament but also enables the Parliament and the general public to appraise government's final replies to the committee's recommendations. This completes the examination of a subject by the committee. With a view to ensure accountability of the executive related to all the issues dealt with in various audit reports, PAC decided in 1982 that the audit reports from 1980–81 onwards be referred to the ministries/departments concerned for furnishing notes duly vetted by audit showing remedial/corrective action taken on all the paragraphs contained therein. Taking note of the inordinate delays and persistent failures on the part of a large number of ministries in reporting to the committee the corrective action taken by them on audit paragraphs, the committee recommended that the Action Taken Notes on all the paragraphs of the report of CAG of India may be furnished to the committee through the Ministry of Finance (Department of Expenditure) within a period of four months from the date of laying of audit reports on the Table of the house and that the Monitoring Cell, Department of Expenditure, may develop and operationalize the Audit Para Monitoring System (APMS) portal for real-time monitoring of the same. At present, due to the persistent efforts of the committee, the entire process of audit para settlement is online. As a result of the initiatives taken by the PAC, the respective ministries/departments have toned up their administrative machinery for timely submission of the remedial action taken notes and the action taken replies on the recommendations made by the committee, pendency figures have drastically come down, and the committee is aiming to achieve zero pendency.

Chairmen of PAC were appointed from the members of the ruling party until 1966–67. Since the committee became a parliamentary committee under the control of the Speaker from January 1950, it has presented 1,596reports till 16th Lok Sabha (Battacharya 2018).

PAC is traditionally considered the most important financial committee of the Parliament in the financial accountability process. It has a wide ambit, it examines the budgetary appropriations and accounts of the government and reports of CAG on the execution of the projects and programmes by the ministries. By convention, the recommendations of PAC are considered as the recommendation of the entire house.

Table 5.1 Number of Reports Submitted by the PAC during various Lok Sabha Tenures

Lok Sabha Tenure	Number of Reports
1st Lok Sabha 1952–57	25
2nd Lok Sabha 1957–62	43
3rd Lok Sabha 1962–67	72
4th Lok Sabha 1967–70	125
5th Lok Sabha 1971–77	239
6th Lok Sabha 1977–79	149
7th Lok Sabha 1980–84	231
8th Lok Sabha 1984–89	187
9th Lok Sabha 1989–91	022
10th Lok Sabha 1991–96	119
11th Lok Sabha 1996–97	024
12th Lok Sabha 1998–99	011
13th Lok Sabha 1999–04	063
14th Lok Sabha 2004–09	084
15th Lok Sabha 2009–14	100
16th Lok Sabha 2014–19	102

Source: Bhattacharjee (2018)

The number of reports submitted by Lok Sabha tenure is presented in Table 5.1.

5.3.2 Committee on Estimates

Constitution

The Committee on Estimates, constituted for the first time in 1950, is a parliamentary committee consisting of thirty members, elected every year by the Lok Sabha from among its members. The chairperson of the committee is appointed by the Speaker from among its members. A minister cannot be elected as a member of the committee and if a member after selection to the committee is appointed as a minister, the member ceases to be a member of the committee from the date of such appointment. The term of office of the committee is one year.

Functions

The functions of the Estimates Committee are as follows:

- to report what economies, improvements in organisation, efficiency, or administrative reform, consistent with the policy underlying the estimates may be effected;
- to suggest alternative policies in order to bring about efficiency and economy in administration;
- examine whether the money is well laid out within the limits of the policy implied in the estimates; and
- to suggest the form in which the estimates shall be presented to the Parliament.

The committee does not exercise its functions in relation to such public undertakings as are allotted to the CoPU by the Rules of Procedure and Conduct of Business of Lok Sabha or by the Speaker.

Working

Soon after it is constituted, the committee selects such of the estimates pertaining to a ministry/department of the central government or such of the statutory and other bodies of the central government as may seem fit to the committee. The committee also examines matters of special interest which may arise or come to the light in the course of its work or which is specially referred to it by the house or the Speaker. The committee calls for preliminary materials from the ministry/department, statutory, and other government bodies related to the subjects selected for examination and also memoranda from non-officials connected with the subjects for the use of the members of the committee.

The committee, from time to time, appoints one or more sub-committees/study groups for carrying out detailed examination of various subjects. If it appears to the committee that it is necessary for the purpose of its examination that an on-the-spot study should be made, the committee may, with the approval of the Speaker, decide to undertake visits to make a study of any particular matter, project, or establishment, either as a whole committee or by dividing itself into study groups. Notes relating to the institutions/offices to be visited are called for in advance from the concerned ministries/departments and circulated among the members of the committee/sub-committee/study group. When the committee/sub-committee/study group is on study visit, only informal sittings are held at the place of visit. At such sittings, neither evidence is recorded nor any decisions are taken. All discussions held by the committee with the representative of the ministries/departments, non-official organisations, etc. are treated as confidential and no one having access to the discussions directly or indirectly should communicate to the press or any unauthorized person any information about matters taken up during the discussions. Later in the light of informal discussions during study visits, memoranda received from non-official and information collected from the ministry/department concerned and other sources, non-official and official witnesses are invited to give evidence at formal sittings of the committee held in the Parliament House Complex, New Delhi. The observations/recommendations of the committee are embodied in its reports which are presented to Lok Sabha. After a report has been presented to Lok Sabha, the ministry or department concerned is required to take action on the observations/recommendations conclusions contained in the report within a period of six months or as directed by the committee. The replies of the government are examined by the committee and an Action Taken Report is presented to Lok Sabha. The replies to the recommendations contained in the Action Taken Reports are laid on the Table of Lok Sabha in the form of statements.

Achievements

Since its inception in April 1950, the committee has presented 1,121 reports covering almost all the ministries/departments of the Government of India. Out of these, 627 are the original reports and 494 are reports on action taken by the government on earlier reports of the committee as on December13, 2018.

5.3.3 CoPU

Constitution

CoPU is a parliamentary committee consisting of twenty-two members, fifteen of whom are elected by the Lok Sabha every year from among its members according to the principle of proportional representation by means of a single transferable vote and seven members are nominated by Rajya Sabha for being associated with the committee. The chairman is appointed by the Speaker from among the members of the committee. A minister is not eligible to become a member of the committee. If a member after his election to the committee is appointed as a minister, he ceases to be a member of the committee from the date of such appointment. The term of the committee does not exceed one year.

Functions

The functions of the CoPU are mentioned below:

- to examine the reports and accounts of public undertakings specified in the Fourth Schedule to the Rules of Procedure and Conduct of Business in Lok Sabha;
- to examine the reports, if any, of CAG of India on the public undertakings;
- to examine, in the context of the autonomy and efficiency of the public undertakings, whether the affairs of the public undertakings are being managed in accordance with sound business principles and prudent commercial practices; and
- to exercise such other functions vested in PAC and the Estimates Committee related to public undertakings allotted to the committee by the Speaker from time to time.

Working of the Committee

The committee selects from time to time for examination such public undertakings or such subjects that may deem fit and as fall within their terms of reference. The ministry/undertaking concerned is asked to furnish necessary material relating to those subjects for information of the members of the committee. The committee may from time to time appoint one or more study groups for carrying out detailed examination of various subjects. If it appears to the committee that on-the-spot study need to be made for the purpose of its examination, the committee undertakes tours to study any particular matter, project, or undertaking with the specific approval of the Speaker.

Notes relating to the undertakings/offices to be visited are called for in advance from the ministries/undertakings concerned and circulated among the members of the committee. These form the starting point for the informal discussion, which the committee holds at the projects. When the committee/study groups are on study tour, only informal meetings are held at the place of visit, and at such meetings, neither evidence is recorded nor any decisions taken. The members of the committee while on tour may also meet informally the representatives of Chambers of Commerce and Industry, non-official organisations, and bodies that are concerned with the subject under examination of the committee. Later, in the light of these informal discussions of the committee and the memoranda and other information received, non-official and official witnesses are invited to give evidence at formal sittings of the committee held in the Parliament House/Parliament House Annexe. All discussions held by the committee with the representatives of the undertakings/ministries/ departments, non-official organisations, labour unions, etc. are to be treated as confidential and no one having access to the discussions, directly or indirectly, should communicate to the press or any unauthorized person any information about matters taken up during the discussions. The observations/recommendations of the committee are embodied in their reports that are presented to the Parliament. After a report has been presented to the house, the ministry or undertaking concerned is required to take action on various recommendations and conclusions contained in the report. The replies of the government are examined by an action taken sub-committee/committee and an Action Taken Report is presented to the house.

Achievements

The committee, since its inception, has presented 664 reports. Of these, 303 are original reports, and 307 are reports on action taken by the government on original reports of the committee. Out of 303 original reports, thirty-eight are in the nature of horizontal studies on various aspects of working of the public undertakings.

5.4 Effectiveness of the Controls

The Constitution of India has recognized the importance of using public money in a guarded manner and put in place institutional mechanisms to exert control on the use of public money by the executive. In the first instance, public money can neither be raised by way of government revenue nor expended without the authorization of the Parliament/state legislature, which serves as an *exante* control. Once there is Parliament authorization and the funds are spent, there are *expost* checks and balances. There are committees, whose functions are discussed earlier, instituted to examine instances of excess expenditure and the factors responsible for such indulgence in excess spending. An important question, however, is whether these checks and balances are effectively ensuring control of expenditure. Although it is a necessary condition to have these checks and balances in place, it is very essential that these serve well in exerting the much required control, in the absence of which the very purpose of instituting such checks and balances gets defeated. In what follows is an examination of the effectiveness of the control measures in place.

5.4.1 Status of Parliament Discussions on Budget Proposals

Parliament/legislature take up discussion of demands for grants following the budget presentation. Detailed discussion on the budget proposals is the exclusive prerogative of the Lok Sabha, and it is necessary to ensure that the quality and sustainability of public expenditure is ensured right at the stage of approving of the proposals. We have already noted that public expenditure in India has grown enormously and there is a considerable chunk of committed expenditure caused by the innumerable programmes announced by the government from time to time. It becomes critical to have informed debates on the usefulness of new budget proposals not to constrain the fiscal space further in future.

Time Spent on Budget Proposal Discussion

In the first place, it is important to understand the seriousness with which discussion on budget proposals happens in the Parliament. There have been growing concerns overtime about the quality time spent by the government and the opposition, very often the sessions get disrupted by unruly behaviour, leaving a very little time for productive discussion. Nayyar (2017) analysed the status of discussions in terms of number of sittings and the time lapsed in walkouts and disruptions, which have increased sharply over time compared to the useful discourse and debate on issues of national importance that used to be the highlight of the Indian Parliament during the first two decades of the republic, until around 1970. Largely, the author attributed two reasons for this decline: Parliament does not meet or work long enough and there are institutional constraints on its performance while working.

The number of sittings and the time lost in disruptions, in days per year, for the Lok Sabha and the Rajya Sabha during 2012–16 are presented in Figure 5.1, presenting the tenure of two governments in equal parts. Nayyar's (2017) analysis revealed that on an average per annum, the Lok Sabha met for sixty-nine days, of which, twenty days were lost to disruptions and the Rajya Sabha met for sixty-eight days, of which, twenty days were lost to disruptions. In the total number of sittings, disruptions took away 30% of the time in the Lok Sabha and 35% of the time

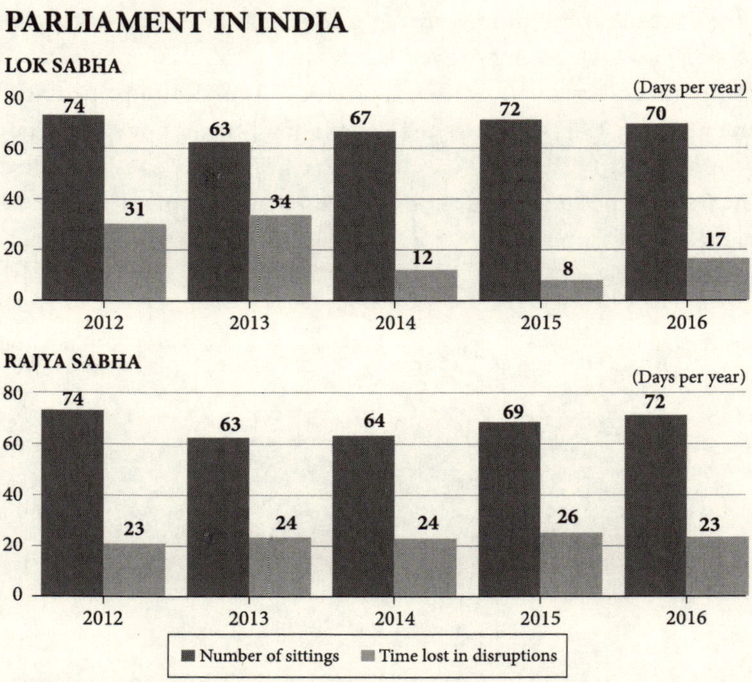

Figure 5.1 Working of the Parliament in India
Source: Nayyar, 2017.

in the Rajya Sabha. Although both houses spent extra hours to make up but in vain as there was more noise than debate, more shouting than listening, and more statements than engagement or debate. In addition, the duration for which the Parliament meets in India is short compared with that in other democracies. In the United Kingdom, both the House of Commons and the House of Lords meet for more than 150 days per year; in the United States, both the House of Representatives and the Senate meet for 133 days per year; and in Japan, the Diet meets for 150 days per year and this is often extended (Nayyar, 2017).

Budget Discussion

Annual budget discussions are very important and essential to streamline public spending into the sectors that need government intervention. It is not adequate to just earmark allocations, making sure that the programmes are working effectively and delivering the results expected is also equally important. Unfortunately, research evidence states that the time spent on discussing the demand for grants has substantially declined over time. Historical analysis pertaining to time taken for general discussion and discussion on demand for grants during 1952–2008 by the Centre for Budget and Governance Accountability (CBGA) reveals that there has been a considerable decline in the time spent on discussing demand for grants since the early nineties (see Figure 5.2).

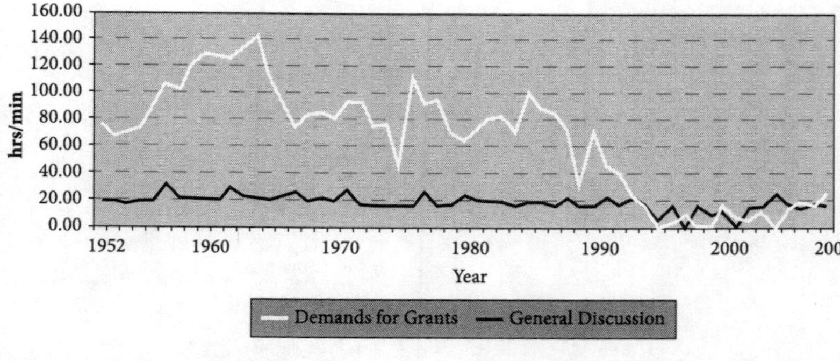

Figure 5.2 Time Taken for General Discussion and Discussion for Demand for Grants

Source: CBGA, 2010.

According to the existing procedures, Business Advisory Committee (BAC) decides time limit to vote on a particular demand and all the demands. At the expiry of the time limit, 'closure' popularly known as 'guillotine' is applied to conclude the discussion and the demand is put to vote. Increasingly, there have been instances, wherein due to time constraints, Parliament has been bunching all the pending demands together and applying guillotine to clear all the pending proposals in one go. Such a practice defeats the very purpose of *exante* parliamentary control on public spending as most of the expenditure proposals are not even scrutinized by the Parliament. It is observed that only three demands of grants on an average were discussed in the Fourteenth Lok Sabha, 90% of the demands from most of the ministries were closed in a few seconds (Table 5.2).

Details regarding the ministries discussed and guillotined during 2004–05 till 2009–10 reveal (Figure 5.3) that demands of the majority of the ministries have been getting guillotined as opposed to hardly three to six ministries getting discussed, which speaks volumes for the efficacy of *exante* control on the budget proposals. Recent PRS study reveals that the situation worsened between 2013–14 and 2018–19 as all demands for grants were guillotined, i.e. passed without discussion (Mandira et.al, 2019; Figure 5.4).

Parliament Authorization vis-à-vis Actual Expenditure: The Evidence

The summary of demands for grants placed before the Parliament/legislature seeks approval for incurring the expenditure proposed in the budget for the respective FY during the course of the year. 'Article 114(3) of the Constitution provides that no money shall be withdrawn from the Consolidated Fund of India except under appropriations made by law. General Financial Rules (GFR), 2017, stipulate that no expenditure shall be incurred which might have the effect of exceeding the total Grant or Appropriation authorized by Parliament for a financial year except after obtaining a supplementary Grant or an advance from the Contingency Fund(CAG, 2019)'.

The expenditure so indicated is supposed to be incurred for the purpose for which approval was sought and also not to exceed the approved limit. On the contrary, in reality, it has been observed that there are numerous cases wherein excess expenditure has been incurred by a number of departments over and above the Parliament authorization

Table 5.2 Statistics of Budget Sessions During UPA Government

No. of Budgets During UPA Govt.	Budget Session (Period)	Time Spent on General Discussion (H/m)	Time spent on Discussion and Voting on Demands for Grants (H/m)	Discussion and Voting on Demands for Grants (No. of Min/ Depts.)	Guillotine Applied (No. of Min/ Depts.)	Time Spent for Guillotine
First	5 July-26 Aug 2004	17h/35m**	NA*	0	52	7 Sec.
Second	25 Feb-13 May 2005	1h/49m	14h/32m	4	48	5 Sec.
Third	16 Feb-23 May 2006	1h/36m	18h/93m	3	50	5 Sec.
Fourth	23 Feb-17 May 2007	17h/27m	15h/45m	3	51	5 Sec.
Fifth	25 Feb-5 May 2008	1h/50m	24h/58m	4	49	6 Sec.
Sixth	2th July-7th August 2009	17h/12m	30h/01m	5	48	5 Sec.

Source: 14th & 15th Lok Sabha Business, Resume of Work, Parliament of India, cited in PILdAT (2010).

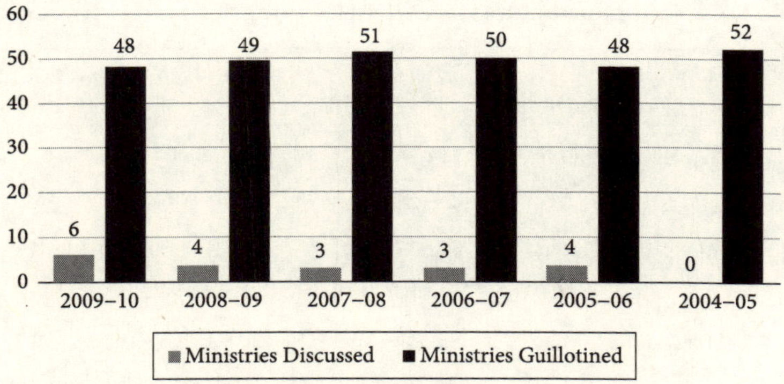

Figure 5.3 Ministries Discussed and Guillotined
Source: PRS, 2010 (http://www.prsindia.org/tags/pac).

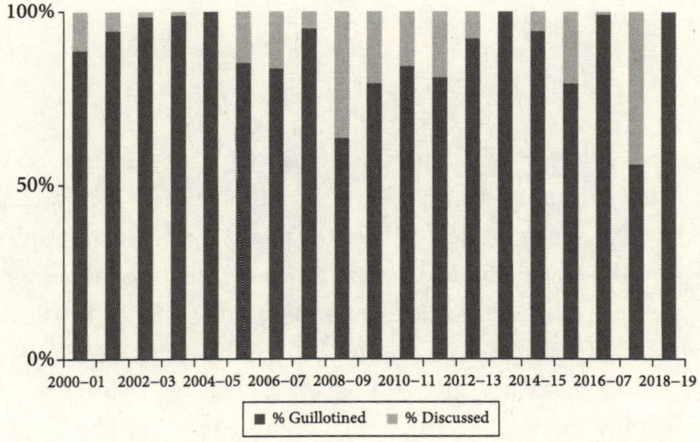

Figure 5.4 Share of Budget Expenditure: Guillotined vs. Discussed (%)
Source: Mandira, et.al, (2019).

and has been a long drawn issue raised in the reports submitted by the PAC. These issues are raised from time to time by the office of CAG every year in their annual publication 'Appropriation Accounts', which provides a comparison of details of accounts of the expenditure, voted and charged, of the central/state government for each FY with the amounts of the voted grants and appropriation passed by the Parliament/legislature. It also ascertains whether the expenditure so incurred is in

Table 5.3 Excess Expenditure Over Grants/Appropriations (Rs. Crores)

Sl. No.	Description of Grant/Appropriation	Total Appropriation	Expenditure	Excess Expenditure
1	20 – Defence Services (Revenue) Revenue (Voted)	198,263.75	201,655.68	3,391.93
2	21 – Capital Outlay on Defence Services Capital (Charged)	341.37	545.72	204.35
3	21 – Capital Outlay on Defence Services-Capital (Voted)	86,339.96	89,892.68	3,552.72
4	38 – Appropriation – Repayment of Debt Capital (Charged)	5,780,270.94	5,872,604.63	92,333.69
5	39 – Pensions Revenue (Voted)	40,895.00	41,022.62	127.62

Source: CAG (2019), p. 14.

conformity with law, relevant rules, regulation, and instructions. The CAG has brought out a number of issues supported by facts and figures where there have been repeated cases of unauthorized expenditure, excess expenditure over the appropriation, increased recourse to supplementary grants often left unutilized, rush of year end expenditure, etc. 'Audit of the Appropriation Accounts revealed failure of the accounting authorities from the highest to the lowest levels to enforce accountability, resulting in violation of the principles enunciated above, leading to an excess expenditure of Rs. 99,610 crore over Parliamentary authorization during 2017–18 (CAG, 2019).

Excess expenditure in select cases as observed by the CAG in the Appropriation Accounts is presented in Table 5.3.

Such excess expenditure over grants approved by the Parliament is in violation of the parliamentary procedures and thus accounts for laxity in the execution of expenditure control procedures instituted. It is also a matter of grave concern as such irregularities of excessive expenditure have been persisting despite being raised by the CAG time and again and no effective steps have been taken to rectify.

Poor Budgetary Planning—Fiscal Marksmanship

Expenditure estimates submitted for parliamentary approval year-on-year are expected to be realistic, and any large savings or excess expenditure reflect poor budget planning by the respective ministry/department. In technical terms, this is called 'Fiscal Marksmanship', indicating the extent of accuracy in the budgeted revenue or expenditure estimates, larger the variation weaker is the budget planning. Appropriation Accounts reports of CAG have observed time and again that the ministries/departments did not prepare estimates of expenditure on a realistic basis and the mechanism of holding pre-budget meetings and scrutiny by the Ministry of Finance for ensuring realistic budgetary projections did not have the desired effect. Poor budget planning is resulting in situations where certain departments end up with huge unutilized resources leading to savings, even when the much required funds are denied to the other needy departments owing to hard budget constraints. CAG report brings out details of savings in the appropriations, which are quite large as reflected in Table 5.4, which account for poor budget planning. CAG report highlights that during 2017–18, out of total savings, savings of Rs.100 crore or more amounting to Rs.247,227 crore (98.80%) had occurred in seventy-two segments of fifty-four grants. Of these, persistent savings of Rs. 100 crore or more occurred in thirty-eight segments of thirty grants/appropriations for three years, i.e. 2015–16 to 2017–18 (Table 5.4).

PAC observes that such deviations reflect faulty budget estimation and lack of financial discipline in abiding the financial rules by the ministries/departments concerned. PAC further observes that savings of Rs. 100 crore or above are indicative of defective budgeting as well as shortfall in performance in a grant or appropriation. In view of the persistence of such deviations, PAC suggests that an effective mechanism be put in place by the Ministry of Finance for imposing financial discipline on all the ministries/departments to prevent recurrence of such serious lapses (CAG, 2019).

Supplementary Provisions

Ministries seek additional/supplementary grants from the Parliament to meet additional expenditure that may arise when budgetary sanctions fall short of required expenditure or need additional funds for a new service

Table 5.4 Details of Large Savings in Grants/Appropriations (Rs. Crores)

Sl. No.	Grant No. and Name	Total Grant/ Appropriation	Expenditure	Savings (as % to Total Grant)
1	80 – Ministry of Railways	432,244	381,568	50,676 (11.72)
2	16 – Department of Food and Public Distribution	205,015	156,787	48,228 (23.52)
	Major savings occurred under sub-head 'Subsidy payable to Food Corporation of India and others on food grains transactions'.			
3	40 – Transfer to States	157,201	128,577	28,624 (18.21)
	Major savings occurred under sub-heads 'NDRP for calamities of severe nature', 'Transfer to National Disaster Response Fund', 'Grants for Centrally Sponsored Schemes', 'Rural Bodies Grants (States)', 'Urban Bodies Grants (States)', and 'Special Assistance (States)'.			
4	33 – Department of Revenue	124,097	99,493	24,604 (19.83)
	Major savings occurred under sub-head 'Compensation for revenue loss to States'.			
5	14 – Department of Telecommunications	40,188	31,055	9,133 (22.73)
	Major savings occurred under sub-heads 'Compensation to Service providers', 'Transfer to Universal Service Obligation Fund', and 'Investment in Hemisphere Properties India Ltd'.			
6	24 – Ministry of Drinking Water and Sanitation	36,333	27,339	8,994 (24.72)
	Major savings occurred under sub-heads 'Swachh Bharat Abhiyan (Gramin)'and 'Transfer to RashtriyaSwachhtaKosh'.			

7	97 – Ministry of Urban Development	38,038	31,405	6,633 (17.44)
	Major savings occurred under sub-heads 'MRTS and Metro Projects', 'Swachh Bharat Mission', and 'Urban Development Construction'.			
8	I – Department of Agriculture, Co-operation, and Farmers Welfare	52,668	46,455	6,213 (11.80)
	Major savings occurred under sub-heads 'Interest Subsidy for Short-Term Credit to Farmers', 'Adjustment of Provision', and 'Green Revolution – KrishnonnatiYojna'.			
9	29 – Department of Economic Affairs	15,690	9,490	6,200 (39.52)
	Major savings occurred under sub-heads 'Transfer to National Investment and Infrastructure Fund', 'Purchase of Coins from SPMCIL-Coins', 'New Scheme', and 'Loans to IMF UNDER New Arrangements to Borrow (NAB)'.			
10	42 – Department of Health and Family Welfare	87,486	81,559	5,927 (6.77)
	Major savings occurred under sub-heads			
11	81 – Ministry of Road Transport and Highways	122,898	117,153	5,745 (4.67)
	Major savings occurred under sub-heads 'Grants for State Roads', 'Works under Roads Wing', 'National Highways Original Works', 'Other Highways Related Schemes Financed from Central Road Fund', and 'Transfer to Central Road Fund'.			
12	7 – Department of Fertilizers	94,797	89,788	5,009 (5.28)
	Major savings occurred under sub-head 'Urea Subsidy'.			

Source: CAG, 2019.

not contemplated at the time of budget sanction. These grants are passed by the Parliament before the end of the FY.

There are three types of supplementary grants—cash, token, and technical:

- Cash supplementary is sought when ministry/department requires additional funds over and above the original budget provisions involving Parliament's cash supplementary approval before the end of the FY.
- Token supplementary refers to the practice wherein when a ministry wants to re-appropriate savings from one head to another within a particular segment of the grant.
- Technical supplementary is to be obtained when the ministry/department requires re-appropriating savings available in one segment to other segment of the grant. Token and technical supplementary do not involve outflow of funds from the CFI.

Although these supplementary grants are meant to enable ministries to overcome fund shortage in providing services, in reality, a number of instances have been reported wherein the ministries seek supplementaries even when the originally sanctioned amount is not fully incurred, resulting in unnecessary cash supplementaries. Instances of such unnecessary supplementaries are borne out by the data presented in Table 5.5.

CAG report observes unnecessary cash supplementary provision at grant level in eighteen cases across fifteen grants, cash supplementary provisions were obtained during 2017–18 in the anticipation of higher expenditure; however, the funds remained completely unutilized. In eleven such cases, cash supplementary aggregating to Rs. 11,017 crore was obtained where the actual expenditure was even less than the original provisions.

In view of the regular recurrence of such instances, PAC observed that the 'Ministry of Finance, should initiate a study of the best international practices on the modalities for ensuring greater conformity of expenditure to the budgetary provisions. The practice of the supplementaries during the fiscal year in addition to the main budget undercuts the sanctity of budgetary provisions. In practice often even known expenditure outgoes are suppressed in the main budget to be provided

Table 5.5 Unnecessary Cash Supplementary Leading to Savings (Rs. Crores)

Sl. No.	Grant/Appropriation	Original Provision	Total Supplementary Grant Obtained	Cash Supplementary	Actual Expenditure	Savings (as % of cash Supplementary)
Civil Grants – Revenue (Voted)						
1	12 – Department of Industrial Policy & Promotion	3,599	2,000	2,000	3,527	2,072 (104)
Large cash supplementary was obtained under 'Budgetary Support under Goods and Service Tax Regime'.						
2	15 – Department of Consumer Affairs	3,723	500	500	3,714	509 (102)
Large cash supplementary was obtained under 'Price Stabilization Fund'						
3	16 – Department of Food and Public Distribution	150,953	3,539	3,487	106,287	48,205 (1382)
Large cash supplementary was obtained under 'Subsidy payable to Food Corporation of India and other on food grain transactions'.						
4	24 – Ministry of Drinking Water and Sanitation	32,333	4,000	4,000	27,339	8,994 (225)
Large cash supplementary was obtained under 'Swachh Bharat Abhiyan (Gramin) and 'National Rural Drinking Water Programme'.						
5	47 – Cabinet	730	20	20	608	142 (710)
Cash supplementary was obtained under 'Office of the Principal Scientific Advisor'.						
6	94 – Ministry of Textiles	6,191	34	24	5,919	306 (1275)
Cash supplementary was obtained under 'Procurement of Cotton by Cotton Corporation of India under Price Support'.						

Continued

Table 5.5 *Continued*

Sl. No.	Grant/Appropriation	Original Provision	Total Supplementary Grant Obtained	Cash Supplementary	Actual Expenditure	Savings (as % of cash Supplementary)
7	96 – Ministry of Tribal Affairs	1,133	9	6	1,081	61 (1017)
Cash supplementary was obtained under 'Secretariat – Ministry of Tribal Affairs'.						
8	97 – Ministry of Urban Development	17,356	1,170	50	15,984	2,542 (5084)
Cash supplementary was obtained under 'Building Lease Charges' and 'Minor Work'.						
9	98 – Ministry of Water Resources, River Development and Ganga Rejuvenation	8,406	1,151	728	5,700	3,857 (530)
Large cash supplementary was obtained under 'National River Conservation Plan', 'Pradhan MantriKrishiSinchaiYojana (HarKhetkoPani)', and 'Border Area Development Programme'.						
10	19 – Ministry of Defence (Misc.)	5,489	500	116	5,036	953 (822)
Large cash supplementary was obtained under 'Coast Guard Organisation'.						
11	97 – Ministry of Urban Development	19,243	86	86	15,288	4,041 (4699)
Cash supplementary was obtained under 'Office Building of Other Ministries/Departments'.						
TOTAL				11,017		

*Source:*CAG, 2019.

for in subsequent supplementaries. The supplementary budget should normally be for unexpected items of expenditure or schemes taken up for compelling public interest. Based on other fiscal federal models, the Finance Ministry should evolve modalities and a framework which will enable the sanctity of budgetary provisions ensuring the reach and superintendence of Parliament on appropriation outgoes (CAG, 2015).'

Similar lapses have been observed by the CAG with reference to 'token' and 'technical' supplementaries leading to injudicious re-appropriation as the final savings under these heads were more than the amount re-appropriated. According to the Appropriation Accounts, there was excess expenditure over total authorization, aggregating to Rs. 1,156.80 crore during 2017–18 across thirteen grants, without obtaining prior approval of the Parliament (CAG, 2019).

PAC has repeatedly raised concerns regarding faulty budget estimation and deficient observances of financial rules by the ministries/departments concerned; it emphasizes the need to enforce strict financial discipline on all ministries/departments and ensure no recurrence of such lapses. It is also important to take note of instances of adherence to the financial rules. During FY 2018–19, Finance Minister Piyush Goyal said, 'This government follows the kind of budget making where there is least deviation between the planned and actual estimates.' Citing an example of the first supplementary demands for grants, it was further added that 'This is the lowest ever in the last 15 years. It is just 0.2 per cent of the total budget compared to 14 per cent in 2008–09 (PTI, 2018).

There have also been issues about injudicious re-appropriation, wherein funds were re-appropriated to various minor/sub-heads without assessing actual requirements. PAC in its eighty-third report (Fifteenth Lok Sabha, 2012–13) noted that re-appropriation of funds can be made only when it is positively known or genuinely anticipated that the appropriation for the unit from which funds are proposed to be transferred will not at all be utilized in full or there is reasonable certainty that savings can be effected in the unit of appropriation(CAG,2019).

Working of the PAC

PRS Legislative Research reveals that PAC has tabled 1,400 reports to the Parliament between the First and the Fourteenth Lok Sabha (PRS, 2010). The average number of reports presented by each of the Lok Sabha regime

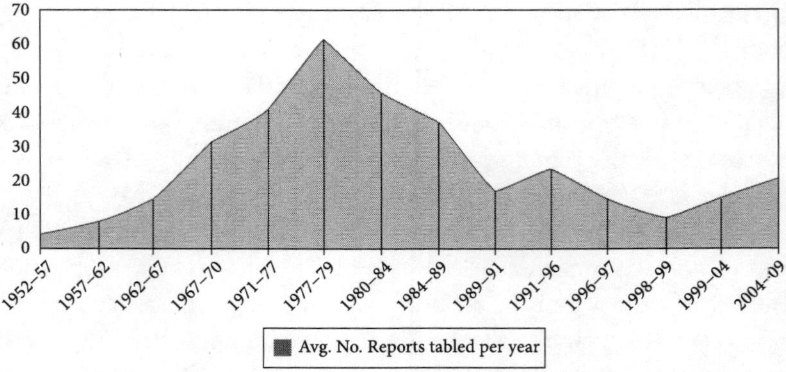

Figure 5.5 Average Number of Reports Tabled Per Year
Source: PRS (2010).

is presented in Figure 5.5. It can be observed that it was during the Sixth Lok Sabha that the highest average number of reports was tabled and the least number of five reports on an average per year was tabled during the first Lok Sabha.

There are concerns expressed about the fact that the two parliamentary committees PAC and CoPU, which are meant to enforce parliamentary financial control and the accountability of executive to the Parliament, are able to examine only a few paras/reviews out of large number of audit reports submitted to them. This tends to defeat the very purpose of such committees. Yet another important issue with reference to the working of PAC is the lapse of enormous amount of time between the CAG audit observations and the PAC reporting to the Parliament. Mukhopadhyay (2002) discussed the time lag and the number of CAG reports taken up for discussion. He observes that discussions of CAG's reports by PAC and finalization of its recommendations have been slow. Instances were reported wherein PAC had selected only 7% of the total 1,197 paras included in CAG's reports on central government in 1998–99 as against which actual examination was confined to 2% of the paras. Large-scale exclusion of items from examination and discussions restricts the effectiveness of parliamentary control on public expenditure. Similar problems were noticed at the sub-national level as in some states, discussions of CAG's audit reports were pending for fifteen years. In UP, the discussions of CAG's reports were observed to be pending for long.

Similar instances were reported by Kalse (2013), wherein out of sixteen reports submitted to the Parliament containing 1,209 paras/reviews the number of paras/reviews selected for examination was 76, out of which, only sixteen could be discussed by the PAC. Indian states too experience similar problems of huge backlog and a limited number of paras get selected for examination in the state legislatures. The study suggests that PAC examines all the reports submitted by CAG and submits its recommendations to legislature within a time limit of say eighteen months to ensure better expenditure control. An important operational issue that has been raised in this regard is the huge number of paras/reviews raised by CAG's audit reports. 'For PAC to function effectively and its members to develop specialisation, the life of PAC be made five years co-extensive with the life of Parliament/state legislature with one-third of members retiring every year' (Kalse, 2013).

There are also suggestions towards fundamental improvements in the functioning of the PAC in India, such as strengthening of the capacity of staff that support the PAC, reviewing the procedures of functioning of the PAC and making PAC discussions public. In fact, it is worth emphasizing here that 'The ultimate impact of the CAG's work depends on the keenness of the legislature to participate and engage with the findings and recommendations of audit reports, fix responsibility and take punitive action' (Asher et al., 2011, as cited in in Acharya et. al, 2014).

Ex Post Control: The Case of CAG

In addition to the *exante* control necessitating Parliament/legislature approval, there is an equally important need to have an effective *expost* control to make sure that the approved expenditure is incurred for the designated purpose and there is no unauthorized or excess expenditure. CAG plays a critical role in the *expost* control.

The CAG of India is an office created by the Constitution of India, which is assigned with the responsibility of audit of accounts of the union and the states. It is the supreme audit institution of the country. It is the duty of the CAG to audit the expenditure and receipts of the union, the states, and the union territory governments as well as various authorities and bodies established by the government (CAG, 2002; Kalse, 2013).

Effectiveness of *ExPost* Audit by the CAG

How effective the operation of the CAG system in the country and how effective the control has been are important aspects to be examined in the context of the working of institutional arrangements meant to ensure public expenditure control in India. There have been a number of issues raised by the National Commission (NCRWC, 2001) that reviewed the working of the constitution in its report on efficacy of public audit system in India. Archarya et al (2014) [4] too has examined these issues, and the following are the key issues based on discussions with some key stakeholders.

The CAG System: Operational Issues and Weaknesses

The CAG audit reports serve as the inputs for the Parliament/legislative committees for discussion and follow-up action. In view of the growing volume and content of the audit reports, the committees has not been in a position to take up all the reports for discussion and only selects a few paragraphs, and it remains an important issue as to whether these represent the core public financial concerns. It has been observed that 'for various reasons, audit reports have grown both in volume and content' over time. Moreover, even the selected audit paragraphs are not fully discussed due to the lack of time and infrequent meetings of the committees (Lakshminarayanan, 2010, as quoted in Acharya et.al, 2014). There has also been an apprehension expressed about the capacity of the supporting staff of the parliamentary/legislative committee who read the reports and support the committees in comprehending the relevant points.

There have also been issues regarding the reader-friendliness of the reports prepared by the CAG for the general public to understand the issues raised in their reports. It is suggested that a non-technical and a concise briefing can be prepared for the general public who cannot understand the technical elements to enhance user-friendliness and also the public engagement in toning up public financial accountability. One of the views in the context of the 'relevance' of CAG's accounts documents (i.e. finance accounts and Appropriation Accounts) for the

[4] This discussion is based on the Acharya et al(2014) assessment of the operational issues of the audit system in India.

general public is that some effort is required for synchronizing their presentation with the budget statements of the government. In order to meet the growing demand for better information and awareness among the general public about government's performance, effective communication of the audit findings is crucial. The findings and opinions provided in the audit reports, as per the conventional process, are expected to reach the public through their representatives in the Parliament and state legislature. However, in practice, the general public in the country is getting to know about audit reports mainly through media coverage of the same. Also, it has been observed by a number of stakeholders that media reports tend to sensationalize audit reports or use audit reports selectively. Hence, a strong perception of many stakeholders is that the CAG needs to explore more popular modes of communication and the reports should be actively made available to the public in a more reader-friendly/attractive format. Some basic dissemination strategies, like sending out the hard copies of the union audit reports to the libraries of all universities across the country and those of state audit reports to the libraries of universities in the state, could also be considered. Moreover, Accountant General (AG) and audit officials could also be encouraged to interact with academia and policy researchers a lot more, which could be a process of mutual learning and sharing of relevant information (Acharya et.al, 2014).

An important corrective measure in ensuring public financial accountability lies in the executive's compliance with the audit observations and effecting the necessary course corrections, which currently seems to be weak and needs to be toned up. These lapses have resulted in a situation where the CAG tends to continue to repeat the same observations time and again leading to wastage of time and resources and weak impact of the audit observations. In addition, PAC should take up the most important audit observations for discussion and ensure compliance from the executive. Better dissemination of the PAC discussions to the public could be ensured to tone up public financial accountability. It is aptly stated, 'The ultimate impact of the CAG's work depends on the keenness of the legislature to participate and engage with the findings and recommendations of audit reports, fix responsibility and take punitive action' (Asher et al., 2011, as quoted in Acharya et.al. 2014).

The effectiveness of the audit while observing violation of law, rules, and regulations by departmental officers lies in taking an effective action to prevent them. A classic case of Bihar fodder scam is illustrated by the National Commission (NCRWC, 2001:11) in its review of the working of the constitution. The commission in its review of the efficacy of the public audit system observes, 'The Accountant General (AG) Bihar could not detect the irregularity in time as Treasury officers suppressed the vouchers through which money was drawn and did not transmit them to AG thus preventing its audit. C&AG has been making mention of excess drawl over voted provision in its Audit Report presented to Bihar Legislature but Public Accounts Committee, it is said did not even meet to discuss the report leave apart take preventive action. After the scam became public knowledge, C&AG has produced a well-documented Audit Report but it is more a case of getting wise after the event—after crores of public money has been looted and shutting the stable door after the steed has been stolen.'

There have also been issues raised about the fact that PAC has not been able to discharge even the constitutional obligation of regularizing 'excess expenditure' over budgetary grants in many states. Kalse (2013) observes that under Article 205(b) of the Indian Constitution, if any money has been spent on any service in excess of the amount granted for that service in the AFS, it would need regularization by the legislative assembly. Under the rules of business framed by the legislature, PAC examines the explanatory notes furnished by the ministry/department and the circumstances leading to such excess and presents a report to the legislature recommending regularization of excess expenditure. As on March 1999, excess expenditure of the order of about Rs.94,314 crore has not been regularized in various states.

Thus in almost all the states, a huge amount of public money has been spent in the violation of budgetary control envisaged in the constitution and fraught with the risk of misappropriation of public money.

Even though there is a need to bring in timely corrective measures based on the audit observations, issues raised by the administrative departments regarding the functioning of the audit department cannot be ignored. It is often observed by them that audit often takes trivial objections and has a negative fault finding approach rather than coming out with solutions to the problems being faced by the administration. Kalse (2013) states audit 'is also criticised for preparing reviews on the working of scientific and technical departments and on issues relating to economic policy making about which it has no expertise. There is considerable merit in these observations. Much of the problems arise due to the existing structure of Indian Audit and Accounts Department (IAAD), which is highly centralised with all powers concentrated with C&AG in person or in his headquarter office with very little delegation to State Accountants Generals or Principal Directors of Audit who perform all the accounting and auditing functions. This tells upon the efficiency of the State Accountant's General and other field outfits and effects their morale.'

Kalse attributes the lack of quality to unwieldy structure of the CAG. To quote him, 'If Indian Audit and Accounts Department (IAAD) is to be given more teeth to be effective it must ensure very high standards of performance. The problem can be seen from the fact the C&AG personally approves about 20 Audit Reports for Union Government and 75 Reports for State Governments. In addition C&AG has to certify Finance and Appropriation accounts of the Union government as well as each of the State governments and UT's having a separate legislature before they are placed in their respective Houses. Each of about 100 odd Audit Reports of the Central and State governments which the C&AG produces annually runs into 200 to 250 pages. It is humanly not possible to read through 20000 to 25000 pages of highly technical literature dealing with subjects as complicated as taxation laws, purchase of defence equipment etc., least of all to give any direction regarding meaningful conduct of audit. It is time to do some serious thinking on the issue and develop a more decentralised functioning of the institution of C&AG' (Kalse, 2013).[5]

There are certain items of expenditure incurred by the governments at the central and the state levels that do not form a part of audit by the CAG. These include grants that are made to autonomous bodies and institutions, when not very substantial, NGOs. Even though utilization

[5] For a more detailed discussion on the issues related to Indian audit system and the international best practices, read Kalse (2013).

certificates are produced, the results of such grants (as very often they are meant to provide the services that the government should have provided otherwise) are not known to the government, let alone the public. It is worthwhile an exercise to examine the quantum of such expenditure in the form of grants to such agencies on a year-on-year basis. Even in the cases, which receive substantial grants that fall within the jurisdiction of CAG audit, are not submitting their annual accounts for audit in time, and there is a time gap of two to three years. Hence, all such expenditure incurred by the government is escaping even procedural audit, let alone performance audit.

The Financial Audit report of CAG (2015) gives an account of the steady increase in grants-in-aid expenditure. Grants-in-aid have emerged as a significant mode of spending for the union government for delivery of public goods. The report further states that over a period of time, grants-in-aid have constituted, with the exception of debt repayments, the single largest item of expenditure for the union government. Grants-in-aid are payments in the nature of assistance, donations, or contributions made by one government to another government, body, institution, or individual. Grants-in-aid are given by the union government to state governments and/or panchayati raj institutions. Union government also gives substantial funds as grants-in-aid to other agencies, bodies, and institutions. Similarly, the state governments disburse grants-in-aid to agencies, bodies, and institutions such as universities, hospitals, co-operative institutions, and others. The grants so released are utilized by these agencies, bodies, and institutions for meeting day-to-day operating expenses and for creation of capital assets, besides delivery of services.

The expenditure on grants-in-aid (as per e-lekha data base) was Rs.423,789 crore (28%) of the revenue expenditure of Rs. 1,534,120 crore (excluding railways) in 2014–15. Out of this, Rs.317,228 crore was plan grants and Rs.106,561 crore was non-plan. Of the total expenditure on grants-in-aid in 2014–15, union government transferred Rs.258,292 crore as central plan assistance to state/UT government. At the end of March 31, 2015, in twenty-six ministries/departments from where the information was received, 37,569 utilization certificates aggregating to Rs.51,527.10 crore were outstanding in respect of grants released up to March 31, 2014. 'The analysis of grants-in-aid in two Ministries showed deficiencies in internal monitoring system such as non-conducting of external peer reviews of grantee organisations and other attached offices, non-submission of performance-cum-achievement reports by the grantees, non-reporting of details to Parliament through annual reports by the Ministry, etc.' (CAG, 2015, 144).

There are also other issues such as bunching or rush of expenditure during the last quarter of the FY resorted to by the spending departments to utilize the budgetary sanctions for the respective FY. As per Rule 56(3) of GFR, 2005, rush of expenditure, particularly in the closing months of the FY, is regarded as a breach of financial propriety and should be avoided. The Ministry of Finance has also issued instructions to ministries/departments in September 2007 to restrict expenditure during the month of March and the last quarter of the FY to 15% and 33%, respectively, of the budgeted estimates. Studies have shown that although such bunching phenomenon did not happen for non-plan expenditure as a major part of it is in the nature of committed expenditure, a major portion of the plan component of expenditure was incurred in the last quarter (Gayithri, 2014b). Such a rush of expenditure not only amounts to violation of rules but also ineffective implementation of programmes that very often leads to poor results.

Sub-National Issues

There are similar set of issues prevailing at the sub-national level: Sub-national governments have been having issues of containing the supplementary budgets. The supplementary budgets are not fiscally neutral and tend to affect the budget-execution process. They tend to distort the process of fiscal consolidation. Some fiscally progressive states like Karnataka have made useful resolutions as recommended by Fiscal Management Review Committee to reduce the number of supplementary estimate passed through the year to one and limit approvals to a minimum of second installment of supplementary estimate. Instances of defective re-appropriation from one grant voted by the legislature to another such grant, from voted items of expenditure to charged items of expenditure, from capital to revenue and vice versa are also indicated by the CAG. Bunching or rush of expenditure in the last quarter is also widely prevalent.

Way Forward

Mere existence of rules is not tantamount to effective control; there is need for stricter enforcement of the same while executing the budgets. India has both the *exante* and *expost* control systems in place, however, there is need to review the adequacy and clarity of these rules such that there is a very limited possibility to bypass the same and strengthen the institutions that enforce public expenditure control.

6

Elections and Government Expenditure

Evidence from Fourteen Major States of India (with Dr Ananatha Ramu)

Political business cycle is one of the most tested concepts in the political economy literature.[1] In times of elections, politicians try to maximize their chance of winning and gain political mileage using the public spending to woo the voters. The preference may be based on ideology, interest groups, level of competition, and so on. Incumbents would try to increase the overall spending or composition of spending in the election years. However, the empirical evidence on this issue is mixed.

India is one of the fastest growing countries in the world. It is also the largest democracy in the world. In a democracy, elections play a major role, and the outcomes play an important role in shaping up the growth and development of a nation. India is a diverse nation in terms of language, religion, region, etc., and public finances are used in gaining maximum political mileage, especially during election times.

India has a three-tier government; central government, state governments, and local bodies. Elections are held once in five years for all these governments. In this chapter, an attempt is made to examine the behaviour of public expenditure at the sub-national level in and around election years. There are a few studies in which state level elections and expenditure changes have been modeled. However, there is no particular study to assess how public expenditure varies in election years at different income level of states. This chapter attempts to examine if elections tend to have differential behavioural impacts on public expenditure across high-, middle-, and low-income states in India.

[1] This chapter is based on an unpublished work jointly prepared with Dr Anantha Ramu.

Public Expenditure in India. Gayithri Karnam, Oxford University Press. © Oxford University Press 2022.
DOI: 10.1093/oso/9780192857569.003.0006

6.1 Theoretical Background

Political business cycle theory by Nordhus is the major and an important theory in political economy. It states that governments are assumed to stimulate their economies with expansionary fiscal policies before elections, and it is based on an assumption of adoptive expectations (Schuknecht, 2000). In short, government expenditure would increase in the election years. An extended version of this theory is rational political business cycle. It argues how politicians can influence voter behaviour by short-term policy manipulations via budget (Sen and Vaidya,1996). In these models, both voters and parties are assumed to be rational utility maximizing agents with same utility function. These models imply a cut in capital expenditure and a rise in government consumption expenditure in election years.

The 'Electoral Theory of Spending' encompasses two core hypothesis: Electoral consequence hypothesis and the legislator insecurity hypothesis. The former states that support for public spending programmes improves the representatives' electoral showing and the latter states that greater electoral insecurity leads representatives to be more in favour of spending programmes (Payne, 1991).

Many a time ideological differences would lead to changes in the composition of expenditure. The 'Partisan Cycles' theory argues that left-wing parties assign greater value to low unemployment, whereas right-wing parties value low inflation more highly (Schuknecht, 2000). It is also argued that the Nordhus approach is more suitable for developing countries than the 'Partisan Cycles' theory as typical right and left party distinction is not exhibited.

6.2 Literature Review

There are many studies in the international context that tested the existence of political business cycles. Katsimi and Sarantides (2012) investigated the impact of elections on the level and composition of fiscal instruments. By taking data on nineteen established democratic and developed Organisation for Economic Co-operation and Development (OECD) countries for the period 1972–99, they tested rational political business cycle. Using the panel fixed effect model they found no evidence of electoral cycle for government deficit and expenditure. However, elections found to be having a negative impact on the capital expenditure. When they considered only the endogenous election dates, the current expenditure was found to be increasing immediately before elections and even deficit increased by 0.46% of GDP.

The electoral cycles in developing countries can be expected to be somewhat different from that in developed countries. In an empirical analysis on twenty-four developing countries for the period 1973–92, Schuknecht (2000) tested the Nordhus political business cycle and Partisan Cycle under three basic hypotheses. The first hypothesis was that elections are preceded by expenditure increase rather than lower revenues. Secondly, election-oriented policies raise capital expenditure more strongly than current expenditure. Finally, the government wage bill is likely to increase before elections. The empirical result fully supported the first two hypotheses and third hypothesis was found to be insignificant.

Shi and Svensson (2006) empirically examined whether political budget cycle differs across developing and developed countries. By considering the data sets of eighty-five countries for the period 1975–95 and using the fixed effect model and also the Generalized Method of moments (GMM) estimation method, they found that on an average, fiscal deficit increases by 1% of GDP in elections. They found that there was a systematic difference between developed and developing countries as political budget cycles are larger in the latter than the former.

It is believed that politicians try to alter voters' preference through the use of fiscal and monetary policy tools during elections. In an attempt to study the same, Peters (2010) took up an empirical analysis on the Caribbean governments for the sample period 1970–2005. Using dynamic panel GMM estimator, they found that government expenditure increased by 1.93% and fiscal deficit by 3.58% during election years. Revenue does not show any electoral cycle. Even though evidence suggests that there was electorally timed intervention by governments, there was no reversal of policies aftermath the elections.

There are very limited studies that analysed the impact of elections on government spending using time series econometric techniques. Payne (1991) tested two hypotheses, namely the electoral consequence hypothesis and the legislator hypothesis in the United States. However, the data supported neither of the hypotheses. There is another study by Kohno and Nishizawa (1990) on Japan using quarterly data between 1965:1 and 1981:1. Using the ARIMA model, they found no significant manipulations of government expenditure during election years. However, they found that government has taken advantage of government spending on public construction for electoral purpose.

Ideology also plays a major role in spending during elections. In a time series analysis on Norway, Fiva and Natvik (2013) investigate how politicians' re-election probabilities affect their investment in physical capital. In Norway, political system is mainly dominated by two fronts, left leaning socialist and right leaning conservative camp. Authors found that a higher re-election probability tends to stimulate investment. Right bloc incumbents raise aggregate investment, whereas left bloc incumbents raise child care investments. Surprisingly, current expenditure was found to be unaltered by both the blocs. In a panel analysis on twenty-three OECD countries, Potrafke (2011) examined whether government ideology has any influence on the allocation of public expenditure. Analysis was conducted for two different data sets, one from 1970 to 1997 and the other from 1990 to 2006. They found no significant influence of ideology on budget composition. However, left-wing governments increased spending on education in election years.

There are several important studies that tested political business cycles in the Indian context. Sen and Vaidya (1996) tested political business cycle theory, particularly rational political business cycle theory in the Indian context. This model implies an increase in deficits and a decrease in capital expenditure during elections; however, the results were not significant. However, there was a surge in monetization of deficit during election time. Contrary to this result, Chhibber (1995) has found that the Government of India does manipulate policy instruments in the time of elections. Using the ARMA model and considering a time frame between 1952 and 1983, the author found that there is significant increase in real government expenditure on revenue and capital account during election years. Under expenditure categories, the allocation for subsidies increased during election years. The evidence was also supportive that central government used political considerations to disburse resources to states.

Khemani (2000) tested the existence of political business cycles in fourteen major Indian states. The author analysed the effect of state legislative assembly elections on the policies of state governments. The time frame of the study was from1960 to 1994. Using panel data analysis, the author found that, in the time of election, incumbent state governments lowered taxes, not on items of mass consumption but on a selection base consisting of manufacturers and producers. There was significant increase in capital spending in election time, whereas the current spending declined. As a result of reduction in current spending, there was no significant effect of elections on state deficit. There was no evidence of a Nordhus type model. It was also found that state governments significantly increased spending on roads.

Government spending composition in the election years many a time also depends on party system. Chhibber and Nooruddin (2004) analysed the same for the Indian economy by using macroeconomic data from 1967 to 1997 on fifteen major states and also conducted the post-election voter surveys on six states. They considered development expenditure as proxy for public good and expenditure on salaries as club good. Multiparty states found to be having higher level of expenditure on club goods or civil administration spending than their counterparts. On ideological competition, both right centre and centre left found to be spending more on salaries, whereas coalition governments are less likely to spend more resource on salaries. Authors argued that parties facing competition from many parties are more likely to mobilize support from specific groups and allocate club goods to those particular groups. In two-party systems, political parties require support from many social groups and hence spend more on public goods to win elections.

After the late 1980s, India saw many coalition governments at the central level, whereas coalition governments at the state level existed since the 1950s. As Lalvani (2005) points out that there were forty-three coalition governments at the state level between 1966–67 and 1998–99. It has been observed that the spending is more by coalition governments than the single-party governments as each player has more veto power to break the government, and enforcement mechanism among coalitions partners is often very weak (Roubini and Sachs,1988). Using data on fourteen Indian major States from 1981–82 to 1998–99, Lalvani (2005) attempted to examine the impact of change in government form single-party to coalition on the economy. Using pooled cross-section time series Generalized least squares (GLS) method, the author found that coalition government has a positive impact on capital outlays. The per capita capital expenditure on social service was insignificant. The revenue expenditure was also found to be significantly increased by coalition governments in election years. On the revenue front, revenue receipts and also the revenue deficit increased in election years. On the same lines, Chaudhuri and Dasgupta (2006) examined how government fragmentation or coalition governments change public spending and revenue receipts in election years. They used fixed effect error component method for the analysis. The data was on fourteen major Indian states for the years starting from 1974–75 to 1994–95. On the revenue front, commodity tax revenue declined in election years and own non-tax revenue declined when there was coalition government. On the expenditure front, current expenditure of state governments was lower in election years than other years. There was clear evidence that current expenditure and development expenditure declined in election years under coalition governments. There was no election year decline in capital account. However, they observed election year spurt in capital account developmental expenditure and capital account education expenditure. The fragmented governments were found to be spending less on education than single-party governments in election year.

Including all the political characteristics, namely electoral cycle, forms of government, and ideology, Dash and Raja (2012) examined whether it has any influence on government expenditure in election years. The study was conducted on fourteen major states for the time frame from 1980–81 to 2006–07. Using panel correction estimation method, they found that when a government's ideology shifts from relatively right wing to relatively left wing position, percapita current expenditure increases and the same result follows when governments become more fragmented. Ideology and electoral cycle did not have any significant effect on capital expenditure. It was also found that more fragmented the government, higher is the capital expenditure. There was significant increase in total expenditure in election years when ideology shifted towards left wing from right wing and also when the government was fragmented.

Chowdhury (1993) developed a political economic interaction model for India to test the political surfing over the economic cycle. The sample period was from 1960 to 1991. The annual fiscal data series was converted into quarterly figures based on movements of quarterly Index of industrial production (IIP) data. The model was estimated by single equation Ordinary least squares (OLS) and probit method. Results indicated that the probability of having election increases as time elapsed since last election and GDP found to be significantly determinant of election. The result was supportive of political surfing concept as government waits for next economic boom for elections. However, there was no evidence to say that fiscal and monetary policy got manipulated during election time.

The literature review reveals clearly that there is mixed evidence on public spending and revenue receipt variations in election and non-election years. There are some evidences that are supportive of the Nordhus electoral business cycle model. The result varies across countries; it is different for developed and developing countries. This chapter has tried to analyse whether political business cycles are different across the states with different income level by dividing fourteen major Indian states into high-, middle-, and low-income states.

6.3 Data and Methodology

The period of the study is from 1993–94 to 2013–14. The data on election years was taken from election commission (GoI, 2015). Data regarding government expenditure and receipts were collected from the RBI publications (RBI, 2015a,b). There are many attempts to study the spending behaviour in election years using the panel data method. However, there is a serious shortcoming in using the panel regression. As the elections, mainly the assembly election, would not happen in a regular and fixed time period for all the states at once, it is very difficult to capture the time effect from the model. Hence, this analysis relies on descriptive statistical analysis, particularly growth rate for the analysis. The annual growth rate was calculated for each year and an average is taken separately for election years and non-election years.

Fourteen major Indian states have been considered for the analysis. Based on the finance commission classification, the states have been divided into high-, medium-, and low-income states. The high-income states are Gujarat, Haryana, Maharashtra, and Punjab; the middle-income states are Andhra Pradesh, Karnataka, Kerala, Tamil Nadu, and West Bengal; and the low-income states are Bihar, Madhya Pradesh, Orissa, Rajasthan, and Uttar Pradesh.

Table 6.1 provides the economic profile of the fourteen major Indian states that are classified based on percapita income level. There is no difference in GSDP growth between the high- and middle-income states, whereas it is much lesser for the low-income states. The difference can be clearly seen in percapita income across states. Fiscal deficit as percentage of GDP is comparatively less for the high-income states. However, for all the categories, fiscal deficit is more than 3% of GSDP. In recent years, the state governments are trying to keep fiscal deficit below 3% of GSDP by following the rule-based fiscal correction mechanism (FRBM Act). Interestingly, the revenue deficit of the low-income states is lesser than that of the middle- and high-income states. It is probably because of the high transfer of fiscal resource to the low-income states from the central government. The debt level is the highest among the low-income states, whereas the middle- and high-income states have almost the same level of debt.

The data is in annual series. It is very important to decide which years should be considered as the election years. Among the existing studies, a few consider the year in which election is scheduled as election year and several other studies consider previous year of election to test the variation in spending. In certain studies, the election year is decided based on the month of election held. In India, assembly elections for state governments is scheduled to happen once in five years, but in unavoidable circumstances like shortage of majority or fall of government, the election commission calls for mid-term polls. We are considering two years,

Table 6.1 Growth Rate of GSDP, PCI, and Fiscal Indicators

States	GSDP (GR)	PCI	FD (% of GSDP)*	RD (% of GSDP)*	Debt (% of GSDP)
High-Income States	6.90	39,110.18	3.26	1.24	27.20
Middle-Income States	6.90	29,483.08	3.45	1.65	27.18
Low-Income States	5.84	15,994.93	3.86	0.92	37.68

Source: RBI database, 2015.

i.e. year in which election was held and previous to that year, as election years. It is expected that incumbents start preparing for elections a year before to the scheduled time and try to alter the public spending to retain the power with the majority of votes. The years during which a state was under the President's rule at least for six months are not considered for the analysis.

The analysis was first conducted on total expenditure and then on its components, namely revenue expenditure and capital outlay. The analysis was followed by the next level of classification, namely social service and economic service, expenditure and further to other important categories of expenditure like education expenditure, health expenditure, rural and urban development expenditure, social welfare expenditure, and expenditure on SC and ST population.

6.4 Results Discussion

Figure 6.1 provides average growth rate of total expenditure in election and non-election years. It is very much clear that only with the

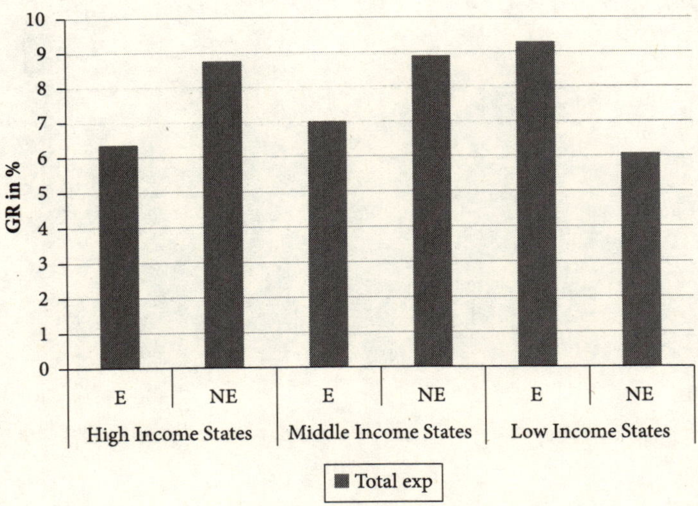

Figure 6.1 Growth Rate of Total Expenditure in Election and Non-Election Year

low-income states, the total expenditure increases by 9% in election years and growth rate is around 6% in non-election years. There is no evidence of hike in aggregate spending in election year for both the high- and middle-income states. It is mostly because there is strict rule (FRBM Act) to check the deficit and keep it under control. The fiscal rule is followed by many high- and middle-income states, whereas many low-income states are not following it in an effective way.

Even though there is less variation in aggregate expenditure, the composition of expenditure may reveal some variations across the groups of states. In the next level, revenue expenditure (current expenditure) and capital outlay have been considered. The growth rate of revenue expenditure declines in election years, whereas the capital outlay increases among the high-income states (see Figure 6.2). The variation is huge mainly with regard to capital outlay. Surprisingly, there is a decline in both the variables for the middle-income states. For the low-income states, there is a sharp increase in revenue expenditure and the capital outlay declines in election years.

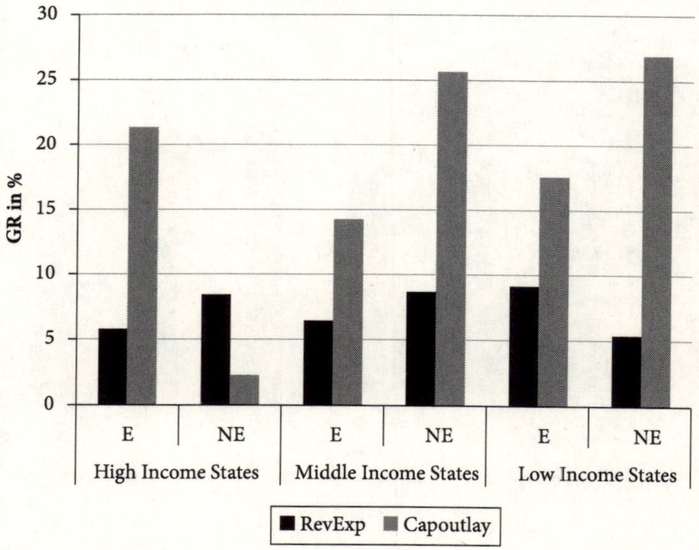

Figure 6.2 Growth Rate of Revenue Expenditure & Capital Outlay in Election & Non-election Years

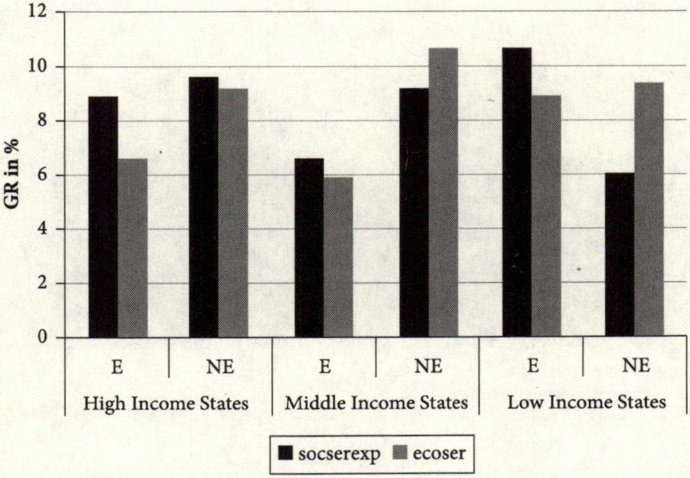

Figure 6.3 Growth Rate of Social Service & Economic Service Expenditure in Election & Non-Election Years

In the next category of expenditures, development expenditure, which comprises of social service expenditure and economic service expenditure are examined and non-development expenditure were considered. There is no huge variation of these two categories of expenditure in election and non-election years among the high-income states (see Figure 6.3), but surprisingly, both declined for the middle-income states. There is a clear trend of sharp increase in social service spending in election years among the low-income states. It is observed here that due to low level of development, politicians try to please the voters with social spending in place of capital spending, which always works with a lag.

Health and education spending are considered to be main components of social service expenditure. However, there is no such variation found among the high- and middle-income states, there was a huge increase in both education and health expenditure in election years among the low-income states (see Figure 6.4).

Other important categories of development expenditure are SC–ST expenditure and social welfare expenditure. These two categories of expenditures are politically very important. The politicians try to please certain interest groups and lower caste people. As the education level

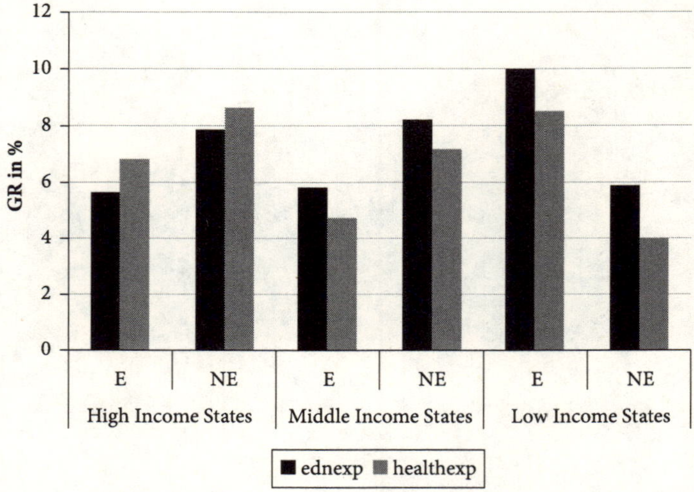

Figure 6.4 Growth Rate of Education & Health Expenditure in Election & Non-Election Years

of these people is lower, politicians try to attract these groups by higher spending in election years. There is no variation among the higher-income states on these two categories of spending (see Figure 6.5). There is only a minimum increase of SC–ST expenditure among the middle-income states. Among the low-income states, social welfare expenditure has increased very sharply in election years.

Another important category of expenditure, which is politically more vibrant, is urban and rural development expenditure. Surprisingly, rural development expenditure saw a decline in election years under all the three groups of states (see Figure 6.6). The urban development expenditure growth is the highest for the high-income states and there is no major change in growth rate among the middle-income states. Even the low-income states try to please the urban population by increasing the expenditure in election years.

It is also observed in the literature that there are chances of reduction in taxes to please voters. To check the same, total revenue receipts, tax revenue, and also the own tax revenue of state governments are included in the analysis (see Figure 6.7). Results do not account for such variation in tax collections found in election and non-election years

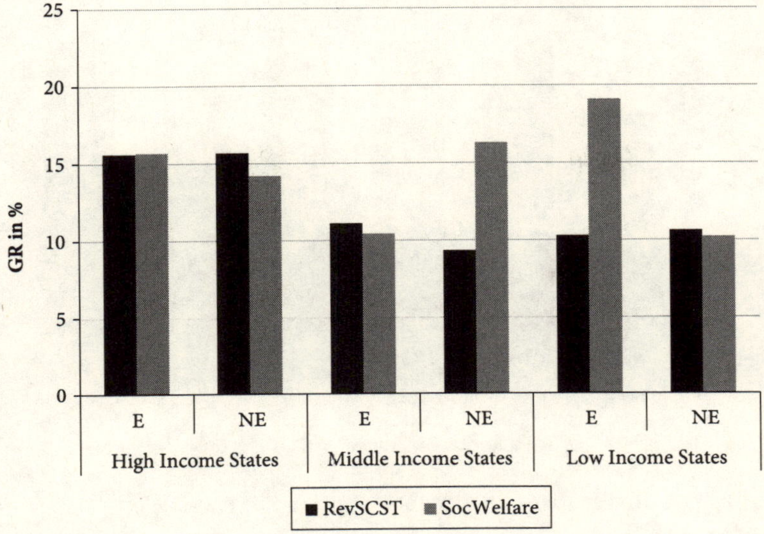

Figure 6.5 Growth Rate of SC-ST & Social Welfare Expenditure in Election & Non-Election Years

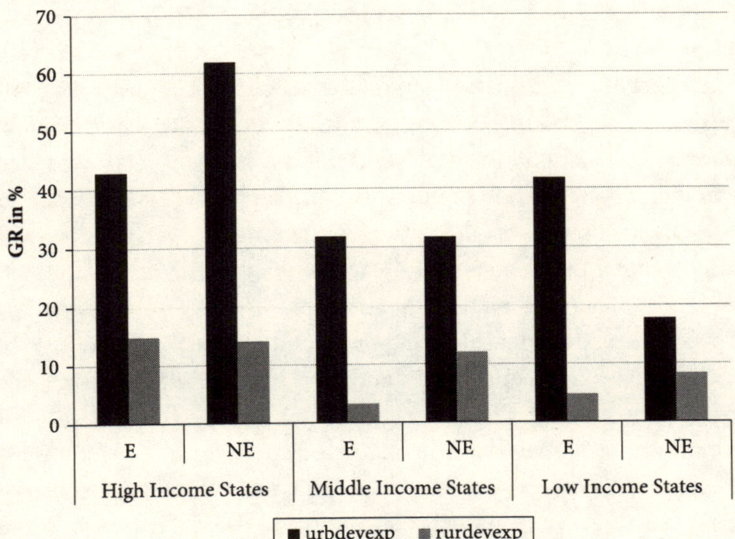

Figure 6.6 Growth Rate of Urban & Rural Development Expenditure in Election & Non-Election Years

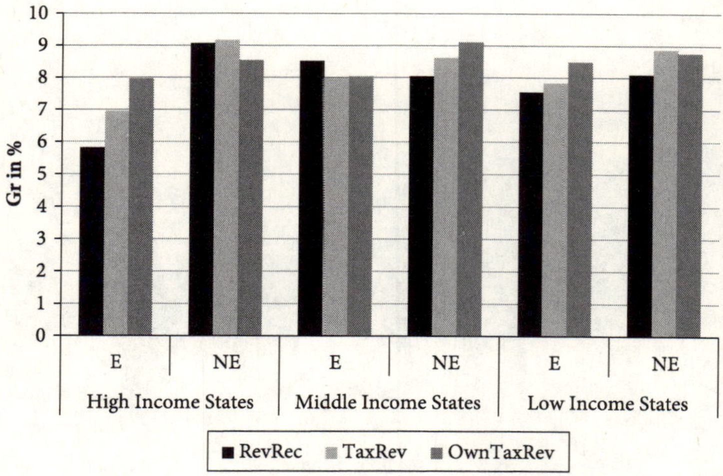

Figure 6.7 Growth Rate of Revenue Receipts in Election & Non-Election Years

among the middle- and low-income states. However, there is a decline in tax collection among the high-income states in election years. It seems that developed states try to please the voters by lowering taxes in election years.

The effect of higher spending is on the deficit level. Figure 6.8 provides the fiscal deficit level in election and non-election years. The fiscal deficit variation is less among the high- and middle-income states irrespective of whether it is an election or non-election years, whereas the deficit level is more in election years among the low-income states. Higher spending among the low-income states in election years has affected the deficit level, and it is clearly depicted in Figure 6.8.

The above analysis revealed that the spending level varies across three groups of states in election years and also among different expenditure categories. It was clearly observed that the high-income states spend more on capital outlay than the revenue expenditure in election years. The low-income states spend more on revenue expenditure, social welfare, and social services, namely education and health. There was no such variation observed among the middle-income states. The revenue collection was found to be declining in election years for developed states than other two categories. It is clearly observed that the deficit level is

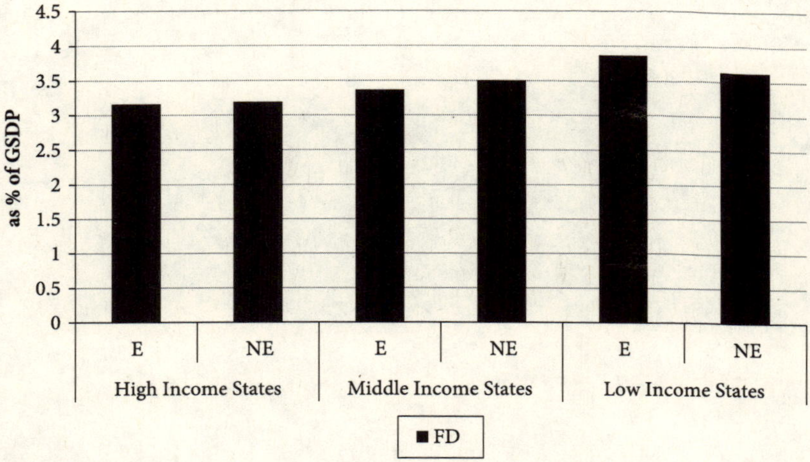

Figure 6.8 Fiscal Deficit in Election & Non-election Years (as % of GSDP)

the highest for the low-income states than the high- and middle-income states. This analysis proves that the political business cycle exists in the Indian context and varies across states with different income levels and the categories of expenditure. It is observed to be stronger among the low-income states.

7

Public Financial Accountability Issues in India

Globally, there has been growing awareness and demand for understanding the consequences of government financial operations rather than merely knowing the size and quantum of the outlays made by the government. This attains special importance in the context of a large-scale financial presence of government in the process of providing many goods and services to the society. Accountability for expenditure has long been viewed as spending budget allocations that have legal sanction. However, of late, accountability is rated more in terms of the efficiency with which public funds are expended, services delivered, and the extent to which the targeted output and outcomes are achieved than the quantum of financial allocations made year on year.

Many countries have addressed these issues through the means of performance evaluation and strengthening the control on the utilization of public funds. In India too there have been some efforts in this direction. The then Union Finance Minister, Mr Chidambaram had emphasized on the need to prepare 'outcome' budgets in order to track the impacts of public programmes on the citizens in 2006. The Government of India has been preparing Outcome Budgets since then; however, the adequacy of these reports to assess the impacts of government programmes has been an important concern.

The World Bank (1997) observes 'Sustainable development generally calls for formal mechanisms of restraint that hold the state and its officials accountable for their actions. To be enduring and credible, these mechanisms must be anchored in core state institutions.' This is a form of accountability that the state imposes on itself through the creation of public institutions whose mandate is precisely to act as a restraint on the government, this form of accountability is termed as horizontal accountability

Public Expenditure in India. Gayithri Karnam, Oxford University Press. © Oxford University Press 2022.
DOI: 10.1093/oso/9780192857569.003.0007

(Schacter, 2005). Hence, the institutions that are responsible for ensuring accountability play an important role in disciplining the use of public funds.

This chapter makes an attempt in the direction of examining the issues that are of concern for India in the areas of financial accountability slated to achieve through the institutions that are responsible for ensuring accountability. The analysis focuses on the working of the current systems in place to ensure public financial accountability in India, their inadequacies, and some corrective measures.

7.1 Current Systems in Place

One of the important indications of the presence of a sound public financial accountability in a country is when its legislative committees and audit committees provide for its citizens crucial oversight of the country's public finances. A country may be financially accountable publicly, if it maintains internal control and performance reporting systems that make the results of public operations transparent to the citizens and corrective actions initiated wherever public funds are not efficiently used. In the Indian context, checks and balances are imbibed on the government financial operations in the form of internal controls, external auditing, and legislature reviews of the government financial operations, which have become a part of the system attempting to ensure accountability on a regular basis.

7.2 External Control

External control mechanisms on public spending have been laid out in the Indian constitution. The office of the CAG of India is the agency that oversees the compliance of the laws by the executive. The office of the CAG is an independent constitutional agency and derives its authority from Article 148–152 of the constitution. Further legal basis for powers and duties of the CAG is provided in the CAG's Act of 1971. External control on public financial operations is in the form of auditing by the CAG of all receipts and expenditure of the government, which is conducted throughout the year based on which audit reports are prepared. These reports highlight many important observations regarding government financial operations, which get tabled in the Parliament/legislature. Legislative bodies such as PAC and Committee on Public Sector Undertakings (CoPU) examine these reports and question the departments concerned. Reports of PAC and CoPU are submitted to the Parliament/legislature. These procedures are very well streamlined over the years, and auditing goes on a regular basis and can be broadly termed as procedural/regularity audit.

An important question that needs to be addressed in the context of prevailing mechanisms to imbibe public financial accountability is whether these have ensured effective control on the use of public funds and public financial accountability. There are three aspects that throw some light on the above question: Firstly, whether the current control mechanism captures entire public spending; secondly, adequacy of the control mechanism in terms of providing insights on the results of public expenditure; and thirdly, response to the CAG audit findings.

7.3 Partial Coverage

CAG has powers under its Act 1971 (CAG Act 1971), Section 13, 16, and 17, to audit all expenditure from and receipt into the CFI and the state. CAG has the authorization under Sections 14, 15, and 20 to audit receipts and expenditure of bodies or authorities substantially financed by loans or grants union or state or union territory (NCRWC, 2001).

There are certain items of expenditure incurred by the governments at the central as well as at the state level that do not form a part of audit by the CAG. These include grants that are made to autonomous bodies and institutions, when not very substantial, NGOs. Although utilization certificates are produced, the results of such grants (as very often they are meant to provide the services that the government should have provided otherwise) are not known to the government, let alone the public. It is worthwhile an exercise to examine the quantum of such expenditure in the form of grants to such agencies on a year-to-year basis. Even cases that receive substantial grants that fall within the jurisdiction of CAG audit are not submitting their annual accounts for audit in time and there is a time gap of two to three years. Hence, all such expenditure incurred by the government is escaping even procedural audit, let alone performance audit.

With the seventy-third and seventy-fourth amendments of the constitution, the local bodies have been playing a greater role in the provision of services, for which substantial transfers take place from the central and state governments. Very often these are direct transfers from the central government, and their magnitude has substantially increased in the recent years. There is a need to develop satisfactory audit systems of these local bodies (some states have developed these already).

7.4 Tax Expenditures

Until the recent past, state governments in India have indulged in fierce competition with one another in attracting industries to their respective states by resorting to fiscal incentives. Even though the financial implications of direct subsidy is available in black and white in the budget documents, the tax incentives doled out by the governments, which result in loss of revenue to the government, popularly known as 'tax expenditures', is a gray area. Strictly speaking, these incentives are offered to fulfil specific objectives, and there is every need to assess the results of such tax expenditures. Although the CAG audit look into any improprieties associated with such incentive schemes, it is very important to know the impact of such schemes vis-à-vis the objectives with which such incentives are provided. A study carried out at the Institute for Social and Economic Change (Gayithri, 2004) reveals that although the revenue loss on account of sales tax concessions to the mega industries alone in Karnataka increased in a very substantial way from Rs.7.38 crore in 1994–95 to Rs. 514.51 crore in 2002–03, the total revenue loss during the above period was Rs. 1,946.52 crore, the results are not very satisfactory. In addition, medium, small, and tiny units had also availed such concessions. In case of many states, these do not even get estimated; however, in Karnataka, tax expenditures are reported in the overview to the budget on an annual basis. There are many other concessions of this nature provided through the other departments, the fiscal implications and the results of such fiscal operations are not known. Similarly, studies reveal that (Gayithri,

2003a) programmes like capital investment subsidy have not really aided much in the dispersal of industry to the backward areas, the objective with which the scheme was originally conceived. On the contrary, it has inadvertently helped the industries in the industrially developed regions.

Hence, public financial accountability does not make sense if the results of complete fiscal operations of the government are not captured. There is a need to subject all government spending to external scrutiny to ensure efficiency and effectiveness in spending.

7.5 Insights into Impact of Public Spending

There are currently two means of getting to know the impact of public spending, CAG reports and Performance Budget reports of development departments.

7.5.1 CAG Source

CAG carries out two types of auditing: Procedural/regularity auditing and performance audit. Procedural/regularity audits are undertaken largely to verify whether the expenditure has been authorized, disbursements sanctioned, and whether rules and regulations have been followed. The issue of whether value for money is ensured and whether the results are in consonance with the objectives of the government are not addressed in the procedural audits. On the contrary, an efficiency-cum-performance audit seeks to evaluate whether the objectives of the expenditure have been met at the lowest cost, and whether the expenditure made has been able to deliver what was expected. However, the performance audit is taken up only for select schemes and, thus, its coverage is very limited. This acts as a major limitation on the checks and balances that we have on the performance/results of the financial operations of the government.

An important issue that largely escapes the attention is with reference to the wastage and improper use of public funds caused by multiplicity/duplication of government schemes in achieving the certain objectives of the government. Instances are evident from many sectors like education, housing, rural development, etc. Even though there are schemes existing to fulfil a particular objective, more are introduced without having a clear understanding of the need for such new additions, there by resulting in inefficient use of scarce public funds. Instances of this kind are evident even in a state like Karnataka that has introduced a number of fiscal reforms. Housing subsidy is one such scheme on account of which there has been a substantial increase in the expenditure by the government. It has been observed that (Gayithri, 2003b) in view of the multiplicity of schemes and the involvement/participation of many departments in providing the service, problems like keeping track of total investments made for the purpose and the total impact of such financial operations by the government crop up. Some of these problems were resolved with the establishment of Rajiv Gandhi Housing Corporation. The compartmentalized tracking of targets vis-à-vis achievements of the housing subsidy schemes sponsored by the central and state governments has led to a situation where excess houses have been built under social housing schemes in Karnataka in certain districts (Gayithri, 2014a). To the best knowledge of the author, none of the agencies are addressing these kinds of issues. However, some such evidences may come to limelight based on some evaluation studies carried out by independent agencies, these obviously will be the only stray cases that are taken up for study, whereas a large number of other programmes may not be evaluated at all for their usefulness to the citizens that the programmes are serving. Similarly, there are some agencies/autonomous institutions, such as Public Affairs Centre, Bangalore, that have used Citizen Report Cards to assess the quality of public services provided by the government, these again will be focusing on limited number of themes. Thus, a major component of expenditure falls outside the scrutiny of public usefulness. Agencies that have some constitutional backing and cover a wide gamut of control on public finances, such as CAG, would be the appropriate agency to address such issues.

7.5.2 Performance Budget Source

Performance budgeting is a system introduced based on the administrative service commission recommendation in the seventies, as per its directives, departments have to report performance of their programmes on an annual basis to the legislature. These are often taken up for discussion by the subject committees, which have the powers to seek explanation for non/poor performance. This is yet another good practice that has been in existence for over two decades.

However, there are many weaknesses associated with this system. The current performance budgeting largely presents financial targets vis-à-vis achievements and physical targets vis-à-vis achievements. Even though it is important to know whether money allocated is spent or not, outlays cannot be treated as outcomes. It is important to know the impacts of government expenditure rather than knowing about the quantum of expenditure itself. Although these issues are addressed to some extent under the physical targets and achievements, these are largely with reference to the outputs rather than the outcomes. Outputs basically indicate the work carried out by the departments in the process of delivering some final product to the public. In essence, what is highlighted is the activity that has been undertaken and not the impact. Yet another weakness of the system is that performance reporting is largely limited to the plan programmes and centrally funded schemes (at the state government level), and the huge non-plan expenditures is left outside the purview.

Citizens will not be interested in knowing how many pulse polio camps have been conducted or how much has been spent on procuring polio vaccine; they will be interested in knowing about how safe their own wards are from the polio menace. Similarly, the interest is not in knowing about what the government has been spending on law and order situation, rather they would be concerned about the safety to their own lives and property, which is largely dependent on the crime rate in the society. Governments are accountable to the public in the delivery of services and the effectiveness with which they are delivered. There is currently a big information gap with reference to the impacts of government programmes on the citizens. Although CAG attempts an evaluation of this nature in its performance audit, the coverage is very small and there is an urgent need to address this issue. The government has been experimenting with various frameworks, which are seriously lacking in assessing the impacts. RFD has been yet another recent failed effort on the part of the government.

7.5.3 Response to CAG Audit Observations

The third issue in the context of finding an answer to the effectiveness with which the existing institutions are ensuring public accountability pertains to the response that the CAG audit observations evoke on the executive. It has been observed by a number of reports that the impact of auditing is not very effectively felt as indicated by the poor response the audit observations evoke on the executive and resultantly no corrective actions taken. Responses to a large number of paras raised in the civil audit reports are not provided and a very large pendency is reported. Yet another problem relates to the fact that responses to such audit reports are not disclosed. This happens even after legislative review, where the departments are expected to provide their response to PAC's reports after they have been reviewed by the legislature.

Schedler (1999, 334) very aptly summarizes the attitude of the governments to the control imposed by the institutions 'Who is eager to respond to nasty questions in public? Who yearns for punishment for misbehavior? Governments usually do not. They understand that institutions of accountability limit their freedom of action and they contain the potential to bring them into painful and embarrassing situations. So why should they be interested in establishing them? This could be the attitude of the executive of the yesteryears; however, the recent thinking has changed, and countries like New Zealand have proved through the enactment of legislations that these types of lapses can be corrected. Strict accountability could also be ensured by having fixed term and output-based contracts for the heads of the departments.

8
Public Expenditure Reform

The ever expanding role of government in a developing country like India and its diverse roles in the pursuit of development and redistribution are justifiable; however, the need to ensure expenditure efficiency needs no reiteration in pursuits of sound fiscal management. In addition, there is every need to review the growth and composition of public spending vis-à-vis the changing societal needs and preferences from time to time. Public expenditure adequacy, efficiency, and effectiveness too need to be periodically reviewed. The following is a list of key questions that need to be addressed:

- Whether the country's public spending is adequate to fulfil and in sync with the professed objectives?
- Is the public spending reviewed both at aggregate and disaggregate levels periodically to address the changing needs and effect mid-course corrections?
- Can the government sustain the spending in the medium-to-longrun, if not identify the alternative sources of financing the same?
- Has the public spending been incurred efficiently, in other words achieving value for money, are there alternative ways of providing public services at a lesser cost without compromising on the quality?
- Has the public spending been effective in terms of delivering the outcomes?
- Is there an institutional mechanism in place to track the results of government spending and factor back the progress achieved into the public expenditure decision-making process to enable informed decision-making possible?

Such a review should not be conceived as a onetime task and be done with it. Howlin, the minister for Public Expenditure and Reform of Ireland,

Public Expenditure in India. Gayithri Karnam, Oxford University Press. © Oxford University Press 2022.
DOI: 10.1093/oso/9780192857569.003.0008

while presenting his budget for the FY 2014 stated, '... the examination of spending plans before the money has been spent. This should bring about a qualitative difference in our debate about spending over the next few years. Our first task upon taking office as a new Government was to undertake a Comprehensive Review of Expenditure. This was not a once off measure. The review of what we do, how we do it and whether we are using our resources appropriately and achieving our policy goals has become the new normal' (The Irish Times, 2013).

It is often noted in policy debates that it is very rare to come across abolition of any scheme by the governments in India both at the central and state government levels(Sharma, 2019). Some progressive sub-national governments in India like that of Karnataka have attempted merging of schemes to arrest duplication. A number of studies have highlighted issues of duplication of schemes and there is also a considerable amount of overlap between the central and state schemes, leading to issues of fungibility by the sub-national governments (Duggal, 2009;Gayithri, 2012). The incremental growth in government expenditure on the ongoing schemes, coupled with constant addition of new schemes, can lead to fiscal unsustainability sooner or later. India has time and again appointed a number of committees to examine issues of tax reforms to enhance tax revenue, the most recent major indirect tax reform being the introduction of GST. On the contrary, the issue of expenditure reform is inadequately addressed barring some political statements in budget speeches. It is time to recognize that no amount of growth in tax and non-tax revenue will be sufficient to meet an unbridled growth in expenditure. The government can create sustainable fiscal space only by an optimal use of revenue resources. This holds well in case of all countries. International financial institutions reiterate the need to achieve long-term fiscal sustainability, 'Despite the different circumstances, the common denominator across these country groups is the need to balance the provision of needed public services with the goals of ensuring long-term fiscal sustainability and maintaining a tax burden that does not harm growth' (IMF, 2014, 21). Expenditure reform should not be a one-off measure; it should be built into the budgeting process as a continuous process by undertaking periodical evaluation of the programmes and the insights should guide the informed decision-making process. The importance of assessing the scheme effectiveness is echoed by both the academic and policy circles time and again. The expert group constituted to review the classification system recommends that the 'Government may undertake periodical benefit–incidence analysis of its programmes/schemes to assess their impact on the targeted beneficiaries' (Government of India, 2004).

8.1 Expenditure Reforms: The Need and Importance

Singh (2009) emphasized the importance of spending well and wisely through expenditure reforms in one of the essays included in 'Not by Reason Alone: The politics of change'. He argues that public expenditure reform has been a very slow process. The intention is not to suggest rushing through any reform without a proper discussion or debate. For instance, the debate to scrap 'plan' and 'non-plan' distinction was longstanding. Singh had suggested constituting a high-level group jointly with the CAG for reclassification of government accounts to go into the oft-repeated distinction on plan and non-plan expenditure in 2009. The high-level group appointed in 2011 chaired by Rangarajan had recommended scrapping of plan and non-plan break up of expenditure in view of the fact that the results of public spending emanate from the total spending and not by the individual plan and non-plan components. Finally the decision to scrap the distinction took effect from the FY 2017–18. Singh (2009) also suggests that 'The classification between capital and revenue expenditure with value judgment attached to one form of expenditure vis-à-vis the other is based on questionable assumptions. Treating devolutions to states for health and education as revenue expenditure, designed to be discouraged, are some examples.' Regarding subsidy administration in toning up tracking of beneficiaries, he suggests, 'Enlarging the bouquet of choice for the intended beneficiaries in seeking the benefit from competing sources like alternative ration shops, public or private schools, through food stamps or education stamps, and creating competition to secure a larger share of available finance, need encouragement.'

The Standing Committee on Finance, chaired by Yashwant Sinha, submitted its fifty-ninth report on the 'Current Economic Situation and Policy Options' on August 30, 2012. The report summarized the economic situation, highlighted challenges, and policy options were recommended. The report states, 'The fiscal deficit of 5.9% of GDP is a source of great concern for the committee. To achieve fiscal consolidation, the government is urged to formulate a coherent and effective disinvestment policy as specified in earlier Standing Committee reports. In addition, the committee recommends that the government prepares a specific action plan which should enhance efficiency in expenditure management; achieve 10% mandatory reduction in non-plan expenditure; rationalize capital expenditure; re-examine the under recovery calculation methods for oil marketing companies; plug loopholes in the tax system and improve the general quality of public expenditure. The committee also calls for better targeted subsidies as they believe a significant share of subsidized products is being used by richer sections of society (Padmanabhan, 2012).'

8.2 History of Public Expenditure Reforms in India

The need to reap optimal benefits from public expenditure was felt by the policymakers quite early in India's planned development effort. Analysing the public expenditure reform initiatives in India and Malaysia, Toye (1981) gives an account of performance budgeting, a form of expenditure reform contemplated by the Estimates Committee way back 1957–58 and 1958–59. A more serious thought was given in 1965 by the Planning Commission's plan projects committee in the context of examining the achievements of planned intervention. The final decision to present Performance Budget by four central ministries was an outcome of the recommendations of the Administrative Reforms Commission (ARC), 1966–70, based on a study of performance budgeting system by a working group set up by the ARC.

Commenting on the usefulness of performance budgeting system introduced in India, Toye (1981,127) observed, 'It seems very unlikely that they are generating significant benefits at the moment. We simply do not know how many legislators read the performance budgets that are produced, or what are the consequences of their doing so. What we do know is that, in their present form, the documents do not and cannot serve as a tool for the improvement of project management, with the result that there is no steady flow of savings of government expenditure which might have more than offset the resource cost of performance budgeting.' Even though the Performance Budget framework has not undergone major correction since that point of time, it remains a fact that, this report continues to be prepared till date by major development departments both at the central and some state governments, including Karnataka, Mahrashtra, Tamil Nadu, and Goa. A more detailed discussion on the performance frameworks used in India is provided in Chapter 9.

Expenditure Reforms Commission was constituted during 1999–2000 to review the excessive growth of non-developmental expenditure incurred by the government. Announcement of the Expenditure Reforms Commission to serve as a tool for combating this unnecessary expenditure was made in the budget speech of 1999–2000 by the then Union Finance Minister Yashwant Sinha while presenting the budget for the FY 1999–2000. Content outline of the Expenditure Reforms Commission reports is presented in table 8.1.

Also, while establishing this commission, the Finance Minister proclaimed about appointing an eminent and experienced person apt for carrying out this task. It was also stated that there would be a complete restructuring of the administrative unit of the expenditure department under the Government of India. This was soon followed with the Government of India (2000)[1] notification for setting up Expenditure Reforms Commission under the chairmanship of Shri. K.P. Geethakrishnan and an eminent members with the following Terms of References:

- Keeping in view the evolving role of the government, the need to foster convergence and avoid overlap in the functions of different central government ministries, departments, and attached organisations and the role of the state governments, suggest a road map for reducing the functions, activities, and administrative structure of the central government;

[1] https://dea.gov.in/sites/default/files/Govt_Note.pdf. Accessed on September 3, 2019

Table 8.1 Content Outline of the Expenditure Reforms Commission Reports

Reports	Contents
First Report (July 10, 2000)	Grants for food supply
Second Report (September 20, 2000)	Optimizing the manpower of government employees Detailing on the functions, activities, and structures of the coal government Offering of fertilizer subsidies Justifying the functions, activities, and structures related to the information and broadcasting department under the Government of India
Third Report (December 23, 2000)	Presents a detail report on the functionalities and role played by the Department of Economic Affairs
Fourth Report (September 20, 2000)	Displays particulars on the small-scale industries along with agro and village industries in the country Presents detail on the Heavy Industry Department Gives a report on public organizations in India
Fifth Report (March 7, 2001)	Elaborated on autonomous institutions Supply department Department of posts
Sixth Report (June 20, 2001)	Presents a report on the activities carried out in the Department of Fertilizers Details on the Ministry of Petroleum and Natural Gas Presents an elaborate report on chemicals and petrochemicals Report on the Government of Steel
Seventh Report (2003–04)	Reports on the Standing Committee on Information Technology
Eighth Report (September 18,2001)	Reports on the Ministry of External Affairs Presents particulars on Agriculture and Cooperation Department Details on the Ministry of Rural Development Programmes
Ninth Report (September18, 2001)	Presents a detailed report on the Ministry of Human Resource Development Presents particulars on the Environment and Sports Department Reports on the Road Transport and Highways Ministry Elaborates on the Department of Culture Presents a report on the Ministry of Youth Activities and Sports Details on the Department of Commerce Details on Ministry of Shipping and Cargo Industry

Table 8.1 *Continued*

Reports	Contents
Tenth Report (September 25, 2001)	Focuses upon the Department of Tourism Details on Ministry of Tribal Affairs Reports on Urban Development and Poverty Reduction in India Presents a report on civil aviation Hands out information on various industrial policies and promotion Reports on the Expenditure Department Presents particulars on the Ministry of Public Grievances, Personnel, and Pension Schemes

Source: Maps of India (n.d.). Expenditure reforms commission, Retrieved from https://bit.ly/3wCho2o , on April 08, 2021.

- Review the framework of all subsidies, both explicit and implicit, examine the economic rationale for their continuance and make recommendations for making subsidies transparent and suggest measures for maximizing their impact on the target population at a minimum cost;
- Review the framework for determination of user charges of departmental and commercial entities and suggest an effective strategy for cost recovery through user charges;
- Review the adequacy of staffing under central government ministries, attached offices, and institutions and suggest measures for rationalizing the staff and cadres of different services. In this context, also review the existing arrangements for re-deployment and re-training of surplus staff to ensure that any additional manpower for new areas of government activities are met by re-deployment;
- Review the procedure for setting up of government-funded autonomous institutions and their pattern of funding and suggest measures for effecting improvement and reducing budgetary support for their activities; and
- Consider any other relevant issue concerning expenditure management in government and make suitable recommendations

8.3 High-Level Expert Committee on Efficient Management of Public Expenditure

The committee constituted under Chairmanship of Dr C. Rangarajan on Efficient Management of Public Expenditure (Government of India, 2011a) has recommended the removal of plan and non-plan distinction in the budget. The report submitted to the Planning Commission also suggests that the process of preparing five-year plan may be continued.

Other recommendations of the group include the following (Government of India, 2011a):

- The annual budgetary component of the plan of the centre and states will have one-to-one correspondence with government budgets of the centre and states, respectively.
- There should be shift in budgeting approach—from a one-year horizon to a multi-year horizon and from input-based budgeting to outputs and outcomes.
- The shift to holistic view of expenditure would require changes in organizational structure, mandates, and processes as well as appropriate interventions in human resource development, information technology, etc.
- The role of the Ministry of Finance, Planning Commission, administrative ministries, and the state governments has been redefined.
- Planning Commission made responsible for consolidation of the five-year plan over all services based on the inputs from the Ministry of Finance.
- The Ministry of Finance made responsible for the preparation of annual budget based on the inputs from the Planning Commission.
- The committee recommends changes in annual budget process comprehensive framework of transfers to states.
- The various problems/issues in the current budget and accounting classification in presenting comprehensive view of central transfer to states may be addressed through the new multi-dimensional budget and accounting classification by a committee headed by Controller General of Accounts (CGA).
- The proposed classification should provide uniform codes for central programmes, sub-programmes, and schemes being implemented in the states.

- The Central Plan Scheme Monitoring System (CPSMS) should be extended to enable tracking of expenditure for all central schemes using both treasury route and society route. This may require interface of CPSMS with core banking solution of banks and systems of state treasuries and AG offices.
- Citizen can also be empowered with information on flow of resources and utilization through a portal, thereby promoting transparency and accountability.
- The treasury mode of transfer of central plan fund is recommended.
- A suitable accounting methodology to be worked out by CGA and CAG to distinguish between final expenditure and transfer and to enable viewing a final expenditure through the books of account.
- Switchover to the complete treasury mode may be made from the Twelfth five-year plan for all new schemes.
- Revenue capital classification should continue. Capital expenditure should relate to the creation of assets and be determined by ownership criteria.
- While all transfers should be treated as revenue expenditure in accounts, the merit of classifying revenue expenditure by end use is also considered for FRBM compliance, and grants for creating assets may be classified as capital grant.
- An adjusted revenue deficit is recommended only for the purpose of FRBM compliance. FRBM may require some amendments to allow for adjusted revenue deficit.
- The central or state plan should continue to include investment outlays (funded by Internal and Extra Budgetary Resources (IEBRs) of Central Public Sector Enterprise (CPSEs) and State Public Sector Enterprises (SPSEs), respectively. Consolidated information on the resources and expenditure of rural and urban local bodies may be provided as special supplement of the budgets.

8.4 Expenditure Management Commission

In the 2014–15 budget speech, Finance Minister Sri. Arun Jaitley announced the constitution of Expenditure Management Commission (EMC). The commission had been conceived as a recommendation body with the primary responsibility of suggesting major expenditure reforms that will enable the government to reduce and manage its fiscal deficit at more sustainable levels. EMC was formed as a five-member body composed of the former RBI Governor Sri. Bimal Jalan, who has been appointed to Head of the Commission, former Finance Secretary Sri. Sumit Bose, former Deputy RBI Governor Sri. Subir Gokarn, and two other members. The commission was mandated to evaluate proposals for reducing the three major subsidies (i.e. food, fertilizer, and oil). The commission was to submit an interim report before the presentation of the budget for 2015–16. The final report was to be submitted before the 2016–17 budget.

The terms of reference of the commission include reviewing all matters related to central government spending, including suggesting space for increased developmental spending, reviewing the budgeting process and norms under the FRBM Act, and suggesting ways to meet a reasonable proportion of spending on services through user charges. It also includes recommending ways to achieve a reduction in financial costs through better cash management, greater use of information technology, and improved financial reporting systems.

The commission is anticipated to give the following broad proposals in the report:

- Ways for the government to cut administrative costs
- Suggest ways to spend budgetary allocation effectively
- Study delivery mechanisms, technology, and accounting methods

The EMC submitted its first interim report in January 2017. The broad proposals suggested ways for the government to reduce administrative costs and disburse funds for various schemes more efficiently. The committee also studied various government schemes, programmes, acquisitions, and projects for which centre's spending was substantial. The three other broad areas the commission examined were the delivery mechanism of programmes, the technology being used to implement these, and the accounting methods used by the government.

The commission studied the pros and cons of the cash-based accounting system, through which income is counted when cash (or a check) is actually received, and expenses are counted when actually paid, and accrual-based system, wherein transactions are counted as they happen, regardless of when the money is actually received or paid.

8.5 Public Expenditure Reform: Context and Issues

Given the incremental budgeting practice that the governments both at the central and sub-national levels are adopting in the framing of year-on-year expenditure estimates, the country has experienced unabated growth in the absolute size of public expenditure over time. New schemes that get added from time to time add to the fiscal pressure. The revenue-driven reform initiatives at the sub-national level have helped in their fiscal consolidation process; however, this cannot last forever sans a corresponding expenditure review and consolidation. On the contrary, the fiscal consolidation effort at the central government has faltered and has gone through revised fiscal consolidation timelines a number of times. Commenting on the fiscal consolidation success, Rao states, 'The attitude towards fiscal consolidation by successive governments has been ambivalent,' ... 'Up to 2007–08, thanks to high buoyancy in income tax revenues, due to the induction of technology through tax information network and service tax due to wider coverage coupled with buoyant economy, there was considerable reduction in both revenue and fiscal deficits. However, after 2008–09, there has been a slippage due to increased spending on subsidies and transfers and inability to adjust the prices of petroleum products commensurate with rise in crude oil prices (Rao as quoted in DH, 2016).'[2]

8.6 Expenditure Planning

A historical review of the expenditure planning process in India reveals that although the plans are all guided by laudable objectives, the programmes are not based on data-based understanding of the societal needs, partly caused by poor databases and partly on account of the haste

[2] April 18, 2016.https://www.deccanherald.com/content/541072/is-fiscal-consolidation-distant-mirage.html.

with which the programmes get announced at the spur of the moment by the political parties in power to enhance their political mileage. These tendencies are all the more visible when elections are round the corner. Other occasions included the Independence/Republic Day celebrations. The NYAY scheme conceived by the United Progressive Alliance (UPA) during 2019 Lok Sabha election is a classic example, wherein the cost implications were not clearly understood and it also amounted to duplicating similar initiatives already in place. The expenditure estimates too are adhoc and not holistic in the sense they do not cover all the cost elements and the likely mid-course cost escalations. These ill-planned expenditure programmes are the ones that lead to unsustainable fiscal outcomes. A key element that adds to the fiscal pressure is the practice that the political parties have adopted from times immemorial is not to discontinue any scheme. Expenditure review to discontinue any scheme duplicative in nature is also a rarity resulting in unbridled growth in expenditure.

8.6.1 Adhoc Cuts on Planned Programmes

Adhoc cuts are the means used by the incumbent governments in temporarily halting such unbridled growth in expenditure as they pose serious fiscal challenges in meeting the fiscal deficit targets. Such adhoc cuts can totally distort the planned development process and result in the wastage of scarce resources. Items of expenditure that are vulnerable to such adhoc cuts have been the capital projects; social sector expenditure that tend to adversely affect the development process even while the non-plan[3] heads of expenditure continue to be protected in view of their downward rigidity. IMF(2014, 22–3) while addressing the issues of public expenditure reform options stated, 'The scope and timing of spending reforms should be in tune with each country's circumstances, but generally, reform efforts should stay clear of across-the-board cuts; tackle major spending items such as the public wage bill and social protection programs; seek gains from better targeting and efficiency-enhancing rationalization;

[3] Non-plan expenditure is largely committed in nature. The plan and non-plan distinction has been abolished from FY 2017–18.

arrest the trend decline in public capital stocks; and mobilize appropriate institutional and political support.'

It further recommends that 'In those countries where fiscal realities call for inevitable reductions in spending, *across-the-board cuts should be avoided*. This approach may seem expedient, but it is neither efficient nor welfare enhancing, and can affect the economy's long-term growth potential, in addition to hurting low-income population groups. Fiscal adjustments are more durable when attained through reforms that reflect well-thought-out strategic choices that protect programmes with high marginal social benefit' (IMF, 2014, 23).

8.6.2 Execution of Expenditure Programmes

Empirical evidences reveal a number of issues relating to poor execution of expenditure programmes that often have resulted in poor outcomes coupled with issues of 'inclusion' and 'exclusion' errors, literature refers to the former as a problem of extending benefits to people who are not eligible for the programme and the latter as excluding the benefits to the people who are entitled to get the benefits.

8.6.3 Efficiency Gains

Gains from improving efficiency are potentially large and could prevent spending restraint from affecting the quantity or quality of the services delivered. In health and education in particular, greater competition and adoption of practices currently used by the private sector have the potential to address cost pressures and, at the same time, generate savings so that coverage can be expanded where needed (IMF, 2014, 24).

8.6.4 Way Forward

Central and state governments have embarked on fiscal consolidation through legislation such as FRBM Act; however, this legislation prescribes limits on the deficit size amounting to the fact that the prescribed control occurs after the expenditure is incurred. Instead, if the government can go to the source, i.e. even before incurring the expenditure, it can set a prescribed level for the growth, which tends to be much more effective. There are variant forms of expenditure rules.

8.6.5 Expenditure Rules

Expenditure rules are of late being increasingly used by the governments to make informed decisions regarding the size, growth, and nature of public expenditure to be achieved. The rule can be extended to the expenditure in totality or limited to certain components alone. For instance, in a developing country like India, where infrastructure requirements are huge, such investments can be exempted from the expenditure rule. On similar lines, social sector investments essential for human development can also be excluded. Hence, the government can use its discretion based on expert advice as to which items of expenditure need to be subjected to control and which ones need to be protected.

There could also be jurisdictional considerations, wherein expenditure targets can be set only for select layers of administration. In India, as we are aware, the third tier, i.e. the urban and rural local bodies account for a very small share in the country's fiscal resources and expenditure. Their dependence on the higher levels of government, i.e. the state and central governments, is also huge; imposing further restrictions on expenditure is meaningless.

Expenditure targets could be set either on the rate of growth of expenditure or on the absolute size and could be in nominal or real terms.

Advantages of expenditure rule lie in the fact that the fiscal correction happens at the source as opposed to deficit targets, which is an end product, hence poses difficulties in the fiscal consolidation process. Canadian government achieved fiscal surplus by resorting to Spending Control Act in the mid-nineties (Gayithri, 1998).

The experiences of the country are detailed in the DICE report. The majority of EU member countries, fourteen out of twenty-five of them, have installed such rules to keep the expenditure side of their budgets under control (see Table 8.2 for details). Germany introduced expenditure rules way back in the beginning of the 1980s itself, with other EU

Table 8.2 Rules for Public Expenditure, EU Countries, 2003: Basic Characteristics

	Expenditure item	Definition of target	Level of application	Date of introduction	Time span
Austria	Administrative expenditure	Cuts in personnel, mostly through not replacing civil servants leaving for retirement.	Central government.	Previous rule: 2000; forthcoming rule: 2003.	End of legislation period (previous rule: 2003 in the ory but government collapsed in 2002; for forthcoming rule: end of 2006).
	Total expenditure	Budget balance rule. However, budgetary targets can be attained cia expenditure side measures only.	Regional and local governments.	2001	End of the current financial equalisation.
Belgium	Primary expenditure	Annual real growth rate to 1.5% in medium terms.	Originally: federal government and social security (entity 1). From 2001 onwards: federal government.	First mentioned at end of 1998 as 'point of reference'.	Medium term (time frame as covered stability programme).
Denmark	Public consumption	Annual real growth rate to 1% on average during 1999-2005.	Central government.	First mentioned in 1997, but became fully binding in 1999.	Multi-annual rule (three years).
Finland	Total expenditure	Freezing real central government spending all the level of 1999 out come.	Central government on-budget expenditure excluding extra budgetary funds (pension, etc.)	1999, but annual frames for central government spending were designed already at the beginning of 1990s.	Cabinet period (latest: 1999-March 2003).
France	Total expenditure	Cummulative real growth rates. As established each year for the next 3 years.	Mainly central government.	1997	Medium term, rolling.

(continued)

Table 8.2 *Continued*

	Expenditure item	Definition of target	Level of application	Date of introduction	Time span
Germany	Overall expenditure	Annual nominal growth rate to be agreed on yearly basis by Finanz plamungsrat (FPC).	Central, regional and local governments.	Beginning of 1980s.	Current and following four years.
Greece	Compensation of employees	Recruitment norm 5:1 (one new recruitment for every five civil servants leaving services). Except for health, education and armed forces where the norms is 1:1.	Central government.	1997	Indefinite
Ireland	Total expenditure	Annual nominal growth of 4% on average during 1998-2002.	Central government.	1997	5 years of the government's term: 1998-2002.
Italy	Primary expenditure	Nominal cellings or "safeguard rules" for all provisions included in all legislation introducing new and higher expenditures.	General government.	End 2002	Indefinite
	Current primary expenditure of regions	In 2002, +4.5% compared to 2000 engagements. In 2003, 2004 and 2005: 2002 absolute value + target inflation.	Regions.	End 2001	2002-2004
Italy	State funding of health care expenditure	Celling on expenditure by regions over a 3-year period. Revised in 2001: celling of € 71.3 billion in 2001, with annual increases in 2002-2004 equal to nominal GDP growth as estimated in the medium- term plan.	Regions.	2000	2000-2003(revised target for 2001-2004).

Netherlands	Expenditure as defined by the ceilings	Medium term real expenditure ceilings, translated each year into nominal amounts.	General government.	First introduced in 1994: adapted in 1998 and 2002.	Medium term: coverage according to cabinet period.
Portugal	Compensation of employees	No new labour contacts in the central administration are to be signed unless authorised by the Minister of Finance.	Central government.	2002	Current legislature (2002-2005).
Spain	Non financial expenditure	Fixed ceiling set up annually in the budget Law.	Central government.	2003	Annually
Sweden	Primary expenditure plus expenditure for the old-age pension system outside the budget.	Annual ceiling on nominal expenditure: expenditure covered by the ceiling should not rise faster than (projected) nominal GDP.	Central government.	1997	3 years ahead, rolling.
United kingdom	Departmental Expenditure Limits (DEL)a)	Government Department sets spending plans for the level of nominal expenditure for three years ahead in so-called Comprehensive Spending Reviews (CRS). Parliamentary authority to spend must still be obtained each year.	Government Departments.	First launched under the 1998 CSR for the period 1999-2002. A new batch of three years was set in the 2000 CSR and again in the 2002 CSR.	3 years. The CSR take place every two years – the third year of the previous exercise becomes the first year of the succeeding exercise.

[a] The two main parts of the UK's budgeting and control framework are DEL (Departmental Expenditure Limits) and AME (Annually Managed Expenditure). Government departments are given three-year spending limits: the DELs. Any spending that cannot reasonably be subject to such multi-year limits is included in AME. (e.g. social security spending, net payments to the EC). All AME projections for future years are estimates which are updated twice-yearly in the Budget and Pre-Budget Reports. Together, AME and DEL sum to Total Managed Expenditure (TME). a national accounts measure defined as public sector current expenditure plus net investment plus depreciation. In tables 1 and 2, only DEL spending is included, since this is the only part of TME which is subject to multi-year limits.

Sources: European commission (2003), Public Finances in EMU 2003, Brussels (COM (2003) 283 final); also published in: European Commission (ed.). (2003). European Economy No 3/2003.

countries following suit ten to twenty years later. In some countries, such rules have been introduced in reaction to the Stability and Growth Pact of Maastricht. In many countries, expenditure rules relate to total public expenditures, but there are also cases where a specific subset of expenditures is addressed, e.g. primary expenditures in Belgium, Ireland, and Italy; public consumption in Denmark; and compensation of public employees in Greece. In Austria and Italy, two and three targets, respectively, are in force. Most countries formulate their expenditure rules only for the central government sector, while borrowing restrictions hold for lower government levels. An exception is Germany, where expenditure rules albeit soft ones apply to all levels of government. The specific way in which an expenditure target is expressed differs widely in EU countries. All the above-mentioned four possibilities occur. A target of a real or nominal growth rate is widespread, but some countries put ceilings on (absolute) levels of certain expenditure items (e.g. Italy, Spain, Sweden, and the United Kingdom). There is also a wide variety concerning the time span for which the rule applies. The majority of countries have installed a multi-year framework, but its concrete definition differs. Most expenditure rules do not have a legal basis but rest on a political commitment, their enforcement is also weak. This is reflected in the absence of prescribed actions in case of non-compliance to the rules in most countries where neither enforcement measures nor sanctions are specified *exante*. An exception seems to be Austria, where for total expenditures (not for administrative expenditures), similar sanctions apply as are foreseen in the 'excessive deficit procedure' of the Maastricht Treaty. An effective rule must specify possible sanctions in case the target is not met (CESifo. 2004).

8.6.6 Effectiveness of Expenditure Rules: The International Experience

IMF (2015, 1) study 'Expenditure Rules: Effective Tools for Sound Fiscal Policy?' provides empirical evidence on the effectiveness of expenditure rules. The analysis is based on a dataset covering all countries with national and supranational fiscal rules, including thirty-three expenditure rules, between 1985 and 2013. This analysis is a comprehensive assessment of compliance with rules and of the potential role of expenditure rules, particularly regarding long-term sustainability. It also analyses whether expenditure rules are associated with changes in public investment and its efficiency.

The study's results reveal that countries comply more often with expenditure rules than with other fiscal rules. As per the IMF study, the expenditure rules have worked well on account of two important situations under which the countries comply more often:(a) if the expenditure target is directly under the control of the government; and(b) compliance with expenditure rules is higher if the rule is enshrined in law or in a coalition agreement. Yet another important finding of the study relates to the fact that expenditure rules have a better compliance record than budget balance and debt rules. High performance of emerging market economies with debt rules is observed to be an exception.

IMF (2015, 11) observed, 'Besides, expenditure rules are most directly connected to instruments that the policymakers effectively control. By contrast, the budget balance, and even more so public debt, is more exposed to shocks, both positive and negative, out of the government's control. One of the desirable features of expenditure rules compared to other rules is that they are not only binding in bad but also in good economic times. The compliance rate in good economic times, defined as years with a negative change in the output gap, is at 72 percent almost the same as in bad economic times at 68 percent. In contrast to other fiscal rules, countries also have incentives to break an expenditure rule in periods of high economic growth with increasing spending pressures. For instance, Iceland never managed to comply with its expenditure rule during its economic boom in the 2000s. The financial and economic crisis of 2009 would have been the first time that Iceland complied with its rule. In the United States, spending pressures also undermined the expenditure rule in good economic times. Belgium and Canada gave up their expenditure rule during periods of relatively high economic growth.'

9

Outlays to Outcomes

Programme Performance Assessment—Theory and Practice

9.1 Background

The need and importance of tracking results for public investment was felt in India way back in the first five-year plan itself, which states, 'With increased investment on development, much more attention to the systematic assessment and evaluation of results from public expenditure is now called for than was probably necessary in the past. . . . With every important programme provision should always be made for assessment of results. . . . Systematic evaluation should become a normal administrative practice in all branches of public activity. With the object of developing the techniques of evaluation a beginning has now been made with the establishment of an independent evaluation organisation under the Planning Commission for community projects and other intensive area development programmes' (Planning Commission, 1951).

Even though there has been repeated emphasis on the need to have the results generated, which was revealed by a number of policy statements such as budget speeches, plan documents, etc., an effective framework is yet to be put in place, and identification of appropriate outcome indicators and generation of data remain a distant dream albeit some centrally sponsored programmes being an exception. The Government of India has rolled out frameworks such as 'Performance Budget', 'Zero-Based Budgeting', 'Outcome Budget', and 'RFD' with the purpose of reporting performance. A more detailed discussion of these frameworks is presented subsequently in this chapter.

Public Expenditure in India. Gayithri Karnam, Oxford University Press. © Oxford University Press 2022.
DOI: 10.1093/oso/9780192857569.003.0009

Poor translation of outlays to effective outcomes related to a number of programmes has been evidenced in the existing research attempting programme evaluation for a number of programmes. The poor results are due to varied factors.

9.2 Monitoring Performance: Meaning and Definition

Monitoring performance is 'a systematic attempt to measure program coverage, the extent to which a program is reaching its intended target population and program process, and the extent to which the service being delivered matches what was intended to be delivered' (Rossi and Freeman, 1982,125).

OECD (2002) defines monitoring as 'A continuous process of collecting and analysing data for performance indicators, to compare how well a development intervention, partnership or policy reform is being implemented against expected results (achievement of outputs and progress towards outcomes).' It defines measurement of performance as 'A system for assessing the performance of development interventions, partnerships or policy reforms relative to what was planned, in terms of the achievement of outputs and outcomes. Performance measurement relies upon the collection, analysis, interpretation and reporting of data for performance indicators.'

9.2.1 Performance Assessment and Outcome Monitoring—The Process

An effective performance assessment and outcome monitoring framework is one that captures two key levels of governmental intervention. First, the various schemes that are drafted for the purpose of achieving the multifaceted goals and objectives of the government need to be constantly examined for their input, output, and outcome performance to enable mid-course correction for any pitfalls. The second and equally important level of intervention is in the nature of enhancing the allocative efficiency of public expenditure by making an effective use of the available outcome information in framing informed expenditure decisions. Since the purpose of any performance assessment is to enhance the utility of expenditure interventions, it is important to factor in both the levels in any useful performance assessment framework. The processes involved are discussed below.

In the process of achieving these objectives, the governments make use of financial and manpower resources—performance at this stage needs to be assessed for the inputs using their input indicators (percent of total resources allocated/percentage of resources used/percent increase in resource/percentage of the components to the total); the second important stage relates to the implementation stage, wherein the government undertakes certain activities that result in certain outputs (school/hospital buildings constructed/training conducted). The resultant work outputs need to be assessed further in terms of the 'output indicators' (percentage of the required school/hospital buildings constructed/percentage of officers due for training trained) and finally the intermediate and end outcomes (universalization of enrolment, polio eradication) measured using relevant and appropriate indictors (percentage of children within age group 6–14 years enrolled/pass percentages/dropout rates/percentage of children afflicted by polio). This requires record-keeping and regular data reporting systems. The complete appraisal of the progress from the stage of inception till the attainment of results relates to performance assessment and overseeing/supervising the performance on a continuous basis amounts to monitoring. A meaningful performance management is ideally extended beyond performance assessment at the stage of attainment of results to macro policy review and scheme design in the subsequent points of time. The assessment at each of these stages is largely dependent on the analysis of relevant indicator data collected and analysed at each of the stages. Hence, mere listing of inputs, outputs, and outcomes for the program/scheme does not entail performance assessment. This complete chain is popularly used as 'results framework' to enhance public sector accountability. Thus the performance terminology is highly interlinked with one another—performance assessment is undertaken by tracking the work progress at all stages—inputs, outputs, and outcomes. Mid- and end-term evaluation tools are applied to assess the programme impacts, these programme impacts are in turn monitored for continued policy intervention.

ADB defines monitoring as a process that 'continuously tracks performance against what was planned by collecting and analyzing data on indicators established for monitoring and evaluation purposes. It provides continuous information on whether progress is being made toward achieving results. Monitoring looks at both program processes and changes in target groups and institutions brought about by program activities … the performance information generated from monitoring enhances learning from experience and improves decision making'(ADB,2008a&b).

9.3 Why Performance Assessment and Outcome Monitoring Matter?

Performance assessment and outcome monitoring are very critical for the successful delivery of the services that are intended to be delivered. In addressing the issue of monitoring the key questions that need to be addressed among many others are—Whether the programmes are being designed to adequately reflect the slated objectives? Are priorities well defined to match the objectives? Are adequate resources earmarked? Is effective scheme implementation ensured? Are the services reaching the targeted population? Most importantly, whether the schemes have their intended impact on the targeted population? Are there measurable indicators to measure the results and populated on a periodical basis to attempt any mid-course correction? Most important of all relates to whether these results information is used in expenditure decision-making in the subsequent budget cycles? Some specific reasons cited in the performance literature for performance assessment are to evaluate the programmes, expenditure control, budget planning, celebrate success, promote effectiveness, learn from the pitfalls, and improve future performance.

Raizen and Rossi (1981) state that monitoring information is often as important as or more important than information on programme impact and pertain to the issues of accountability. Various forms of accountability listed by them are presented in Box 9.1.

Box 9.1 Forms of Accountability

- Coverage Accountability: Are the persons served those who are designated as targets? Are there beneficiaries who should not be served?
- Service Accountability: Are proper amounts of outputs being delivered? Are the treatments delivered those that the programme is supposed to be delivering?
- Fiscal Accountability: Are funds being used properly? Are expenditures properly documented? Are funds used within the limits set by the budgets?
- Legal Accountability: Are relevant laws being observed by the programme, including those concerning affirmative action, occupational safety and health, and privacy of individual records?

Source: Rossi and Freeman, 1982,p. 127.

9.4 Performance Measures: A Conceptual Framework

Conceptual clarity regarding what is being measured is an important aspect in any attempt to measure performance and take the required corrective action. A number of terms indicating various forms of performance, such as financial, physical, and impacts, are all defined (OECD, 2002) below. Each of these forms of performance when measured by appropriate indicators and populated has significant implications in the planning and delivery of services. Hence, there is every need to track and review them on a periodical basis to have an understanding of the magnitude of intervention, the activities undertaken, and the results. Debates in the recent past highlight the importance of results and have been advocating that there is need to shift the focus from 'outlays' to 'outcomes'. It is important to note that each of the forms of performance, i.e. inputs, outputs, and outcomes, is important by itself and needs to be tracked in the toning up of expenditure planning and management. There are evidences of all these measures used as 'family of performance measures' in assessing the overall performance of a scheme/programme.

Conceptual Framework for performance Measurement

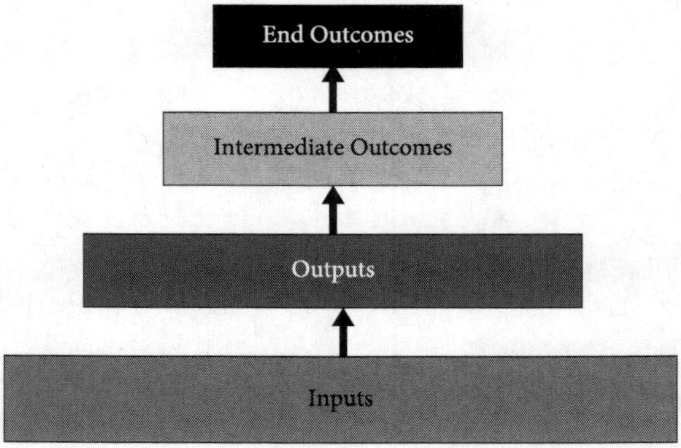

9.4.1 Performance Measures

Results

Results are changes in a state or condition, which derive from a cause-and-effect relationship. There are three types of such changes (intended or unintended, positive, and/or negative), which can be set in motion by a development intervention—its output, outcome, and impact.

Goal

Goal refers to the higher-order objective to which a development intervention is intended to contribute to.

Impact

Positive and negative long-term effects on identifiable population groups are produced by a development intervention, directly or indirectly, intended or unintended. These effects can be economic, socio-cultural, institutional, environmental, technological, or of other types.

Outcome

The intended or achieved short-term and medium-term effect of an intervention usually require the collective effort of partners. Outcomes represent changes in development conditions, which occur between the completion of outputs and the achievement of impact.

Outputs

Outputs refer to the products and services that result from the completion of activities within a development intervention.

Inputs

The financial, human, material, technological, and information resources used for the development intervention are referred to as inputs.

Activity

It refers to the actions taken or work performed through which inputs, such as funds, technical assistance, and other types of resources, are mobilized to produce specific outputs.

Performance

Performance refers to the degree to which a development intervention or a development partner operates according to specific criteria/standard/guidelines or achieves results in accordance with stated plans.

Performance Indicator

Performance indicator is a quantitative or qualitative variable that allows the verification of changes produced by a development intervention relative to what was planned.

Benchmark

Benchmark is the reference point or standard against which progress or achievements can be assessed. A benchmark refers to the performance that has been achieved in the recent past by other comparable organizations or what can be reasonably inferred to have been achieved in similar circumstances.

Results Chain

Results chain is the causal sequence for a development intervention that stipulates the necessary sequence to achieve desired objectives—beginning with inputs, moving through activities and outputs, and culminating in outcomes, impacts, and feedback. In some agencies, reach is part of the results chain.

Results Framework

Results framework is the logic that explains how results are to be achieved, including causal relationships and underlying assumptions. The results framework is the application of the log frame approach at a more strategic level, across an entire organization, for a country programme, a programme component within a country programme, or even a project.

9.5 Performance Measurement in the Public Sector: A Caveat

While performance assessment of government schemes remains important, it has to be borne in mind that the task is very challenging. This is in view of the fact that governmental programmes are quite diverse and designed to fulfil multiple objectives that could at times be not compatible with one another. For instance, it is a very common practice in the government sector to have objectives that may not reinforce one another. For instance, the goals of enhancing the growth and productivity of the manufacturing sector and industrial growth of backward areas are two contradictory objectives that could be coexisting despite them not reinforcing one another, unlike the private sector whose objectives and strategies are in a single direction, i.e. towards maximizing profits/earnings. Similarly, public investments in education are guided by not only advancement in the sector but also by equity considerations, both regional and interpersonal. In view of this, resource use may strictly not happen in the manner that a private company would use, i.e. with the sole objective of maximizing profits. Hence, very often, this results in technical inefficiency (outputs not matching the level of input use) and cost-ineffective service provision. In addition, very often, market completely fails in the production of a number of goods and services that are in the nature of public goods characterized by jointness in consumption and non-excludability.

In view of these multifaceted and divergent roles that governments assume, performance measurement is a more difficult and challenging task in the public sector than in the private sector. This is because performance measurement works best when there is clarity about what is being measured and why. This type of clarity is characteristic of the private sector because the 'bottom line' that private sector managers manage for is clear. Private companies exist to make a profit and create wealth for their owners. There are well-accepted ways to measure whether a private enterprise is achieving these objectives. Indicators in this context include profits, revenue, shareprice, market share, etc. Performance measurement in the public sector is of entirely different nature, because public sector organisations exist for many diverse reasons. The private sector is driven by profit, so that success or failure can be measured in monetary terms.

Notwithstanding the challenges posed by the complex nature of monitoring performance, it still is a very critical component in the provision of public services and public expenditure planning and management. The current levels of performance achieved serve as an important benchmark in planning for the future.

9.6 Monitoring Frameworks and Country Experiments

Many monitoring tools have been evolved over time. These have largely been designed and adopted by the international donor agencies, such as The World Bank, Asian Development Bank (ADB), The Department for International Development (DFID), and United States Agency for International Development (USAID), in the process of monitoring projects funded by them. Although no attempt is made in the present chapter to get into a detailed review of all the approaches, a summary of the various monitoring approaches as discussed in a World Bank (2004) chapter and other studies is presented in Box 9.2. However, following this, we present a detailed discussion of the Logical Framework Approach (LFA), which is observed to be a very effective technique in monitoring the programmes/projects capturing all the important stages involved in the process of the service delivery—starting from objectives till the end results.

These frameworks either independently or in combination were tried out in a number of countries. Mackay (2006) summarizes the practices used in other countries—Brazil has adopted a whole of government approach to the setting of programme objectives and the creation of a system of performance indicators (May et al., 2006),and Columbia

Box 9.2 Approaches for Performance Assessment, Monitoring, and Evaluation

Performance Indicators: Performance indicators are measures of inputs, process, outputs, outcomes, and impacts for development projects, programmes, or strategies. When supported with sound data collection—perhaps involving formal surveys—analysis and reporting, indicators enable managers to track progress, demonstrate results, and take corrective action to improve service delivery. The participation of key stakeholders in defining indicators is important because they are then more likely to understand and use indicators for management decision-making.

Uses: Setting performance targets and assessing progress towards achieving them. Identifying problems via an early warning system to allow corrective action to be taken. Indicating whether in-depth evaluation or review is needed.

Program/Performance/Outcome Budgeting: Performance-based budgeting is an advanced version of the performance indicators approach wherein the current performance information serve as the basis in annual financial allocations, thus aids in the enhancement of allocative efficiency.

Open Coordination Method: The European Union has recently developed a strategy (Pestieau, 2009) for improving the performance of social policy among its member states. The member states agree up on a number of social indicators, which are published on a regular basis to motivate/induce each country to get to the best score and this approach is termed as Open Coordination method. An important aspect of this approach is that inputs are not considered in the assessment of the indicators.

LFA: Logical framework helps clarify objectives of any project, programme, or policy. It aids in the identification of the expected causal links—the 'programme logic'—in the inputs, processes, outputs, outcomes, and impact results chain. It leads to the identification of performance indicators at each stage of results chain, as well as risks which might impede the attainment of the objectives. The log frame is a vehicle for clarifying objectives and designing activities. Log frame serves as an important tool to review progress and take corrective action during programme implementation.

Uses: Improving quality of project and programme design—by requiring the specification of clear objectives, the use of performance indicators, and assessment of risks. Summarizing design of complex activities. Assisting the preparation of detailed operational plans. Providing objective basis for activity review, monitoring, and evaluation.

Theory-Based Evaluation: Theory-based evaluation allows a much more in-depth understanding of the working of a programme activity. In particular, it need not assume simple linear cause-and-effect relationships. For example, the success of a government programme to improve literacy levels by increasing the number of teachers might depend on a large number of factors. These include, availability of classroom and textbooks; the likely reactions of parents, school principals, and schoolchildren; the skills and morale of teachers; the districts in which the extra teachers are to be located; the reliability of government funding; and so on.

Uses: Mapping design of complex activities. Improving planning and management.

Formal Surveys: Formal surveys can be used to collect standardized information from a carefully selected sample of people or households. Surveys often collect comparable information for a relatively large number of people in particular target groups.

Uses: Providing baseline data against which the performance of the strategy, programme, or project can be compared. Comparing different groups at a given in time. Comparing changes over time in the same group. Comparing actual conditions with the targets established in a programme or project design. Describing conditions in a particular community or group. Providing a key input to a formal evaluation of the impact of a programme or project. Assessing levels of poverty as basis for preparation of poverty reduction strategies.

Rapid Appraisal Methods: Rapid appraisal methods are quick, low-cost ways to gather the views and feedback of beneficiaries and other stakeholders in order to respond to decisionmakers needs for information.

Uses: Providing rapid information for management decision-making, especially at the project or programme level. Providing qualitative understanding of complex socioeconomic changes, highly interactive social situations, or people's values, motivations, and reactions. Providing context and interpretation for quantitative data collected by more formal methods.

Participatory Methods: Participatory methods provide active involvement in decision-making for those with a stake in a project, programme, or strategy and generate a sense of ownership in the monitoring and evaluation results and recommendations.

Uses: Learning about local conditions and local people's perspectives and priorities to design more responsive and sustainable interventions. Identifying problems and troubleshooting problems during implementation. Evaluating a project, programme, or policy. Providing knowledge and skills to empower poor people.

Public Expenditure Tracking Surveys: Public expenditure tracking surveys track the flow of public funds and determine the extent to which resources actually reach the target groups. The surveys examine the manner, quantity, and timing of releases of resources to different levels of government, particularly to the units responsible for the delivery of social services, such as health and education.

Uses: Diagnosing problems in service delivery quantitatively. Providing evidence on delays, 'leakage', and corruption.

Cost–Benefit and Cost-Effectiveness Analyses: Cost–benefit and cost-effectiveness analyses are tools for assessing whether or not the costs of an activity can be justified by the outcomes and impacts. The cost–benefit analysis measures both inputs and outputs in monetary terms. The cost-effectiveness analysis estimates inputs in monetary terms and outcomes in non-monetary quantitative terms.

Uses: Informing decisions about the most efficient allocation of resources. Identifying projects that offer the highest rate of return on investment.

<u>**Impact Evaluation**</u>: Impact evaluation is the systematic identification of the effects—positive or negative, intended or not—on individual households, institutions, and the environment caused by a given development activity, such as a programme or project. Impact evaluation helps understand the extent to which activities reach the poor and the magnitude of their effects on people's welfare.

<u>**Uses**</u>: Measuring outcomes and impacts of an activity and distinguishing these from the influence of external factors. Helping in clarifying whether costs for an activity are justified. Informing decisions on whether to expand, modify, or eliminate projects, programmes, or policies. Drawing lessons for improving the design and management of future activities. Comparing the effectiveness of alternative interventions. Strengthening accountability for results.

Source: The World Bank, Some tools, methods and approaches for monitoring and evaluation. Study, World Bank, Washington D.C., 2004.

combined these with rigorous impact evaluations. Australia, the United States, and the United Kingdom have tried out a mix of M&E tools and methods: Including performance indicators, rapid reviews, impact evaluations, and performance audits (Lahey, 2005). Some countries have succeeded in building a whole of government M&E system, while others such as Uganda comprise an as yet uncoordinated and disparate collection of about sixteen separate sectoral monitoring systems (Hauge, 2003) and uses are different. Chile's monitoring and evaluation is cited to be a well-performing home grown monitoring and evaluation system (Mackay, 2006).

The poorest countries, those which are required by multilateral donors to prepare poverty reduction strategies, stress the regular collection of performance indicators to measure the Millennium Development Goals (MDGs) (Mackay, 2006, 4).Mackay (2006) reviewing the monitoring practices in various countries as to whether there is any single model that can be emulated by other countries states that 'As a general proposition, it is dangerous to look for best practice, and perhaps even good practice countries. Each is unique, with particular circumstances and realities, and each government has developed its M&E functions in particular directions for particular purposes'. The usefulness of these monitoring approaches ultimately is dependent on the use to which the performance information is put to. The effective uses could include, among many others, basis for year-on-year resource allocation in the budget process, reprioritization of programmes, department level expenditure planning, management of delivery of services, and better targeting, ensure accountability, or all of them.

9.6.1 Country Experiments

Many countries, as mentioned earlier, have been experimenting with varied forms of result-based frameworks, while the ones initiated in the decades of sixties and seventies did not survive for long, the reforms conceived in the decades of eighties and nineties are designed to sustain the temptation to discontinue the effort. 'There is a growing appreciation within the development community that an important aspect of public sector management is the existence of a results or performance orientation in government. Such an orientation—in effect, an "evaluation culture"—is considered to be one avenue for improving the performance of a government in terms of the quality, quantity and targeting of the goods and services which the state produces' (Mackay, 2006, 1). Chile's monitoring and evaluation system is described in text box 9.3.

Selected features of the International Reform Initiatives Include the following:

- Performance review
- Formal legislations forming the basis
- Budget classification
- Medium fiscal framework
- Performance contracts
- Public spending reviews

9.7 Performance Review

Performance review is an important feature of budget reforms adopted in a number of countries. A number of OECD countries have used special forms of policy evaluation in the context of the budget process under

Box 9.3 Chile's Whole-of-Government M&E System

Chile's M&E system, which is managed by the powerful Finance Ministry, has developed progressively over time, partly in response to fiscal pressures, partly in response to the changing landscape of public sector reforms, and partly in an opportunistic manner (see Guzman, 2003;World Bank, 2005; and Zaltsman, 2006). Major milestones include the following:

- *Ex ante* cost–benefit analysis required for all government projects (1974)
- Performance indicators collected for all government programmes (1994): Regular information is collected on about 1,600 indicators. These are used in the formal reports prepared for the congress, and to provide key data for the various types of evaluation which are conducted.
- Comprehensive Spending Reports (1996)
- Government Programme Evaluations (1996): These are in the nature of programme reviews and about 160 have been conducted so far. They comprise clarification and agreement of detailed programme objectives, preparation of a log frame analysis, desk review, and analysis of existing data. Their average cost is $11,000, and they usually take from four to six months to complete.
- Rigorous impact evaluations (2001). These entail primary data collection and often the use of control groups and difference-in-differences. Fourteen have been completed to date at an average cost of $88,000 and taking up to eighteen months to finish. About 60% of the government's budget has been evaluated by means of either these impact evaluations or the government programme evaluations.
- Comprehensive Spending Reviews (2002): These review all programmes within a particular functional area and look at issues of inefficiency and duplication of programmes. They include desk reviews and have an average cost of $48,000. Five have been completed so far.

Source: Keith Mackey, January 2006. Evaluation Capacity Development.

names such as 'strategic policy reviews' (Australia), 'strategic program reviews'(Canada), 'interdepartmental policy reviews'(The Netherlands), 'spending reviews'(United Kingdom), and the 'Program Assessment Rating Tool (PART)'(United states).Spending reviews in the United Kingdom were aimed at reallocating money to key priorities, change policies so that money is well spent, ensure that departments work better together to improve services, and weed out unnecessary and wasteful spending (Kraan, 2007, 31). The Australia National Audit Office (ANAO) is responsible for review of the reports and the Department of Finance reviews performance and budgeting information. Two independent reviews were commissioned by the Department of Finance 'effective reporting in program performance statements' and 'performance reporting in common wealth annual reports' in the years 1993 and 1995, respectively. The Administrative Tribunal (AAT) and the Ombudsman are the two principal federal administrative review bodies. Contrary to the cases of Australia and New Zealand, which undertake selective reviews, the United Kingdom and the United States undertake reviews of all the programmes on an annual basis. The reviews are used to reprioritize and introduce corrective allocations that would ensure achievement of preset objectives.

9.8 PART

The performance assessment initiated in the United States provides some useful guidelines. The launching of PART in the United States was largely governed by the frustration that 'Washington mentality has generally assumed that program funding should steadily increase with the only question being "by how much?" This type of thinking has wasted untold billions of dollars and prevented the emergence of results-oriented government' (OMB, 2004) reference. An important milestone in the journey towards assessing the performance of government schemes was the announcement of 'Government Performance and Results Act' in 1993. This law required the federal agencies to identify long-term and annual goals, collect performance data, and justify budget requests based on the performance. Each federal programme was required for the first time to explicitly identify measures and collect data to testify the success or the achievement levels of the programmes. However, this effort flawed as there were numerous measures with poor focus developed and thus could not serve the purpose of helping in the budget decisions.

PART was designed with a view to overcome these flaws. PART is basically a performance evaluation tool (questionnaire with thirty questions approximately included—the number varies depending on the type of programme being evaluated) rating the programme/scheme performance in four critical areas. These are purpose and design of scheme, strategic planning, management, and results and accountability. A set of questions ascertaining whether the programme design and purpose are clear and defensible answers the first criteria. Whether the agencies set valid annual and long-term goals is ascertained from a set of questions to answer the second criteria. The third set relates to the financial and programme oversight and performance improvement efforts. The last set of questions address the issue of programme results, which need to be reported with accuracy and consistency.

Performance assessment of each programme is based on the responses for the set of questions pertaining to the four criteria and they are rated using a scale ranging from 0 to 100, where a score of 100 represents the best performance and the converse is zero. Both the scores are combined to rate an agency, and the qualitative rating is categorized as 'effective', 'moderately effective', 'adequate', and 'ineffective'. The programmes that do not have acceptable performance measures or have not collected the performance data are categorized as 'results not demonstrated'. PART serves as a useful tool for the budget allocation dialogue.

These kind of initial problems were faced even in the context of the United States, and the measures adopted to resolve some of these are discussed below. Some of these provide direction to the current performance assessment initiatives planned by governments in India, both at the centre and sub-national levels.

The innate difficulties in attempting to review all the government-run programmes on these lines were realized and a decision was taken to review one-fifth of all programmes every year.

Initially, more than half of the US programmes received the rating 'results not fully demonstrated' due to the lack of either performance measures and/or performance data. The situation was very similar to that of any Indian state, where the majority of programmes had measures that emphasized inputs (such as the amount spent and the number of people a programme served) rather than the outcomes. It was recognized that development of good performance measures is critical for making sure that the programme is generating the intended outcome. PART has now alerted the agencies to identify performance measures for the programmes that currently lack them and also generated performance data required before their next cycle of performance assessment.

Programme 'Outcomes' being a new concept, the need to train the officers in the identification of performance measures was felt and was also introduced. These inputs are also very essential in the Indian context as for a very long period the focus has been on the 'inputs' and to a certain extent 'outputs'.

Understanding the fact that a perfect or an ideal practice cannot be put in place in one go and to continue with refined persistent interventions to achieve positive results in the medium- to long-term is very essential.

For this kind of performance assessment system to remain in place and deliver the desired results, it is very essential that the system is institutionalized to ensure that the departments assess the performance of the programmes at regular intervals and factor in the required changes in the budget process. Whether or not these are used in the budget decision process, the policymakers will certainly have the right kind of information to frame the appropriate policies.

9.9 RFD

Performance monitoring and evaluation system (PMES) has been approved by the Prime Minister of India in 2009 (September11, 2009). RFD was expected to serve two important purposes—move the focus of the organisation from process orientation to results orientation and to serve as a basis to evaluate the organisation's performance.

RFD contains the following sections (Government of India, 2011b, 2):

- Organisation's vision, mission, objectives, and functions
- Inter se priorities among key objectives, success indicators, and targets
- Trend value of the success indicators
- Description and definition of success indicators and proposed measurement methodology
- Specific performance requirements from other departments/organisations that are critical for delivering agreed results.

A number of departments prepared the RFD from the FY 2009–10, which was adopted by a number of sub-national governments also, the Government of India, however, withdrew the RFD practice.

There are some more measures that are worth emulating attempted in the context of other countries that have launched systematic performance assessment of government schemes.

9.9.1 Formal Legislation Forming the Basis

Many nations have resorted to framing of legislation to guide the reform process and their provisions were binding on the government. The financial improvement programme of Australia, one of the forerunners in the budget reforms to achieve better service delivery, featured introduction of a white paper on budget reforms in 1984.This was followed by the framing of an act entitled 'Public Service Reform Act[1] and by many related initiatives. These initiatives spanned over fifteen years.[2]

[1] Starting with the Reid Review and the 1983 White paper for financial improvement program in 1983, Australia undertook a series of measures to address the issue of public services. These included preparation of a white paper on budget reform in 1984 and enacted two legislation—merit protection act and public service reform act. Program management and budgeting (PMB) was introduced in 1987, followed by performance-based pay agreements in 1992. The Public Service Act was reviewed in 1994 and four legislation were framed to address the issue of public service delivery. These were Financial Management and Accountability Act-1997; Common Wealth Authorities and Companies Act-1997; Auditor General Act-1997; and a Public Service Act-1999.

[2] First major reform initiatives in the Australian public sector started with the 1983 Reid Review. Merit protection Act and Public Service Reform Acts were passed in 1984. Financial Management and Accountability Act, Commonwealth Authorities and Companies Act, and Auditor General Act were framed in 1997, and the Public Service Act was framed in 1999.

The Reid Review recommended that 'changes be designed to increase public sector efficiency, devolve responsibility, make public servants more accountable for their actions, free up recruitment procedures for senior managers and increase ministerial control over departments.' The Australian government's public service reform initiatives included government service charters, public performance agreements for agency heads, removal of hierarchical controls, and streamlining of administrative procedures. It is observed that legislative commitment played the role of a critical success factor of Australian public sector reforms.

New Zealand was yet another forerunner in budget reforms. It had a fairly standard budgeting system that was common with the OECD countries until the introduction of reforms. The country began its reform initiatives in 1985, followed by a fiscal crisis in the eighties. A complete change in the public financial management was attempted through a stream of legislative (The Fiscal Responsibility Act 1994) and administrative reforms pertaining to all aspects of service delivery (Scott et al., 1997). 'The primary objective of the Act is to entrench sound fiscal policies and make it difficult for future governments to deviate from them' (OECD, 1997; The World Bank, 1998b). Many other nations such as Canada (Federal Accountability Act, 2006) and France (Organic Budget Law 2001) used the strategy of providing legal and administrative framework to the reforms introduced in their respective countries.

9.9.2 Budget Classification

The line item description practice that normally depicts the expenditure break outs by each line item was brought under reform fold. A number of OECD countries have attempted programmatic reclassification of their central government budget line items. Australia, France, the Netherlands, Sweden, and the United Kingdom offer good examples of reclassified budgets based on programme criteria(Kraan, 2007). These reform initiatives shifted the focus from single line items, which have for long served as the focal points of expenditure control, to grouping of certain related line items that contribute to specified outputs and outcomes. The broad objective of a programme focus is to enable result-oriented public expenditure decision-making.[3]

In Australia, under PMB, expenditures were classified on the basis of a hierarchy of programmes, sub-programmes, and activities, each related to purposes and objectives (as opposed to the lineitem budgeting system previously in use). Management reporting systems to monitor and report on programme achievement were based on this programme structure. The programme format enhanced the alignment of the annual parliamentary appropriations with programme management. Under PMB, performance information was seen as essential. Australian states like New South Wales, Queen's land, and Western Australia introduced similar reforms. In making this possible, a required necessary condition is to factor in an element of discretion and flexibility for the line departments to reallocate resources among the line items. This may pose a threat to the conventional input control; however, by making the line departments accountable for the outputs to be produced for the resources allocated, effective control can be exerted on the utilization of funds. This exercise involves a careful reclassification of the line items into groups that collectively result in certain outputs and outcomes.

9.9.3 Medium-Term Framework

Unlike the traditional budgets that are cast for one out year, the reform initiatives are characterized by a medium-term focus, the term varying from three to five years. It is meant to help assess the costs of public services in a medium term, prepare a realistic resource framework, and ensure better funding predictability. Multiyear estimates have to take into account the future demand for outputs while framing the projections, failing which the projections would not be realistic and become meaningless. Some countries have factored in flexibility for the line agencies to

[3] The programme budgeting concept introduced in the current wave of reforms,i.e. the one introduced in the decades of eighties and nineties, is different from the program budget concept used in the decade of fifties and sixties. The current concept is used to reflect programs within the existing organisational structure of a line department, which makes it responsible for the programs unlike the program budgeting of fifties, which cut across line departments and, hence, posed problems of accountability.

reprioritize and reallocate their authorized resources to suit the sectoral needs. However, multiyear estimates are usually not authorized, thus do not have legal status, but are essential for macro budgetary planning.

9.9.4 Performance Contracts

Singapore has been using budgeting for results from 1996. Public sector managers are delegated more powers to improve performance; however, associated with increased accountability. Public sector organisations are to be managed as autonomous agencies. Resource agreements will specify the outputs and performance targets that these agencies will deliver in exchange for allocated resources. Resources will be allocated on the basis of outputs. The resource agreements will be used as an accountability tool for performance evaluation and resource allocation and details will be agreed between the agencies (The World Bank, 1998b, p.88). The case of New Zealand has formalized the resource allocation mechanism by way of a purchase agreement between the minister and the chief executive of each agency covering the provision of an agreed type, volume, timing, quality, and cost of outputs in return for a specified appropriation.

9.9.5 Use of Performance Information in Budgeting

Measurement and benchmarking of performance of governmental programmes is yet another important feature of performance-based budgeting adopted by almost all the countries that have introduced reforms. In Australia, departments at the federal as well as the state level paid a great deal of attention to develop measurement systems. The measures are qualitative and quantitative, covering inputs, outputs, and outcomes, with a large-scale emphasis on outcomes. Managing for outcomes model of Queensland and output-based management of Western Australia are two good examples of performance measurements. Australia also provides a good example of country cases that have used performance information in the budget process. As a part of the result-oriented budgeting, Finland insists up on the development of performance indicators to be included in the annual reports in the process of financial devolution to the agencies. Countries like Sweden report performance results along with their financial statements in their annual reports.

Although performance information is the key to improving allocative efficiency, it is feared that direct links between the government spending and outcomes is difficult to establish. There are also certain expenditures that typically would require long gestation period to generate the end outcomes, in such cases, the annual reviews have to be restricted to outputs or intermediate outcomes. Despite such problems, the introduction of the performance budgeting practices has resulted in an improved focus on performance and service delivery. Allen Shick observes in the context of New Zealand that 'Departments had a clearer idea than previously of what was expected of them, their output was specified and fully costed, chief executives had broad discretion to manage resources and operations, and ministers had choices in obtaining outputs including policy advice' (Schick, 2001, 2). However, caution has to be exercised in identifying and using the right indicator in reprioritizing allocations (The World Bank, 1998b).

Although not exhaustive, given above are some key reform features adopted by various countries. They have been successfully able to make some difference to the budget process. These serve well as pointers for the nations that are making similar ventures. However, each country has to evolve reform initiatives that suit its needs. Lessons from building country monitoring and evaluation systems are summarized in Box 9.4.

9.10 Operational Issues

There are some important operational issues that need to be considered in the effective formulation of performance assessment.

9.10.1 Defining Performance 'Outputs' or 'Outcomes'

Before putting in place a systematic performance assessment framework, there is need to have clarity as to whether the emphasis should be in tracking the 'outputs' or 'outcomes'. A number of countries including India have extensively resorted to using the 'output' information to report performance of governmental schemes and programmes. The general ease, with

Box 9.4 Lessons from Building Country M&E Systems

- Substantive government demand is a prerequisite for successful institutionalization
- Role of incentives
- Key role of a powerful 'champion'
- Centrally driven, by capable ministry
- Build reliable ministry data systems
- Danger of over-engineering the system
- Utilization is the measure of 'success'
- Limitations of relying on government laws, decrees, and regulations
- Role of structural arrangements to ensure M&E objectively and quality
- A long-haul effort, requiring patience

Source: Keith Mackey, January 2006. Evaluation Capacity Development.

which the outputs can be measured, tracked, and attributed to a particular intervention result in their extensive use. The recent effort by a number of nations to move away from input-based budgeting to outcome-based budgeting had generated a considerable amount of debate to shift the performance assessment of government schemes from 'outputs' to' outcomes'.

9.10.2 Plan and Non-Plan Distinction

For a very long period, i.e. until the abolition of plan and non-plan distinction in the FY 2017–18, tracking of the performance was done by 'plan' and 'non-plan' schemes, which did not meaningfully serve the purpose as individually they did not lead to any outcomes. The need to consider total expenditure in the outcome assessment needs no reiteration.

9.10.3 Programme Approach

On the similar lines, it is common knowledge that individual schemes may at the best have some activities associated with it and some outputs but not the results, and it is a group of related activities that lead to the expected results. Hence, the ideal approach to be adopted is the one where the focal points are 'programmes' and 'sub-programmes' rather than schemes. Three sub-national governments in India, Karnataka, Jharkhand, and Uttarakhand have had the advantage of USAID reform initiative, which had provided a very good programme and sub-programme grouping for certain departments. This approach would also help detect the duplication that exists in the objectives and help avoid scheme multiplicity. This would certainly help conserve scarce resources.

9.10.4 Delineating Monitoring Roles and Time Frame

Figuring out how scheme monitoring has to be attempted in a system that has three administrative layers below the state level, i.e. district, taluk, and panchayat levels, is a very important first step. The monitoring of detailed activities and their progress are best left in the jurisdiction of district and below. It makes sense to monitor all the activities for their progress at the grassroots level at short time intervals such as a month to help initiate corrective action during the programme implementation. Such detailed month-wise and activity-wise reporting at the state level would amount to waste of manpower and financial resources. Such detailed information would add to the woes of officers compiling them as they are already hard pressed for time to discharge their programme implementation duties. At the state level, it is more meaningful to monitor the outputs—district wise on a quarterly or six monthly intervals and outcomes on an annual basis.

9.10.5 Performance Indicators

An important aspect to be noted is that it is essential to have performance indicators for each of the important stages in the results chain—inputs-financial indicators; activities-activity status indicators; outputs-output indicators; and results-outcome indicators. Having too many and inappropriate indicators would again cause greater damage to performance assessment rather than enhancing it. In the present context, where the performance assessment has to be tracked at all the administrative levels, it would also be meaningful to identify two/three key indicators to reflect the financial output and outcome performance and to be used as standard indicators at all the levels, i.e. taluk, district, and state, that would help in comparative analysis and programme intervention.

Literature states performance measures have to be SMART-Diamond's and the description of the same is presented in Box 9.5.

Box 9.5 SMART Performance Indicators

'SMART', which stands for 'Specific, Measurable, Achievable, Realistic (Relevant), and Time-bound'. Strictly speaking, the SMART features do not relate to indicators, but to results (i.e. objectives and outputs).

To be **SMART** means to be:

Specific—Are you precise about what you are going to achieve?

Measurable—Are your objectives quantified?

Achievable—With a reasonable amount of effort and application, can the objective be achieved? Or are you attempting too much?

Realistic—Do you have the resources to make the objective happen? (men, money, machines, materials, minutes)

(Relevant—Can the people with whom the objective is set make an impact on the situation?

Do they have the necessary knowledge, authority, and skill?)

Time-Bound—Is there a completion date clearly stated or defined?

The SMART features make an objective or an output 'monitorable', thus highlighting how formulating good objectives and outputs is essential to the monitoring effort: Without SMART objectives and outputs, it becomes very difficult to choose and formulate relevant indicators for measuring progress. It is therefore worthwhile to formulate—or to seek influence on the formulation of—programme and sector objectives at all levels with a view to make them as SMART as possible.

Source: Diamond, 2006.

9.10.6 Performance Data Collection Issues

Current data availability is largely limited to inputs and outputs and occasionally outcomes. In the results chain, reliable monitoring requires reliable data at all levels to attune the programme design or financing to deliver the end results. Currently, there are large sets of data collected at the grassroots level by almost all the sectors; however, their utility has been an important issue, in other words who uses this information for what purpose and its relevance and accuracy. In a health sector study undertaken by me in the past it was observed that the institutional deliveries reported by the agency for the district is almost two times that of the DLHS survey. Hence, important issues that need to be considered in putting in place meaningful and relevant data collection mechanism are to check whether the data collected is comprehensive, relevant, regular, and reliable. In doing this, it is very important to strengthen the capacity of the officers concerned. Data management, publication, analysis, and use are the other important aspects of effective monitoring systems.

9.10.7 The Cost of Monitoring

The cost of monitoring varies widely depending on the method of data collection. Some might say that not more than 5% of the total programme budget should be spent in this field. It is hard to suggest a standard level of cost for programme monitoring. Does the programme have access to the required data from systems that already collect it for their own purposes, or does it have to collect it itself? In the latter case, are we talking about data that can be extracted from existing (administrative) systems or documents (such as the financial management system or reports from programme units to the programme HQ) or data requiring specific field studies to be collected? There are various ways of reducing costs. One is to choose indicators that can be monitored using available data. This may imply some compromises, such as using less-than-optimal proxy indicators.

Finally, but most importantly, how 'nice to know' is different from what we 'need to know'. This distinction is fundamental in all monitoring but has been neglected too often, giving rise to overly costly and bulky monitoring systems as well as to the collection of huge quantities of information that cannot be processed and is therefore left unused. It goes without saying that considerations of cost and relevance are equally valid when advising on establishing or improving sector or national monitoring systems.

9.10.8 Skills and Mechanism in the Departments

Our experience of working with the departmental officers in the context of several research studies has revealed (and also the content of the reporting formats) that massive capacity building is needed in equipping the skills of officers concerned in the concepts and methodology. No doubt they are very familiar with concepts like 'inputs' and 'outputs'; however, converting these into indicators has been observed to be a difficult task. This capacity building should happen across all the administrative levels—state, district, taluk, and village panchayat. This training should not only be limited to the departmental monitoring officers but also to the state, district, and taluk statistical officers.

9.10.9 Broad Features of an IT-Based Mechanism

There are good IT-based solutions currently available for many of the government monitoring schemes. Tracking of the financial targets and achievement position with reference to the programmes implemented is a good example under the Special Development Plan used by the Planning Department of the Government of Karnataka. This is based on MS Excel and Dashboard analyses. Financial targets and achievement position are being currently tracked at all the three layers, i.e. taluk, district, and state, and the dashboard analysis clearly helps identify the regions by their levels of performance. This could be extended to tracking of inputs, outputs, and outcomes at all the layers, i.e. taluk, district, and state, and enable informed policy decisions.

The second IT-based solution was developed by the USAID REFORM[4] project. This was tailor-made for performance assessment across all the

[4] Three state governments in India viz. Karnataka, Uttarakhand, and Jharkhand were recipients of technical assistance for the State Fiscal Management Programme.

administrative layers and departments. The package is developed using MS Access and has a very neat mapping of schemes into programmes and sub-programmes along with the progress in the indicators and the spending associated with it. This could suitably be modified if required. An important prerequisite to have an effective IT mechanism in place is to first identify appropriate outcome indicators and generate data on a periodical basis.

9.10.10 Central Mechanism to Implementation Process

Many country experiences reveal that success of their effective monitoring and performance assessment was largely attributable to the lead agency, which was the Finance Ministry in many a case, and its proactive role. Based on this international experience, it could be attempted in India both by the central and state governments.

9.10.11 Prerequisites for Effective Performance Monitoring

Effective monitoring and performance assessment is not dependent merely on the usage of good tools and techniques but are enabled by certain prerequisites.

9.10.12 Perusal of the Performance Information

Often a number of countries are anxious to put in place monitoring and performance assessment practices owing to their eagerness to track the results of government interventions and also to the civil society pressures to make the public sector accountable. An important purpose that the performance information serves or is expected to serve is to enable the policymakers to frame informed expenditure decisions and thus enhance the 'allocative efficiency' of government expenditure. This is largely absent in the Indian context with the exception of certain plan programmes. Chile offers a good example (Mackay's [2006] observation based on World Bank evaluation) of intensive utilization of monitoring information and evaluation findings produced by the monitoring and evaluation systems. It is observed that the Chilean Finance Ministry uses the performance information for resource allocation within the budget process. The Finance Ministry also ensures that the performance information is reported completely to the Congress. Australia is yet another country that has used the performance information for expenditure planning in the subsequent budget cycles.

9.10.13 Life Cycle and Annual Monitoring and Monitoring of Infrastructure Projects

Monitoring of infrastructure projects through their life cycle has often been a major challenge. The project management approach offers methodologies to track the progress of the infrastructure projects that go through multiple stages involving multiple activities before project completion before the end outcomes are achieved. Although the activities may vary from one project to another, they go through some important stages that are summarized in Box 9.6 (ERC, 2011).

9.10.14 Project Management Techniques

Some of the techniques used in project management include the use of Earned Value Analysis Technique, Cost Performance Index, and Schedule Performance Index. The Earned Value Analysis Technique objectively measures a project's accomplishments in respect of its performance against time, cost, and quality targets. Thus, in Earned Value Analysis, in the period being measured,

- — Planned value i.e. amount that was planned to have been spent (planned physical progress [in percent] multiplied with the cost of Activity) or financial progress;
- — Earned Value i.e. amount that should have been spent to date based on what has been achieved (actual physical progress [in percent] multiplied with the cost of Activity);

Actual Value i.e. amount actually spent;

Box 9.6 Stages in project management

Project Stage	Activities
Pre-Execution Stage	Identification of project development objectives, i.e. need for the project Financial sources Identification of measurable and monitorable outcome Indicators Calculations for cost–benefit analysis, financial viability, etc. Identification of design parameters/design conditions/design options/contract design
Execution Stage	Selection of vendors Construction Contract management
Completion Stage	Commissioning Handover Preparation of maintenance scheme

These are analysed to calculate variations which include:

— Cost variation, calculated as (Actual Value minus Planned values)
— Schedule variation, calculated as (Earned Value minus Planned Value)
— Schedule delay, calculated as (Number of days required to catch [up or lost] to achieve the difference of Earned value and the Planned Value).

Logical framework is a tool that can be suitably adapted to each of the infrastructure project as here again there cannot be a one size fits all kind of framework. One has to factor in to the LFA detailed milestones relevant to the activities and also specify the time frame for each milestone.

Box 9.7 Key milestones by activities

Activities with milestones
Improved agricultural marketing infrastructure
Slaughterhouses contract package
Prepare tender documents (year 1)
Evaluate bids (year 1)
Award contract (year 1)
Construct slaughterhouses (year 2–4)
Undertake oversight of slaughterhouse construction (year 1 onwards)
Farm collection and marketing infrastructure contract package
Prepare tender documents (year 1)
Evaluate bids (year 2)
Award contract (year 2)
Undertake contract of small scale infrastructure (year 2 onwards)
Undertake oversight of small scale infrastructure construction (year 2 onwards)
Product standards laboratories, Prepare laboratory equipment specifications (year 2)
Prepare tender documents (year 2)
Evaluate bids (year 2)
Procure and install equipment (year 2)
Implement procedures for international accreditation (start in year 2; need 3 years of operation before accreditation)
Project management and capacity support
Project management
Project director appointed by MAIL (start year 1)
Project staff appointed to PMO by MAIL (early year 1)
Equipment for PMO procured and installed (mid-year 1)
Establish MAIL project tender committee (early year 1)
Establish project steering committee (mid-year 1 onwards)
Mobilize international and domestic project consultants (mid-year 1 onwards).
Undertake baseline survey (mid-year 1)
Prepare annual work plans (yearly)

Carry out midterm and completion evaluations and semiannual ADB review missions (continuous)

2.5 Technical capacity support

Farm market infrastructure

Update commodity value chain gap assessment (year 1)

Evaluate priority needs for small-scale infrastructure, technology support, and training (year 1)

Prepare selection criteria

Develop standard infrastructure designs (year 1)

Undertake selection (year 1)

Train agribusinesses, traders, marketers, and MAIL in targeted commodities in market and product management (year 2)

2.5 Product standards development

2.3 Ministry of Agriculture, Irrigation and Livestock (MAIL)

- 2.3.1Assist MAIL in establishing policies, grads, and standards for Project's targeted commodities (year 1–2)
- 2.3.2 Strengthen MAIL capacity in implementing SPS policy and regulatory issues for priority value chains (mid-year 1 to end of project)

Prepare laboratory system design and specification (year 2)

2.4 Ministry of Commerce and Industries (MOCI)

- 2.4.1 Design and implement improved lab system management (year 2)
- 2.4.2 Undertake laboratory technical training (year 2)

2.5 WTO accession

- 2.5.1 Assist MAIL and MOCI in integrating the agriculture sector's needs and special considerations on sensitive products into the WTO accession process (year 1)

Source: ADB—Draft design and Monitoring Framework, Proposed Asian Development Fund Grant Islamic Republic of Afghanistan: Agriculture Market Infrastructure Project, October 2008.

Chart 9.1 depicts the important stages in a project and monitoring, when attempted at each of these levels would help in putting in place a very effective project management.

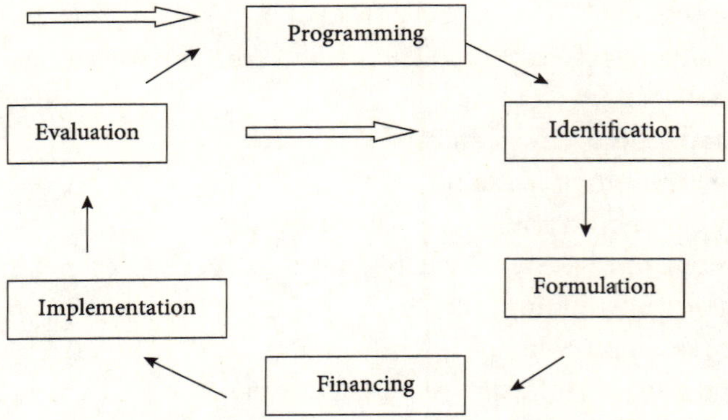

Chart 9.1 The Project Cycle

9.11 LFA as a Practical Tool

LFA was developed as a project planning tool and has been widely used by most donor agencies for many years.

9.11.1 What Is Logical Framework?

Government intervention in the process of providing goods and services involves a number of causal links, including objectives, inputs, processes, and outputs, before it gets translated into end results. LFA provides a useful framework for keeping track of the various links in the 'results chain' of a project or programme, right from the inputs invested to the final impact achieved (Diamond, 2006). 'LFA is an effective technique for enabling stakeholders to identify and analyze problems and to define objectives and activities which should be undertaken to resolve these problems. Using the log frame structures, planners test the design of proposed project to ensure its relevance, feasibility and sustainability. In addition to its role during program and project preparation, the LFA is also a key management tool during implementation and evaluation. It provides the basis for the preparation of action plans and the development of a monitoring system, and a framework for evaluation' (ITAD, 1999, 13).

The LFA typically provides information pertaining to all the key links in the results chain covering the following levels (Diamond, 2006).

Objectives

Objectives of the programmes/schemes are presented in the first column of the log frame. The developmental objectives should narrate the expected long-term or final impact to which the programme/project will contribute. The immediate objectives indicate the outcomes needed for achieving the envisaged development objective.

Outcomes

The outcome of a given intervention would normally be to fulfil its immediate objectives. In the DAC (OECD, 2002) terminology, outcome is defined as 'The likely or achieved short-term and medium-term effects of an intervention's outputs.' Data for monitoring at the outcome level may be found in existing statistics, e.g. on crop yields, service delivery levels, etc. In some cases, it may be relevant to conduct specific surveys as a means of adjusting intervention strategies and activities. Such surveys may be part of the regular work of extension agents or other service providers. Another method is to have the target group conduct surveys of itself, e.g. letting an organisation conduct its own survey of its members' satisfaction. Self-monitoring can also take place at the level of farmers, who register the inputs and outputs in relation to a given activity.

Activities

Activities are the various jobs undertaken by the departments in the process of providing services leading to the fulfillment of the professed objectives. These too are quantitative and verifiable. Activity monitoring oversees the progress of scheduled activities, one by one, and is usually highly quantitative, e.g. construction of embankment, construction retaining walls, etc. At this level, physical and financial progress may easily be compared, matching reports on progress of work with expenditure data. Physical monitoring is normally based on the implementers' reporting on own activities. The activities are akin to the 'outputs' term used in the results framework.

Outputs

These are the direct products, largely tangible, of various activities carried out in the process of delivering the services. Monitoring at the output level relates directly to the 'product' of a given activity, e.g. number of training courses conducted, school buildings constructed, number of polio camps organized, etc. Such data will often be collected anyway as part of routine administration. As the outputs are linked closely to the activities, aspects of budget performance will form part of output monitoring (i.e. assessing the link between money spent and outputs achieved).

Inputs

Inputs include money and material that are needed to carry out the activities. These have to be monitored in terms of their availability, timeliness, quality, and consumption. The accounts are the tool to monitor consumption of financial inputs.

Objectively Verifiable Indicators

Objectively verifiable indicators (OVIs) describe the programmes' objectives in operationally measurable terms and provide the basis for performance measurement. The specification of OVIS acts as a check on the viability of objectives and forms the basis of the project monitoring system (ITAD, 1999, 29). Indicators that can be objectively verified are identified and populated periodically to enable progress verification over time.

Sources of Verification

Sources of data to verify the behaviour of the indicators identified for each level to be specified. Sources of verification (SOV) should also specify the format in which information should be provided, who should provide the information, and with what frequency, monthly, quarterly, or annually, it should be provided.

LFA also stipulates the risks and the assumptions associated with the programme or project between each of the above levels, e.g. the risks that may prevent the achieved outcomes from leading to the expected impact, or the assumptions that need to hold true for the outputs to give rise to the envisaged outcomes.

At each level, LFA will typically include the following: a number of indicators by which to monitor whether the planned impact, outcomes, etc. have actually been achieved, and the means by which each indicator can be measured—the so-called means of verification.

All these elements are usually presented in an LFA matrix.

The LFA thus reminds us that monitoring (or, as phrased in the Paris Declaration, 'performance assessment') of development interventions needs to take place at all levels in order to track the achievement of results, during as well as after implementation. The LFA also provides a terminology to differentiate between the various levels (Diamond, 2006).

Utility of the Log Frame Approach

The logical framework helps clarify objectives of any project, programme, or policy It leads to the identification of performance indicators at each stage of the results chain as well as risks that might impede the attainment of the objectives. The log frame is a vehicle for clarifying objectives and designing activities. Log frame serves as an important tool to review progress and take corrective action during programme implementation. Log frame approach helps in (Diamond,2006):

- Improving quality of project and programme design by requiring the specification of clear objectives, use of performance indicators, and assessment of risks
- Summarizing design of complex activities
- Assisting the preparation of detailed operational plans
- Providing objective basis for activity review, monitoring, and evaluation

ITAD (1999, 34) observes that the 'main output of the LFA is the log frame matrix. (An example of the log frame sourced from ITAD detailing all the steps involved is presented below.) The log frame sets out the intervention logic of the project (if activities are undertaken, then results will be achieved, then project purpose etc.) and describes the important assumptions and risks that underlie this logic. With objectively verifiable indicators and sources of verification, the log frame provides the framework against which progress will be monitored and evaluated.'

An example of a completed log frame is given below.

	Intervention Logic	**OVIs**	**SOV**	**Assumptions**
Overall Objective	Infant & maternal mortality rates reduced.	Mortality rates reduced for under-1s, under-5s & pregnant &nursing mothers from X to Y by19xx.	Dept of Health statistics, analyse d*exante*, mid-term, & *expost*	
Project Purpose	Health status of pregnant & nursing mothers, infants & babies improved.	Incidence of post-partum & neonatal infection within health centers reduced from X to Y by19xx. Rates of infectious diseases (polio, measles, tetanus) among under-5s reduced from X to Y by19xx. Incidence of acute birth complications reduced from X to Y by 19xx.	Hospital & clinic records, analyse d*exante*, mid-term,& *expost* Sample survey of target group conducted &analysed in years 1, 3,&5.	Incidence of infectious diseases in the household reduced.
Results	1. Functioning primary healthcare service established at district level.	Number of villages provided with regular PHC services increased from X to Y by 19xx. Proportion of under-5s vaccinated against polio, measles & tetanus increased from X to Y by 19xx. No. ofbirth complications diagnosed& successfully assisted increased from X to Y by 19xx. Increased patient satisfaction with quality of services provided.	Clinic attendance records, analysed quarterly. Clinic vaccination records, analysed quarterly. Client satisfaction survey, conducted annually.	Mothers willing to attend clinics. Household nutrition improved through increased seasonal availability of high protein foods, & increased proportion breastfed babies. Pregnant & nursing mothers able to access cash to pay for treatment.

	2. Quality & efficiency of secondary healthcare improved.	Number of patients treated increased from X to Y by 19xx. Average cost of treatment per patient reduced from X to Y by19xx. Increased patient satisfaction with standards of care.	Hospital records, analysed quarterly. Client satisfaction survey, conducted annually.	
Activities	1.1 Rehabilitate/replace mobile clinic vehicles & equipment 1.2 Design & implement mobile clinic programme. 1.3 Recruit & train village birth attendants. 2.1 Rehabilitate staff housing. 2.2 Recruit new staff. 2.3 Design & implement new procedures for: Personnel management, vehicle & equipment maintenance, drug storage & control, financial control & cost recovery. 2.4 Design & implement staff training programme for: Patient care, hygiene maintenance, basic accounting, data collection & analysis.	Technical assistance Equipment Medical supplies (See activity schedule).	Lump sum costs Reimbursable.	Department of Health maintains level of funding at pre-project levels in real terms. Suitably qualified staff willing to work in rural areas.
				Pre-condition: Department of Health implements decentralization act to enable provincial health office to rationalize staffing levels.

Source: ITAD, 1999.

Developing the Log Frame for Specified Objectives

Log frame delineates the steps involved in the translation of objectives into the end outcomes and thus can clearly guide the staff involved monitor project implementation using the appropriate indicators for each of the stages. Chart 9.2 describes the process.

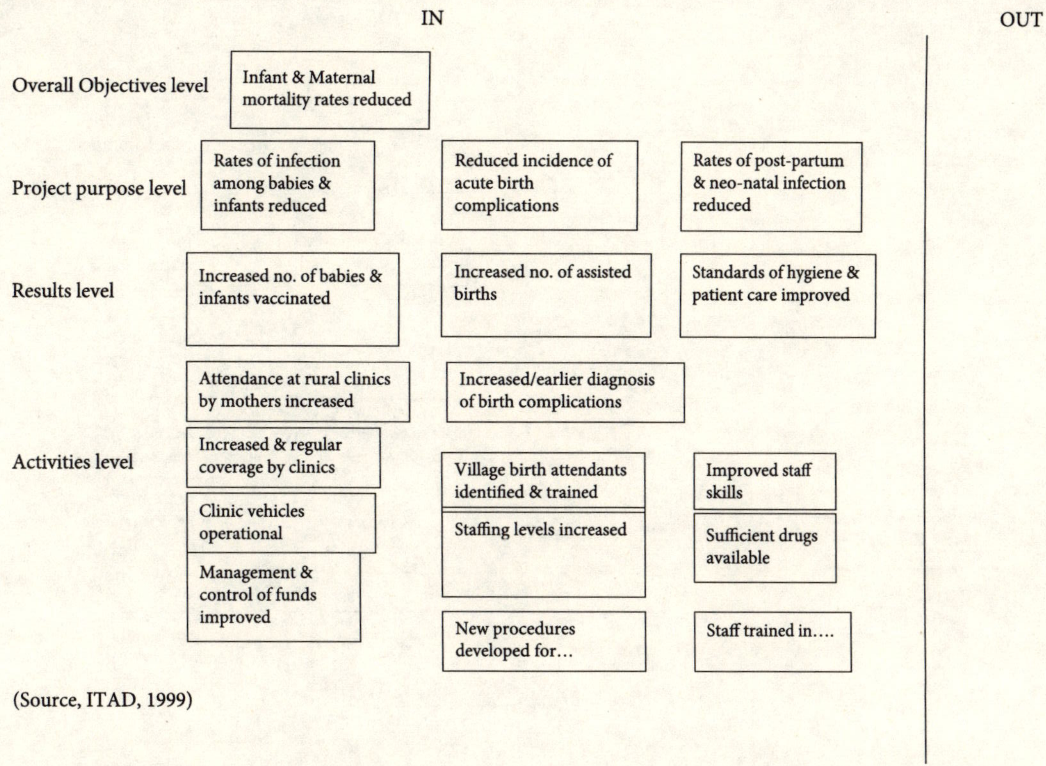

Chart 9.2 Transposing Objectives into the Log Frame

Source: ITAD, 1999.

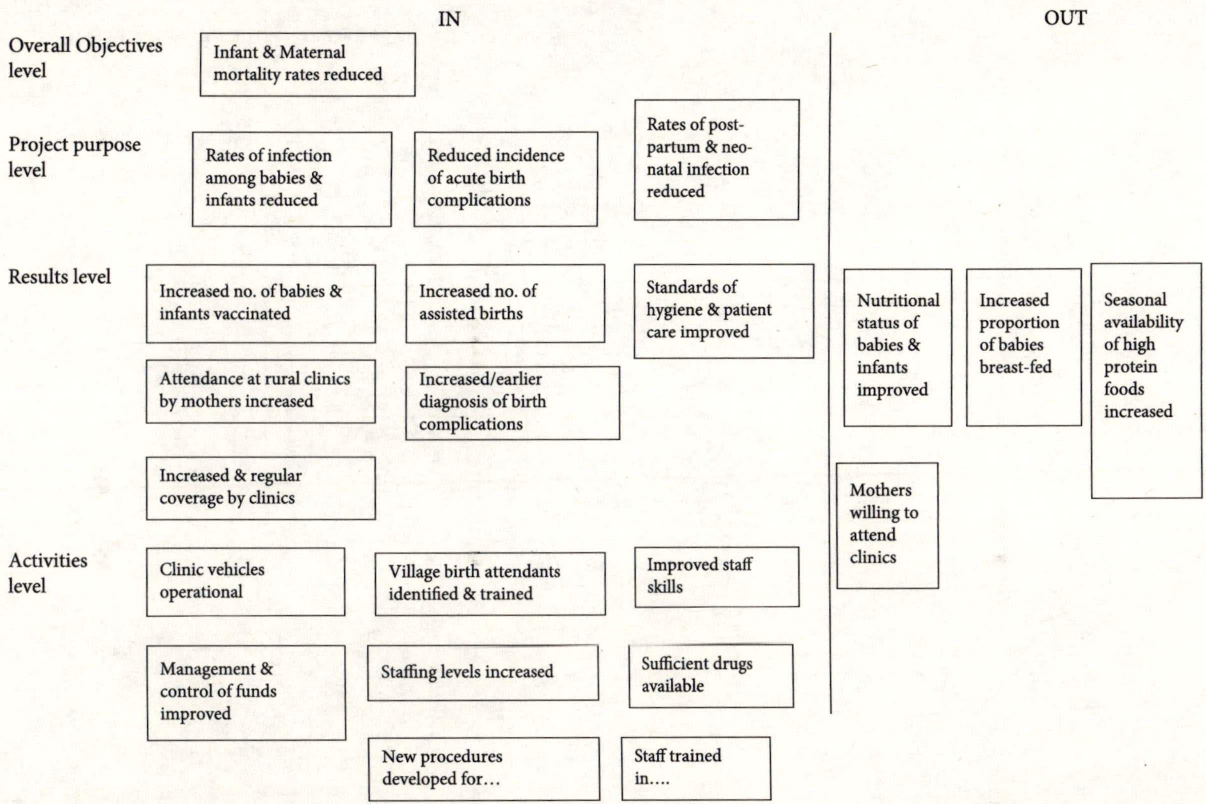

Chart 9.3 Specifying Assumptions

Log frame method also helps in identifying the type of information required by each level of log frame, and the measurement concept and the timing of collection of the information. These steps are presented in chart 9.3.

Level of Log Frame	Type of Information	Timing of Collection	Measurement Concept
Overall Objectives	Substantive development change specific to the sector Measurement based on trends, possibly of key sectoral indicators NOTE: the project is only one of many factors influencing change	Project completion and *expost*	SUSTAINABILITY Continuing the flow of benefits IMPACT Making a difference in the wider environment RELEVENCE Meeting target group needs
Project Purpose	Realistic and sustainable change in target group situation, specific to project intervention	Mid-term and project completion	
Beneficiary Response	Early warning of likelihood of implementation success from opinions of beneficiaries about their access to, use of, and degree of satisfaction with services provided by the project.	Quarterly/yearly (collected as part of results monitoring)	LEADING INDICATORS Proxies for relevant and sustainable change
Results	Quantitative and qualitative measures of physical progress in service delivery Cost ratios and input–output ratios of performance Comparisons of actual achievements with planned targets	Quarterly/yearly	EFFECTIVENESS 'progress towards objectives—doing the right things.' EFFICIENCY 'Efficient implementation—doing things right.'

Level of Log Frame	Type of Information	Timing of Collection	Measurement Concept
Activities	Measures based on activity schedule Comparisons of actual start and completion dates with planned dates Variations from the planned schedule Milestone dates and events	Weekly/monthly	ECONOMY Ensuring the best relationship between cost, quality & time.'
Costs	Measures based on project budget Comparisons of actual against plan Analysis of government, donor and beneficiary contributions Cost variance analysis	Weekly/monthly	

9.12 Way Forward

A number of frameworks have been used by the Indian governments without achieving proficiency in any of the frameworks used till date. Given the international experience and availability of sound frameworks, we need not spend more time and effort reinventing the wheel. A careful review and adaptation of features that suit the Indian situation will help track the results of government intervention. Identification of appropriate performance indicators to be applied all over the country to enable interstate comparison should be followed by generation of sound data. Capacity of the personnel engaged in generating the data has to be built on the data definitions and methods of collection. It is needless to emphasize the importance of analysis of the performance indicators and its usage in framing informed expenditure decisions. This is a very useful way of weeding out expenditure programmes that have outlived their utility and become redundant, and this will automatically pave the way for enhancing the fiscal space.

10

Covid-19 and Public Spending

10.1 Context

As I was finalizing this book, the Covid-19 pandemic broke out, causing havoc to mankind and global economy, and it continues unabated till date. India currently is reporting the second-highest number of cases next only to the United States. Initially, WHO praised India for its swift efforts in adopting lockdown and social distancing, and the country revealed very small number of cases. The disaster brought to light the huge health infrastructure inadequacies and the unpreparedness of the health sector. Stringent measures in the form of lockdown and social distancing adopted to arrest the spread of Covid-19 have seriously impacted the economic growth that was already sluggish. Fiscal policies have a critical role to play in reviving consumer demand, reviving and boosting investor confidence. Many sectors have been adversely affected. The Government of India and the state governments have announced a slew of fiscal policy measures in an attempt to address the human misery and revive the economic activity. This chapter makes an attempt to present an overview of the fiscal measures taken up in India and its implications on government finances, which was already reeling under pressure owing to slower economic growth and limited fiscal space.

10.2 Economic Growth in India: Pre-Covid-19 Trends

The growth of real GDP was on the increase in 2017–18, revealing an increase from 5.1% to 8.7% from the first quarter to the third quarter. Performance of all the three sectors, i.e. agriculture, industry, and service sector, recorded good growth, in particular the manufacturing sector's performance improved significantly from a negative growth of –0.9% in

Public Expenditure in India. Gayithri Karnam, Oxford University Press. © Oxford University Press 2022.
DOI: 10.1093/oso/9780192857569.003.0010

the first quarter to 7.3% in the third quarter. Service sector's performance was good in all the three quarters. Deceleration in growth started in the first quarter of 2018–19 itself, with the real GDP declining from 7.1% to 5.6% in the third quarter; this was largely caused by the industry sector, which declined from 7.5% to 5%. The growth in the service sector remained at 7.4% level during all the three quarters, and that in agriculture declined from 3.8% to 2%. Growth dampened further in 2019–20 from 5.6% and 5.1%in first quarter (Q1) and second quarter (Q2), respectively, to 4.7% for the third quarter (Q3) (Table 10.1). This decline was mainly contributed by the industry sector as its growth declined from 3.8% in

Table 10.1 Quarter Wise Growth of GVA and GDP at Constant Prices 2011–12 **(Percent)**

Sectors	**2017–18**			**2018–19**			**2019–20**		
	Q1	**Q2**	**Q3**	**Q1**	**Q2**	**Q3**	**Q1**	**Q2**	**Q3**
Agriculture, forestry & fishing	**5.9**	**6.2**	**5.7**	**3.8**	**2.5**	**2.0**	**2.8**	**3.1**	**3.5**
Industry	**0.5**	**6.7**	**7.7**	**7.5**	**4.8**	**5.0**	**3.8**	**0.8**	**0.1**
Mining & quarrying	2.6	11.9	5.2	–7.3	–7.0	–4.4	4.7	0.2	3.2
Manufacturing	–0.9	7.8	9.3	10.7	5.6	5.2	2.2	–0.4	–0.2
Electricity, gas, water supply & other utility services	11.2	11.8	10.1	7.9	9.9	9.5	8.8	3.9	–0.7
Construction	0.0	1.3	4.6	6.4	5.2	6.6	5.5	2.9	0.3
Services	**8.4**	**5.8**	**7.5**	**7.4**	**7.4**	**7.4**	**6.9**	**7.3**	**7.4**
Trade, hotel, transport, communication and services	8.1	8.2	8.2	8.5	7.8	7.8	5.7	5.8	5.9
Financial, real estate & professional services	5.9	2.9	5.7	6.0	6.5	6.9	7.1	7.3	
Public administration, defence and other services	14.5	8.7	9.1	8.8	8.9	8.1	8.7	10.1	9.7
GVA at basic price	5.5	6.1	7.2	6.9	6.1	5.6	5.4	4.8	4.5
GDP at market prices	5.1	7.3	8.7	7.1	6.2	5.6	5.6	5.1	4.7

Source: GoI, 2020[a].

[a]GoI, 2020, MONTHLY ECONOMIC REPORT Combined report of March and April 2020 https://dea.gov.in/sites/default/files/March%20and%20April%202020_0.pdf accessed on 17 September 2020.

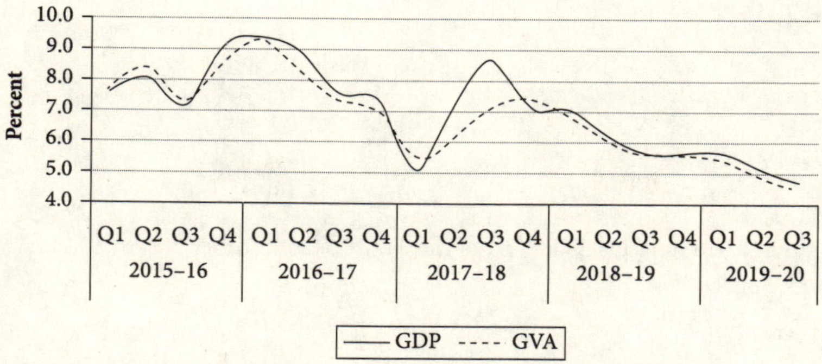

Figure 10.1 Quarter Wise Growth of Real GDP and GVA
Source: Same as Table 10.1.

first quarter to 0.1% in the third quarter. Growth in the services sector improved from 6.9% to 7.4% during the above period. The agriculture sector also had shown some signs of improvement. Quarter-wise growth in real GDP and Gross Value Added (GVA) are depicted in Figure 10.1.

10.2 Fiscal Parameters: Pre-Covid-19 Trends

Gross fiscal deficit of the central government declined from 3.5%in 2016–17 to 3.4% in 2018–19 (Figure 10.2) and further budgeted at a 3.3% level in 2019–20 (BE). However, this budgeted target could not be achieved by the government, and the deficit was revised to 3.8% of GDP in the revised estimates. Adherence to the FY 2020–21 budgeted estimate of 3.5% is next to impossibility and justifiably so, given the significant revenue shortfalls caused by the economic lockdown and additional outlays incurred to revive the economy and social safety measures. The government also could not achieve the targeted revenue deficit of 2.3% as per 2019–20 BE and stands revised to 2.4% in 2019–20 RE.

As per the provisional details on some fiscal parameters provided by the Government of India, gross tax revenue declined by 0.8% to Rs. 16.8 lakh crore in 2019–20 over that of 2018–19. During this period, revenue receipts (net to centre) increased by 8.9% to Rs. 13.8 lakh crore. Tax revenue (net to centre) grew by 1.9% to Rs. 11.1 lakh crore. Non-tax revenue increased by 53.2% to Rs. 2.6 lakh crore. Revenue expenditure grew by

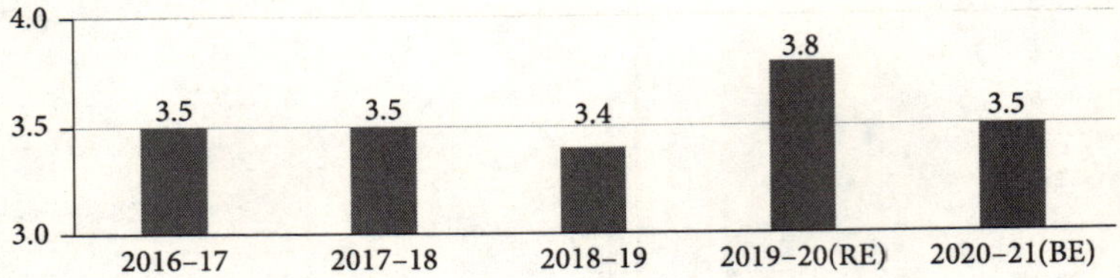

Figure 10.2 Gross Fiscal Deficit of the Central Government (Percent to GDP)
Source: Same as Table 10.1.

12.8% to Rs. 21.6 lakh crore. Capital expenditure increased by 11.4% to Rs. 3.1 lakh crore. Total expenditure increased by 12.6%, amounting to Rs. 24.7 lakh crore (Government of India, 2020).

10.3 Covid-19 Fiscal Measures

Indian government responded to the Covid-19 pandemic very quickly as soon as the first case was reported on January 30, 2020.[1]The government was quick to announce a number of stringent measures to contain the movement of people by imposing travel restrictions, closure of educational institutions, and other public places of mass gathering, such as theatres and malls. A complete lockdown was announced on March 24. With effect from April20, 2020, the government rolled out a number of relaxation measures by gradually opening up select facilities in geographical areas that did not report many cases of Covid-19. The regions with more cases continued as containment zones. State governments were given considerable amount of freedom in taking region-specific decisions. The net result has been a substantial reduction in the pace of economic growth and fall in revenue to the government. Coupled with a reduction in revenue, the rapid growth in public expenditure owing to the number of fiscal measures to boost up demand derailed the fiscal consolidation plans of the government. The sudden onset of Covid-19 changed the course of both the fiscal parameters, government revenue and expenditure, amounting to a serious blow to the fiscal consolidation targets slated for the current fiscal year. This effect is in all likelihood to

[1] For a detailed coverage of Covid-19 policies of all the countries IMF (2020 a & b).

continue beyond the 2020–21 FY. It remains a fact that the initial efforts by the Indian government and the slow growth in the number of cases received the appreciation of international agencies like IMF and WHO. Speaking on the National Technology Day, Swaminathan said, 'I would like to commend and congratulate the minister and colleagues for having contained so far the Covid Pandemic in India and having kept both the number of cases and the number of deaths very low compared to other countries (The Times of India, 2020).' The IMF has supported India's 'very wise' decision to impose a national lockdown to combat the Covid-19 pandemic despite the resulting economic slowdown... Rhee said that India's strict action against the Covid-19 pandemic 'can cause a drop in economic activity (and) growth rate will go down definitely, but I think that is a very wise and important decision to minimise the long-term cost of this disease spread ...' He said that the fiscal stimulus, as well as the monetary policy easing adopted by the Indian government and the Reserve Bank, are in the right direction, but whether they will be enough 'depends on how this containment policy which is just adopted, how successful it will be (Srivastava, 2020).'

10.4 Policy Response

A major decision taken by the government is to become self-reliant (Atmanirbhar), with a slew of measures being announced by the government, some involving direct expenditure to provide immediate relief in the form of food grains, enhancement in the wages of the employment guarantee scheme, pension payments, etc. The government's announcement of the special economic and comprehensive package of Rs. 20 lakh crores is equivalent to 10% of India's GDP. The government also geared up from zero production of personal protection equipment (PPE) before March 2020 to a capacity of producing 2 lakh PPE kits daily, which is also growing steadily.

The five pillars of Atmanirbhar Bharat focus on (Government of India, 2021b):

1. Economy
2. Infrastructure

3. System
4. Vibrant demography
5. Demand

The five phases of Atmanirbhar Bharat are:

- **Phase-I**: Businesses including MSMEs
- **Phase-II**: Poor, including migrants and farmers
- **Phase-III**: Agriculture
- **Phase-IV**: New horizons of growth
- **Phase-V**: Government reforms and enabler

Phase I: Business Including MSMEs:

Pradhan Mantri Garib Kalyan Package (1)

- A relief package worth Rs.1.70 lakh crore under Pradhan Mantri Garib Kalyan Yojana was announced for the poor to help them fight the battle against corona virus.
- Insurance cover of Rs. 50 lakh per health worker.
- 80 crore poor people given benefit of 5 kg wheat or rice per person for next 3 months, which was later extended until Diwali.
- 1 kg pulses for each household for free every month for the next 3 months.
- 20 crore women Jan Dhan account holders get Rs. 500 per month for next 3 months.
- Gas cylinders, free of cost, provided to 8 crore poor families for the next 3 months.
- Increase in MNREGA wage to Rs. 202 a day from Rs. 182 to benefit 13.62 crore families.
- Ex-gratia of Rs. 1,000 to 3 crore poor senior citizens and poor widows.

Pradhan Mantri Garib Kalyan Package (2)

- Front-loaded Rs. 2,000 paid to farmers under existing PM-KISAN to benefit 8.7 crore farmers.

- Building and Construction Workers Welfare Fund allowed to be used to provide relief to workers.
- 24% of monthly wages to be credited into their PF accounts for next 3 months for wageearners below Rs. 15,000 per month in businesses having less than 100 workers.
- Five crore workers registered under Employee Provident Fund (EPF) to get non-refundable advance of 75% of the amount or three months of the wages, whichever is lower, from their accounts.
- Limit of collateral free lending to be increased from Rs. 10 to Rs. 20 lakhs for Women Self Help Groups supporting 6.85 crore households.
- District Mineral Fund (DMF) to be used for supplementing and augmenting facilities of medical testing, screening, etc.

While these were the direct measures, there were many other relaxations in statutory and compliance matters, measures announced by RBI, collateral free automatic loans to MSMEs, equity infusion, and liquidity injection for DISCOMs, etc.

The fiscal and monetary measures have been wide ranging; however, the research evidence hints at the challenges in establishing the actual fiscal costs, both short and long term as some costs may end up as contingent liability on the government. Commenting on the fiscal response of India to Covid-19 Basole and Coutinho (2020) state that, 'However, given the blurring of the distinction between fiscal and monetary components, ensuring comparable and accurate figures for fiscal responses is a challenge. For example, the total Atmanirbhar package is billed at 10% of GDP. The headline number for India's fiscal response in international databases is around 4% of GDP. But we and others have estimated that the new fiscal outlay, including the Pradhan Mantri Garib Kalyan Yojana, of March, the direct fiscal aspects of Atmanirbhar Bharat, and the latest extension of free rations under the Public Distribution System, is around 1.7% of GDP. The one significant demand-side intervention in the Atmanirbhar Bharat package was Rs.40, 000 crore of additional outlay for the Mahatma Gandhi National Rural Employment Guarantee Act (MGNREGA). Most other demand-side measures involve the frontloading, consolidation, or rerouting of existing funds—for example, the recently announced

Rs.50,000 crore Garib Kalyan Rojgar Abhiyan, which consolidates projects of 12 ministries/departments.'

Further providing some examples from other countries they observe cash transfers constitute the largest category of support in other developing countries. 'The World Bank reports that, on average, such transfers amount to 30% of monthly GDP per capita, reaching 46% for lower-middle-income countries, for an average of three months. Countries have also significantly expanded coverage of their cash transfer programmes from pre-COVID-19 levels; Bangladesh and Indonesia have increased the number of beneficiaries by 163% and 111%, respectively. Indonesia's cash schemes now cover more than 158 million people (or 60% of the population). It has even created two new unconditional cash schemes to reach 20 million individuals in urban and rural settings excluded from the current social protection measures. India could take these actions into account in decisions about expanding existing transfer programmes or even creating new ones.'

The fiscal policy measures tend to have varied implications on government finances, while direct relief related expenditure tends to boost demand and enhances unforeseen expenditure, financial support extended will have long-term implications. The likely implications of fiscal measures on public finances are summarized by IMF in the text Box 10.1.

Box 10.1 Understanding the Implication of Different Types of Fiscal Measures for Public Finances

To address the economic and social challenges posed by the COVID-19 pandemic, governments are using fiscal measures that take various forms and have different budgetary and debt-related implications (Figure 1.1.1). Additional spending or tax cuts result in immediately higher budget deficits. Support to companies in financial trouble through loans or equity injections does not impact budgets directly but may increase debt or require additional borrowing. Guarantees do not affect deficits or debt in the near term, but they expose the government to medium- to long-term fiscal risks.

The full cost of most budgetary "above-the-line" measures is reflected in the fiscal balance, government debt, and increased borrowing needs in the short term. These measures include additional spending (for example, health services and unemployment benefits); capital grants and targeted transfers (for example, wage subsidies or direct transfers); or tax measures (for example, tax cuts or other relief) provided through standard budget channels. Deferrals of tax payment and social security contributions have a temporary effect on the deficit and debt, and aim to provide liquidity to taxpayers. Although deferrals create a financing need today, the government will eventually be repaid in the future.

	Today		Tomorrow[1]	
	Budget Balance	Debt	Budget Balance or Net Worth	Debt
Additional spending or tax cuts	↓	↑	Unchanged	
Tax deferrals	↓	↑	↑	↓
Loans[2]	Unchanged	↑	↓ (if firm defaults)	Unchanged
Equity injections[2]	Unchanged	↑	↓ (if firm fails)	Unchanged
Guarantees[2]	Unchanged	Unchanged	↓ (if called)	↑

Figure 1.1.1 Likely Impact of Measures on the Government Budget and Debt
Source: IMF, 2020a.

Note: All transactions are assumed to be financed through debt rather than by drawing on other goernment funds.

[1] Additional effect in the future rather than a combined effect with today's incurrence.

[2] If transactions are reasonably expected to have an economic rate of return. If not, treated like budgetary spending and revenue measures.

"Below-the-line" measures generally involve the creation of assets, such as loans or equity in firms. Equity injections or loans to firms may have little or no upfront impact on the fiscal deficit unless they have a concessional component, but they can increase debt or reduce liquidity. Government guarantees granted to banks, firms, or households usually have no immediate upfront cost in the form of deficit or debt unless the expected cost is budgeted, but they create a contingent liability, with the government exposed to future calls on guarantees. A loan default or loss in equity would reduce the government's assets, whereas a call on a guarantee would increase public debt, as the guaranteed debt is assumed by the government. These would reduce government net worth (assets net of liabilities).

10.5 Covid-19: Impacts on Economy

Adverse impact of Covid-19 on the global economy is clearly borne out by the April–June quarter data. US economy has contracted by 9.1%, the United Kingdom, France, Spain, Italy, and Germany by 21.7, 18.9, 22.1, 17.7, and 11.3%, respectively, with the overall Euro zone contracting by 15.0% and Japan contracting by 9.9%. In comparison to these advanced nations, India's GDP contraction at 23.9% is higher owing to the stringent lockdown measures. Governments were forced into lockdown measures to prevent the spread of Covid-19. 'Government Response Stringency Index' a measure to assess the government response is observed to be the highest among the countries presented in Table 10.2. At 85.6, intensity

Table 10.2 Global Stringency Index, Covid-19 Fatality Rate and Growth in Q2, 2020

	Government Response Stringency Index (0 to 100.100 Implies Strictest)	Covid-19 Fatality Rate (As on August 31)	GDP Growth Rate Year-on-Year in Q2, 2020
G-20 Advanced Economics			
Canada	71.5	7.0	−13.0
France	78.1	10.1	−18.9
Germany	67.3	3.8	−11.3
Italy	70.4	13.2	−17.7
Japan	37.9	1.9	−10.0
Spain	72.5	6.3	−22.1
United Kingdom	74.9	12.4	−21.7
United States	72.0	3.0	−9.1
G-20 Emerging Markets			
Brazil	77.6	3.1	−11.4
China	71.8	5.3	3.2
India	85.6	1.8	−23.9
Indonesia	69.6	4.2	−5.4
Mexico	78.8	10.7	−18.7
Russia	80.1	1.7	−8.5
South Africa	83.3	2.3	
Turkey	72.0	2.4	−9.0

Source: Government of India (2020).

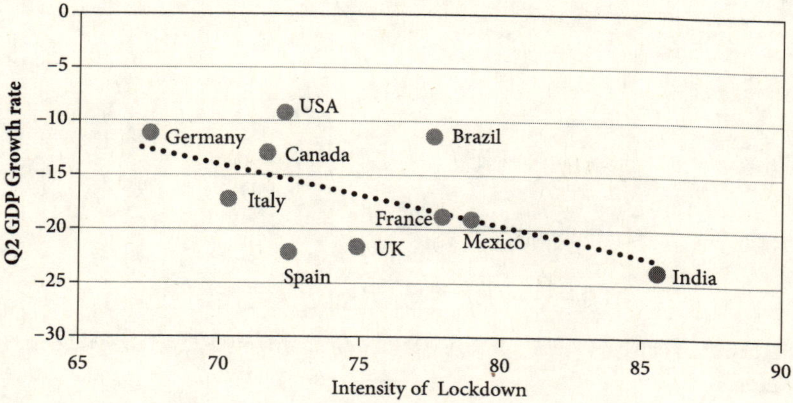

Figure 10.3 Stringent Lockdown Led to Higher Contraction
Source: GoI, 2020. (https://dea.gov.in/sites/default/files/MER_August%202020.pdf. Accessed on September 17, 2020).

of lockdown as measured by the government response strategy index (see Figure 10.3), India proved to have rolled out the strictest measures as compared to Japan with the least stringency. Fatality rate in India is also observed to be one of the lowest, along with Japan and Russia. Due to timely tracing, treatment, and reporting, the number of people recovering from the virus is continuously rising and the active cases, as on date, are 21% of the total cases in the country. India's case fatality rate was at 1.8% as on August 31compared to 3.04% in the United States, 12.35% in the United Kingdom, 10.09% in France, 1.89% in Japan, and 13.18% in Italy (Government of India, 2020).

10.6 Post-Covid-19 Government Finances

The fiscal measures announced by the government have had its impact on the government finances. The budgeted levels of fiscal deficit have been overshot by the actual as presented in Figure 10.4. Indian government's monthly report of August 2020 reveals that fiscal deficit stood at Rs. 8.2 lakh crore by the end July 2020, which is 103.1% of BE compared to 77.8% during the first four months of fiscal year 2019. Net tax revenue collections stood at 12.4% of BE compared to 20.5% in the corresponding period of the previous year. Personal income tax collections up to July end

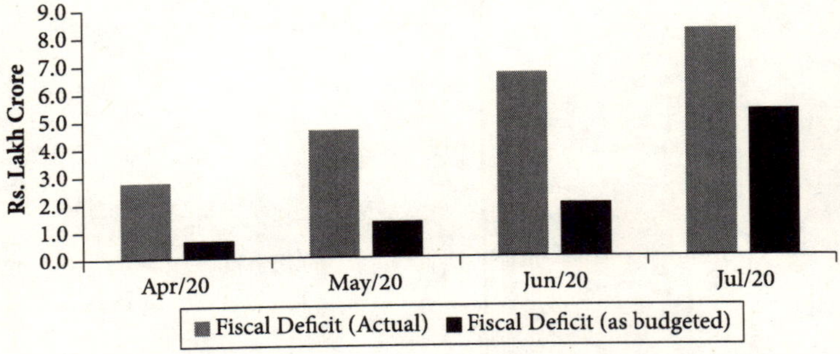

Figure 10.4 Fiscal Deficit of the Central Government: Budgeted vis-à-vis Actuals

Source: Same as Figure 10.3.

amounted to Rs. 0.91 lakh crore, compared to Rs. 1.29 lakh crore in the corresponding period of the previous year. Non-debt capital receipts declined and stood at Rs. 5,458 crore, which is 2.4% of BE compared to 14.2% of last year. On the expenditure side, capital expenditure stood at Rs. 1.12 lakh crore, 27.1% of BE compared to 31.8% of last year. Revenue expenditure was Rs. 9.42 lakh crore, 35.8% of BE compared to 34.3% in corresponding period of 2019–20. Central government's revenue expenditure, net of interest payments, and major subsidies increased by 33.7% in the first quarter of the year (Government of India, 2020).

Governments both at the centre and state levels had to resort to additional borrowings to meet Covid-19-related expenditure, the revenue shortfall accentuated the problem. Gross market borrowings by the centre rose to Rs. 5.84 lakh crore up to August 21, 2020, i.e. 1.72 times the amount raised in the last year. Gross borrowing of states has increased by 58.7% year-on-year till August 21, with Karnataka, Maharashtra, and Tamil Nadu among the top borrower states as presented in Figures 10.5 and 10.6 (Government of India, 2020).

Given the seriousness of the pandemic, the fiscal stimulus became necessary and has also been supported by the international agencies. IMF spokesman Gerry Rice said, 'Given the unprecedented shock, the immediate priority is a coordinated policy response to fight the virus.' He added that the IMF supports the government's responses to the pandemic, including fiscal stimulus with a focus on low-income workers and households. 'We support the monetary easing and liquidity and regulatory measures for the financial

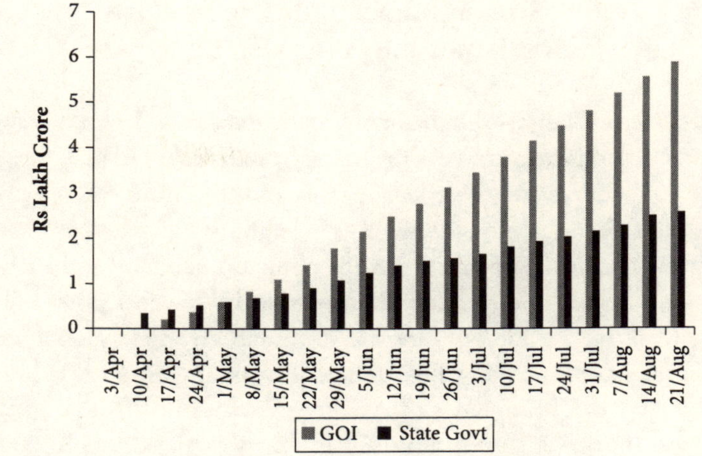

Figure 10.5 Gross Market Borrowings Centre and States

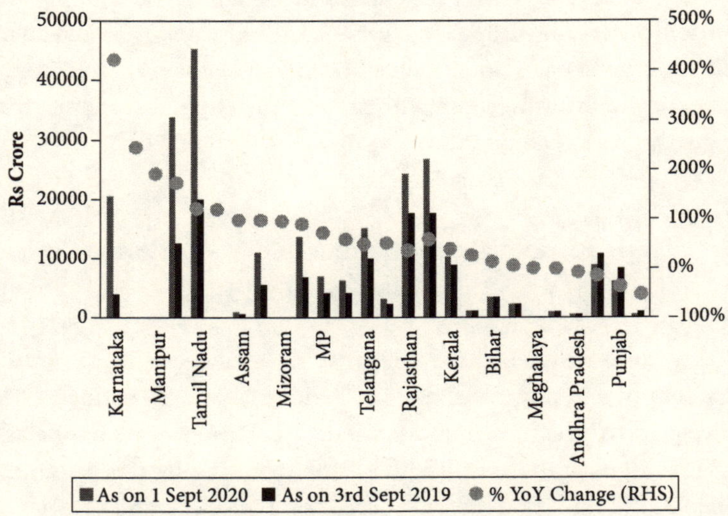

Figure 10.6 State Wise Borrowings Centre and States
Source: Same as Figure 10.3.

sector for borrowers that have taken place. And may be just to add, in this context, we believe further fiscal stimulus is warranted—especially expenditures on health, food, and income support for vulnerable households, and support for businesses (The Times of India, 2020).'

10.7 Streamlining Public Expenditure Policy: Issues and Policy Alternatives

Covid-19 has brought to light many inadequacies and weaknesses in the current policy regime. Lessons learnt from this should help the government in addressing these weaknesses and introduce the necessary structural reforms. Covid-19 has also brought to light the cost advantage India has in the production and supply of medicine and vaccine, which can help restore economic growth. India is also a potential investment venue for foreign direct investment, given the global wrath that China has attracted owing to the outbreak of Covid-19. However, in order to succeed in getting these investments and sustain it in the long run, India has to gear up itself in terms of strengthening infrastructure, skills of manpower, ease of doing business, and create the necessary investment climate. Structural reforms in the factors of production—land, labour, and capital markets—are needed to revive the growth process. The ultimate goal should be to lead the country to high inclusive growth path. Some key public financial issues that need structural policy reforms in leading the country to high and sustained inclusive growth path include the following.

10.7.1 Inadequate and Vulnerable Allocation to the Social Sector

Social sector investments covering areas like education, health, housing, water supply, and poverty alleviation tend to be more conducive to inclusive growth. The most important and a persistent issue has been the low and stagnant share of health sector spending by the government to the GDP. Total expenditure incurred by the centre and sub-national governments together has been around 1.3% of GDP during the period 2008 till 2015 as against the world average of 6%. There have been policy pronouncements to raise it time and again, NRHM had proposed to raise it to 3% but failed to do so, and the latest National Health Policy (2017) proposes to increase this to 2.5% of GDP by 2025. Studies also have observed that health sector spending has been highly vulnerable to the resource position of the government, implying that whenever there are revenue shortfalls the axe falls on the social sectors and in particular the health sector (Gayithri, 2012). The current Covid-19 pandemic is a case reiterating the need to ensure constant preparedness of the governments to face unforeseen health emergencies. There is an imminent need to strengthen the preventive health care to effectively address any health emergencies. Given the importance of health sector, not only from the point of view of economic gains associated with health sector investments but also from the welfare point of view, governments have to insulate health sector spending from revenue shortfalls. While there have been recommendations on the need to assign a particular share in the GDP, this estimate has to be arrived at based on a scientific estimate of the need. It is needless to highlight the differential requirements of regions in a vast country like India, with existing differences in the levels of health sector development. Addressing the question of how much should be spent on the health sector, WHO states, 'This seemingly straightforward question cannot be adequately answered without doing the hard work of addressing these five basic questions together. What health problems do we face? What health status do we aspire to? How effective are our health services, activities and policies? What are the prices of inputs? Are there better uses of funds for other ends' (WHO, 2003, 7)? A plausible solution lies in framing a legal mandate to earmark a prescribed budgetary allocation in per capita terms to the health sector year-on-year, which cannot be bypassed.

10.7.2 Glaring Inter Regional Variations in Public Spending

Sub-national governments in India have a major responsibility in the provision of health services. An analysis of the per capita real health expenditure across fourteen major states reveals huge variation, which also has persisted over a long period and in some cases has increased too. While the per capita expenditure in Kerala was 2.92 times more than that of Bihar in 2007–08 by the FY 2014–15, it increased to 4.16 times. The per capita expenditure in 2007–08 ranged between Rs. 100.1 in Bihar, representing the lowest and Rs. 292.5 in Kerala, the highest among all states. Their relative positions continued to remain the same in 2014–15,

Table 10.3 Real Per Capita Expenditure on Health—Revenue Account (in rupees)

Period	2007–08	2008–09	2009–10	2010–11	2011–12	2012–13	2013–14	2014–15
AP	211.6	223.5	242.9	270.0	304.7	275.5	294.7	319.0
Bihar	100.1	99.7	103.4	95.3	103.2	92.6	101.9	147.2
Gujarat	167.1	173.3	219.9	250.1	240.4	296.6	271.9	347.6
Haryana	165.4	200.5	258.6	243.7	255.7	311.9	306.6	377.8
Karnataka	186.0	202.9	200.8	225.5	263.3	290.7	298.5	340.5
Kerala	292.5	328.9	336.9	378.6	475.9	508.5	533.7	612.9
MP	118.1	128.7	152.4	169.2	185.2	215.1	214.3	283.9
Maharashtra	196.5	207.6	234.6	254.5	264.5	296.6	317.9	375.9
Odisha	122.9	148.0	171.4	158.0	158.7	185.4	190.6	275.1
Punjab	210.1	210.9	229.4	255.3	309.2	333.3	329.6	394.1
Rajasthan	152.6	196.6	202.5	191.8	204.3	218.4	241.9	257.9
TN	184.3	220.0	267.4	329.4	318.5	339.6	339.9	371.7
UP	124.6	126.5	137.8	148.4	145.5	154.8	156.5	167.7
Bengal	153.7	158.8	215.9	212.7	209.5	214.9	208.8	247.4

Source: Gayithri, et. al. 2020.

with Kerala spending Rs. 612.9 as compared to Bihar, which increased to Rs.147.2 (Table 10.3).

10.7.3 Efficiency of Public Spending

Given the extremely limited fiscal space that currently government has in meeting the unforeseen expenditure without disturbing the fiscal consolidation efforts, there is need to review public finances and weed out the duplicative expenditure programmes and also the ones that have become redundant and outgrown their utility. Mrs Nirmala Sitharaman, the present Union Finance Minister, makes a reference to review of schemes in the 2021–22 FY budget speech, this task needs a serious and immediate action. This will help the government to achieve some savings. Toning up public expenditure efficiency also can generate savings. Efficiency here is defined as quantum of output achieved per unit of input. Studies have used Data Envelopment Analysis (DEA) to estimate

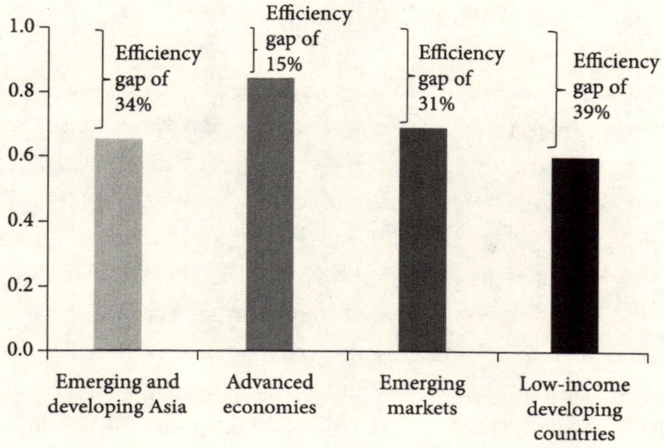

Figure 10.7 Public Investment Efficiency Scores
Source: Ha Vu et al. (2020), p. 129.

the level of efficiency; inefficiency indicates excess use of resources/inputs to achieve the outcomes. Research evidence in the Indian context bears out the poor efficiency of expenditure. Analysing the efficiency of public spending in the Indian context in the social sector spending by the Indian states, Mohanty and Bhanumurthy (2017) found that the spending of Indian states on education is more efficient than on health and overall social sector spending. The study uses DEA for twenty-seven Indian states during 2002–03, 2008–09, and 2015–16.The study emphasizes the importance of good governance in yielding good outcomes from public spending.

Estimating the efficiency of public investment on infrastructure development, IMF observes that on average, countries lose over one-third of their resources in the public investment process owing to inefficiencies (IMF,2020c).[2] An efficiency gap of 34% was observed in the public investment on infrastructure in the emerging and developing Asia, where efficiency gap measures the relative difference between a country's performance and best performers (India is included in this group). A comparative efficiency gap with other group of countries is presented in Figure 10.7.

[2] IMF, 2020. Well Spent: How Strong Infrastructure Governance Can End Waste in Public Investment.

10.7.4 Capital Investments

It has been observed in Chapters 3 and 4 that revenue expenditure has been growing over time and the share of capital investments, which is crucial in building infrastructure, has significantly declined. A glaring reflection of health infrastructure inadequacy is currently seen. Research evidence has it that the multiplier effect of capital spending is much higher than the revenue expenditure. Given the huge infrastructure deficit that the country has, government cannot achieve the goal of attracting and sustaining investments. IMF states, 'In a range of countries, high-return public investment could act as a bridge to sustainable, resilient, and inclusive economic growth, including by lifting productivity, creating jobs, and spurring private sector investment ... In many emerging market and developing countries, infrastructure bottlenecks are impediments to long-term development' (IMF, 2020c). In the wake of Covid-19, there has been a considerable emphasis on achieving self-reliant India (Atmanirbhar Bharat). Increasing capital investment is constrained by the huge committed expenditure, which has actually been cutting into a large portion of borrowed funds, leaving a little room for capital investments. This situation is further accentuated by the current fiscal deficit and debt targets laid down to achieve fiscal consolidation. This is especially true for the central government, as state governments have managed to achieve surplus in revenue account after the introduction of FRBM. In the current Covid-19 pandemic context, which has necessitated huge additional expenditure by the government, the 3%fiscal deficit limit needs policy review. Relaxing the fiscal deficit limit, however, should not lead to uncontrolled and irresponsible spending spree. Expenditure rules to restrict the growth in revenue expenditure successfully used by a number of countries could be a way out, coupled with strictures that fiscal deficit in its entirety be used for capital investments. Given the social distancing measures, IMF suggests that countries can use short-term capital works like upkeep of the infrastructure rather than resorting to major new capital projects. 'At the current juncture, the scope for large public investment is limited considering supply disruptions (lockdowns and quarantines). Since public investment has a long lead time, however, efforts should start now to review the pipeline, identify bottlenecks, and prepare a set of ready-to-implement projects that can be deployed. Maintenance and repairs can be quickly scaled up as part of broad-based stimulus when supply disruptions ease. Some governments (Australia, Ireland, New Zealand, and Norway) have a rolling pipeline of public infrastructure projects within a budget constraint over the long term, which provides details on the timing, sequencing, and scale of future public investment at different levels of government. In downturns, implementation of smaller projects can be accelerated' (IMF, 2020c). In addition to low public capital investment, there are a number of other issues that the government has to address, such as cost and time overruns of capital projects, strict application of scientific project appraisal for capital projects, monitoring, and evaluation.

10.7.5 Targeting

Research evidence highlights a number of public service delivery issues such as reaching benefits to wrong beneficiaries, leading to inclusion errors, and excluding the ones who need them, leading to exclusion errors. Public resources tend to get wasted even while the intended results are not achieved. An added reason for waste of resources lies in the duplicative nature of the programmes. The government should attempt a complete rehaul of its social safety net interventions. Real-time testing of eligibility is very important in netting out ineligible beneficiaries; South Korea uses its information network in verifying the eligibility. Such measures can help achieve substantial savings and enhance fiscal space.

10.7.6 Translation of 'Outlays' into 'Outcomes'

There has been a shift in global thinking from 'outlays' to 'outcomes'. It is important to recognize that the public funds need to be spent efficiently to achieve the desired outcomes and the information on the outcomes should be used to frame informed expenditure decisions in the ensuing budgets. There have been concerns expressed about poor translation of outlays into outcomes in the Indian context. Poor service delivery, especially in the health sector, has been observed by Singh (2009). The study further observes that the variation in the HDI across fourteen Indian states did not decrease over time, and the per capita health expenditure did not have a positive correlation with the HDI. The overall functioning of the government, including factors like corruption and over spending in subsidies and salaries, led to inefficiency in service delivery.

References

Acharya, N., Das, S., Agrawala, T., and Samy, P. (2014). *Reporting in public interest: Value and impact of CAG's audits*. New Delhi: Centre for Budget and Governance Accountability. Retrieved from https://bit.ly/3sSttgB.

ADB (2008a). *Project performance and the project cycle. Special evaluation study reference number: SST: REG 2008-38*. Manila: Asian Development Bank.

——— (2008b). *Proposed Asian development fund grant Islamic Republic of Afghanistan: Agriculture market infrastructure project. Draft design and monitoring framework*. Project number: 39370. Manila: Asian Development Bank. Retrieved from https://www.adb.org/sites/default/files/project-document/67731/39370-afg-dmf.pdf.

Ahluwalia Committee (2011). Report on Indian Urban Infrastructure and Services, The High Powered Expert Committee for Estimating the Investment Requirements for Urban Infrastructure Services, (Chairperson: Isher Judge Ahluwalia). New Delhi: Ministry of Urban Development, Government of India.

Alok, V.N. (2019). *Design of intergovernmental fiscal transfers in India to rural local governments: A report of the study sponsored by the 15th Finance Commission*, New Delhi, IIPA.

Anantha Ramu, M.R. and Gayithri, K. (2017). Fiscal consolidation versus infrastructural obligations. *Journal of Infrastructure Development*, 9(1), 49–67.

Aschauer, D. (1989). Is public expenditure productive? *Journal of Monetary Economics*, 23(2), 177–200.

Asher, M., Patnaik, A., and Sheikh, S. (2011). *Enhancing CAG's role in public financial management*. CFO Connect.

Badunenko, O, Fritsch, M., and Stephan, A. (2006). Allocative efficiency measurement revisited: Do we really need input prices?, No 2006,7, *Working Paper Series, European University Viadrina Frankfurt* (Oder), The Postgraduate Research Programme Capital Markets and Finance in the Enlarged Europe, https://EconPapers.repec.org/RePEc:zbw:euvgra:20067.

Basole, A. and Countinho, J. (2020). The COVID-19 fiscal response and India's standing. The Hindu, July 22, 2020. Retrieved from https://bit.ly/3cZR36M, on April 8, 2021.

Basu, K. (2016). *An economist in the real world: The art of policy making in India*. New Delhi: Penguin Viking.

Bhattacharjee, G. (2018). Parlimentary oversight of CAG: Auditor and PAC – An uneasy relationship, *Common Cause*, XXXVII (3), Retrived from (http://14.139.53.35/jspui/bitstream/1/2756/1/Parliamentary%20oversight%20of%20CAG.pdf) on 30 September 2021.

Bird, R.M. (1970). The growth of government spending in Canada. Canadian Tax Papers no 51, pp. xv, 333. Toronto: Canadian Tax Foundation.

Bose, S. and Bhanumurthy, N.R. (2013). *Fiscal multipliers for India*. NIPFP Working Paper125. New Delhi.

CAG (2002). *Parliamentary control over public purse in India*. New Delhi: Comptroller and Auditor General of India. Retrieved from https://bit.ly/328VPZr. Also available in Kalse 2013.

——— (2015). *Report of the comptroller and auditor general of India for the year 2014–15. Union government accounts of the union government No. 50 of 2015 (Financial Audit)*. New Delhi: Comptroller and Auditor General of India. Retrieved from http://dgace.cag.gov.in/pdf/Report%20No.%2050_English.pdf on April 08, 2021.

——— (2019). *Report of the comptroller and auditor general of India for the year 2017–18*. Union government accounts of the union government No. 2 of 2019 (Financial Audit). New Delhi, Comptroller and Auditor General of India. Retrieved from https://bit.ly/3mqWBdx, on April 08, 2021

Center for Policy Research (2014). Rural local body core functions and finances, a study undertaken for the Fourteenth Finance Commission. New Delhi; Center for Policy Research.

CESifo (2004). Expenditure Rules, CESifo DICE report: *Journal for Institutional Comparison*, 2(4), pp.60–65. Retrieved from https://www.ifo.de/en/node/29180, 1st October 2021.

Chatterjee, P. (1997). *A possible world: Essays in political countries*. New Delhi: Oxford University Press.

Chaudhuri, K. and Dasgupta, S. (2006). The political determinants of fiscal policies in the states of India: An empirical investigation. *The Journal of Development Studies*, 42(4), 640–661.

Chhibber, P. (1995). Political parties, electoral competition, government expenditures and economic reform in India. *The Journal of Development Studies*, 32(1), 74–96.

Chhibber, P. and Nooruddin, I. (2004). Do party systems count? The number of parties and government performance in the Indian states. *Comparative Political Studies*, 37 (2), 152–187.

Chowdhury, A.R. (1993). Political surfing over economic waves: parliamentary election timing in India. *American Journal of Political Science*, 37(4), 1100–1118.

Corbridge, S. and Harriss, J. (2000). *Reinventing India: Liberalization, Hindu nationalism, and popular democracy*. Cambridge: Polity Press.

Dash, B.B. and Raja, A.V. (2012). Political determinants of the allocation of public expenditures: A study of the Indian states. NIPFP Working Paper No. 2012–10. New Delhi: National Institute of Public Finance and Policy.

Dash, J. (2018). States spend lower than their budgeted estimates: PRS Legislative Research. The Business Standard. Digital Edition, published on April 3, 2018. Retrieved from https://bit.ly/3cV1GYm, on April 08, 2021.

Devarajan, S., Swaroop, V., and Zou, H.F. (1996). The composition of public expenditure and economic growth. *Journal of Monetary Economics*,37(2), 313–344.

Dev, S.M. and Mooij, J. (2002). *Social sector expenditures and budgeting: an analysis of patterns and the budget making process in India in the 1990s*. CESS Working Paper, 43. Hyderabad: Centre for Economic and Social Studies.

Diamond, J. (2006). *Establishing a performance management framework for government IMF*. Working paper, WP/05/50.

Duggal, R. (2009). Sinking flagships and health budgets in India. *Economic and Political Weekly*, 44(33), 14–17.

Fabricant, S. and Lipsey, R.E. (1952). *The trend of government activity in the United States since 1900*. New York: National Bureau of Economic Research.

Farrell, M.J. (1957). The measurement of productive efficiency. *Journal of the Royal Statistical Society*, Series A (General) 120 (III), 253–281(290).

Fiva, J.H. and Natvik, G.J. (2013). Do re-election probabilities influence public investment? *Public Choice*, 157(1–2), 305–331.

Gayithri, K. (1988). Growth and pattern of state expenditure a case study of Karnataka, A Ph.D. dissertation submitted to Mysore *University*. Mysore: University of Mysore. Unpublished manuscript.

——— (1998). Macro-economic impacts of spending control measures in Canada, a report submitted to Shastri Indo Canadian Institute. Unpublished manuscript.

——— (2003). Housing subsidies in Karnataka, in: M.G. Rao (ed). *Volume and composition of budgetary subsidies in Karnataka*, ISEC Monograph Series1. pp. 174–209, Bangalore: Institute for Social and Economic Change. Retrieved from http://www.isec.ac.in/Monograph%201.pdf, 1stOctober, 2021.

——— (2004). *Spin off effects of industrial incentives in Karnataka, a study of mega industrial units*. Unpublished manuscript, Bangalore: Institute for Social and Economic Change.

——— (2012). District-level NRHM funds flow and expenditure: sub-national evidence from the state of Karnataka. *The Indian Economic Journal*, 60(2), 95–118.

——— (2014a). Housing subsidies, in: K. Gayithri (ed). *Government subsidies in Karnataka*, ISEC Monograph Series 34. Bangalore: Institute for Social and Economic Change.

——— (2014b). Evaluation of Karnataka state finances: A report prepared for Government of India, Fourteenth Finance Commission. Unpublished manuscript.

——— (2018). Public expenditure in India: some issues and concerns, in: K. Gayithri (ed). *Public Budgeting in India: Principles and Practices.*: 91–108. Springer. New Delhi.

——— (2019). Monitoring and evaluation of government programs in India and Canada, in: K. Gayithri, B. Hariharan, S. Chattopadhyay (eds). *Nation-building, education and culture in India and Canada*, 171–185. Singapore: Springer https://doi.org/10.1007/978-981-13-6741-0_12.

Gayithri, K. and Madheswaran, S. (2015). Bengaluru region finances: A design for restructuring, Unpublished manuscript, Bangalore: Institute for Social and Economic Change.

Gayithri, K., Acharya, V., Singh, S., and Nagesha, G., (2017). Gram Panchayat Finances in Karnataka: *A Regional Perspective*. DOI:10.13140/RG.2.2.33447.04001

Government of India (1948). *Budget speech* (Finance Minister Shri. R. K. Shanumgam Chetty). New Delhi: Ministry of Finance.

——— (1991). *Budget speech* (Finance Minister Dr N Manmohan Singh). New Delhi: Ministry of Finance.

——— (1999). *Union budget speech* (Finance Minister Shri Yashwant Sinha). New Delhi: Ministry of Finance.

——— (2000). *Resolution No. 1(30)/E. Coord. /2000 for setting up economic reform commission*. New Delhi: Ministry of Finance. Retrieved from https://bit.ly/3wzArKF.

——— (2004). *Report of the expert group constituted to review the classification system for government transactions*, New Delhi: Ministry of Finance. Retrieved from https://bit.ly/3t0WR5s, on September 5, 2019.

——— (2005). *Budget Speech of 2005–06* (Finance Minister, Sri P. Chidambaram) New Delhi: Ministry of Finance.

——— (2009). *Report of the Thirteenth Finance Commission 2010–15*, New Delhi: Government of India, Retrieved from https://fincomindia.nic.in/TFC/

——— (2011a). *Report of the high-level expert committee on efficient management of public expenditure*. New Delhi: Planning Commission. Retrieved from https://bit.ly/3dMSHJf.

——— (2011b). *Result Frame-work Document (RFD)*. New Delhi: Ministry of Finance.

——— (2015). Election Commission of India. New Delhi.

——— (2019). *Key to Budget Documents—Budget 2019–20*. New Delhi: Ministry of Finance. Retrieved fromhttps://bit.ly/3wAeIlV, on April 08, 2021.

——— (2020). *Monthly Economic Reports, March to September*, New Delhi: Ministry of Finance. Retrieved fromhttps://bit.ly/3nlg27K, on September 17, 2020.

——— (2021a). *Union budget speech 2021–22*. (Finance Minister Mrs. Nirmala Seetharaman), New Delhi: Ministry of Finance.

——— (n.d.a.). *Parliament committee's introduction*. New Delhi: Parliament of India, Lok Sabha. Retrieved fromhttps://bit.ly/2OuRV9P, on April 08, 2020.

——— (2007, 2010, 2015). *Indian Public Finance Statistics* (issues 2006–07; 2009–10; 2014–15), New Delhi: Ministry of Finance, Retrieved from https://bit.ly/2QVusj7

——— (2021b). Building Atmanirbhar Bharat and overcoming Covid-19. Retrieved from https://bit.ly/3mueZSF, on April 8, 2021.

Gupta, M. and Chakraborty, P. (2019). State Finance Commissions: How successful have they been in Empowering Local Governments? *NIPFP Working Paper Series No. 263*, New Delhi: Institute of National Finance and Policy.

Guzman, M. (2003). Systems of management control and results-based budgeting: the Chilean experience. Santiago: Ministry of Finance, Government of Chile.

Ha, V., Olivier, B., and Masahiro, N. (2020). Boosting infrastructure in emerging Asia, in: G. Schwartz, M. Fouad, T. Hansen, G. Verdier (eds). *Well spent: How strong infrastructure governance can end waste in public investment*. Pp. 125–153, Washington D.C: International Monetary Fund. DOI: https://doi.org/10.5089/9781513511818.071

Hauge, A. (2003). The development of monitoring and evaluation capacities to improve government performance in Uganda. Document No. 38270, pp. 1–41. The World Bank.

Hemming, R., Kell, M., and Mahfouz, S. (2002). The effectiveness of fiscal policy in stimulating economic activity: A review of the literature. IMF Working Paper No. WP/02/208.

IGNOU (unknown). Unit 9: Classification of government expenditure. Retrieved from https://bit.ly/3fNOTZH on April 8, 2021.

ICRIER (2019). State of Municipal Finances in India A Study Prepared for the Fifteenth Finance Commission, New Delhi: Indian Council for Research on International Economic Relations.

IMF (1991). *Public expenditure hand book: A guide to public policy issues in developing countries*. Washington DC.

——— (2014). *Public expenditure reform: Making difficult choices, Fiscal monitor April*. Washington DC: International Monetary Fund.

——— (2015). *Expenditure rules: Effective tools for sound fiscal policy*. Washington DC: International Monetary Fund.

——— (2020a). *Policies to support people during the COVID-19 pandemic, Fiscal monitor*. Washington DC: International Monetary Fund.

——— (2020b). *Policy response to Covid-19*. Washington DC: International Monetary Fund. Retrieved from https://bit.ly/2Qwdwj5on September 18, 2020.

——— (2020c). *Well Spent: How strong infrastructure governance can end waste in public investment*, Washington DC: International Monetary Fund.

The Irish Times (2013). Full budget speech of Finance Minister for public expenditure and reform. Published on October 15, 2013. Retrieved fromhttps://bit.ly/3fXz Wo1, on April 08, 2021.

ITAD (1999). *Project cycle management training handbook*. West Sussex: Information Training and Agriculture Development Ltd. Retrieved from https://bit.ly/3sUm68y.

Jacobs, D. (2008). A review of capital budgeting processes. *IMF Working paper 08/160*.

Jacobs, D., Hélis, J.L., and Bouley, D. (2009). *Budget classification: Technical notes and manuals*. Washington DC: International Monetary Fund.

Jha, S., Mallick, S., Park, D., and Quising, P. (2010). *Effectiveness of countercyclical fiscal policy: Time-series evidence from developing Asia*. ADB Economics Working Paper Series211. Pp. 1–25, Manila: Asian Development Bank. Retrieved from https://www.adb.org/sites/default/files/publication/28268/economics-wp211.pdf, October 1st, 2021.

Joshi, V. and Little, I.M.D. (1994). *India: Macroeconomics and political economy: 1961–1991*. The World Bank.

Kalse, A. (2013). *Financial control: The comptroller and auditor general of India*. Mumbai: Maharashtra Legislature Secretariat, Government of Maharashtra. Retrieved from https://bit.ly/3sZj43D, on April 25, 2019.

Katsimi, M. and Sarantides, V. (2012). Do elections affect the composition of fiscal policy in developed, established democracies? *Public Choice*, 151(1), 325–362.

Khemani, S. (2000). *Political cycles in a developing economy: Effect of elections in the Indian states*. The World Bank Working Paper 2454.

Khundrakpam, J.K. (2003). *Public sector spending and economic growth in India, MPRA Paper 51105*. Germany: University Library of Munich.

Kohno, M. and Nishizawa, Y. (1990). A study of the electoral business cycle in Japan: Elections and government spending on public construction. Comparative Politics, 22(2), 151–166.

Kraan, D.J. (2007). Programme budgeting in OECD countries. *OECD Journal on Budgeting*, 7(4), 7–46.

Kumar, R. and Vashisht, P. (2009). *The global economic crisis: Impact on India and policy responses*. ADBI Working Paper 164. Tokyo: Asian Development Bank Institute.

Lahey, R. (2005). A comparative analysis of monitoring and evaluation in four selected countries: Canada, United States, Australia, and United Kingdom. Unpublished manuscript.

Lakshminarayanan, S. (2010). Audit reports—A few thoughts. Indian Journal of Public Audit and Accountability, 4(1& 2),34–39.

Lalvani, M. (2005). Coalition governments: Fiscal implication for the Indian economy. *American Review of Political Economy*, 3(1), 127–163.

Mackay, K. (2006). *Institutionalization of monitoring and evaluation systems to improve public sector management* (ECD Working paper series, No 15, No. 37828, pp. 1–26). The World Bank.

McKinsey (2010). India's urban awakening: Building inclusive cities, sustaining economic growth, Mckinsey global institute.

Mandira, K., Mann, G., and Tiwari, S. (2019). *Overseeing public funds: How to scrutinize budgets*. New Delhi: PRS Legislative Research. Retrieved from https://prsindia.org/budgets/primers/overseeing-public-funds-how-scrutinise-budgets on 30 September 2021.

Maps of India (n.d.). Expenditure reforms commission. Retrieved from https://bit.ly/3wCho2o, on April 08, 2021.

May, E., Shand, D., Mackay, K., Rojas, F., and Saavedra, J. (2006). Towards the institutionalization of monitoring and evaluation systems in Latin America and the Caribbean. In *Proceedings of a World Bank/Inter-American Development Bank Conference*. The World Bank.

Mohanty, P.K. (2016). Financing Cities in India: Municipal Reforms, Fiscal Accountability and Urban Infrastructure, Sage Publications, New Delhi.

Mohanty, B., Bhanumurthy, N.R., and Ghosh Dastidar, A. (2017). What explains regional imbalances in public infrastructure expenditure? Evidence from Indian states. *Asia-Pacific Development Journal*, 24(2), 113–139.

Moharkan, F. (2016). Is fiscal consolidation a distant mirage? Deccan Herald, April 18, 2016.

Mukherjee, S. (2019). *State of public finance and fiscal management in India during 2001–16*. Working paper no. 265. New Delhi: National Institute of Public Finance and Policy.

Mukhopadhyay, P.K. (2002). Parliamentary control over public purse in India. *Journal of Management and Training*, Vol.21 (April 2002–December) 2002, 1–10.

Mundle, S., Chowdhury, S., and Sikdar, S. (2016). *Governance performance of Indian states 2001–02 and 2011–12*. NIPFP Working Paper no 164. New Delhi: National Institute of Public Finance and Policy.

Mundle, S. and Rao, M.G. (1991). Volume and composition of government subsidies in India, 1987–88. *Economic and Political Weekly*, 26(18), 1157–1172.

——— (1992). Issues in fiscal policy, in: B. Jalan (ed). *The Indian economy: Problems and prospects*. New Delhi: Penguin Books India Pvt Ltd.

Musgrave, R.A. and Peacock, A.T. (1967). *Classics in the theory of public finance*. UK: Palgrave Macmillan.

Nayyar, D. (2017). *Vibrant democracy: Dormant parliament*. New Delhi: Livemint digital edition, July 14, 2017. Retrieved from https://bit.ly/3gCSBG0.

NCRWC (2001). *National commission to review the working of the constitution effectiveness of public audit system in India: Reforming the institution of the Comptroller and Auditor General (CAG)*. New Delhi: Ministry of Parliamentary Affairs.

OECD (2002). *Glossary of key terms in evaluation and results-based management*. Retrieved from https://www.oecd.org/dac/evaluation/2754804.pdf.

OMB (2004). *Budget of the United States Government, Fiscal Year 2004*, Budget Speech of President George W. Bush, Washington DC: Office of Management and Budget,

USA Government, pp. 47–54, Retrieved from (https://www.govinfo.gov/content/pkg/BUDGET-2004-BUD/pdf/BUDGET-2004-BUD.pdf), on 30 September 2021.

Padmanabhan, V. (2012). *Standing committee report summary current economic situation and policy options*. New Delhi: PRS Legislative Research. Retrieved from https://bit.ly/2ZzGtyN, on Sept. 29, 2021.

Panagariya, A. (2005). India in the 1980s and the 1990s: A triumph of reforms, in: W. Tseng, D. Cowen (eds). *India's and China's recent experience with reform and growth. Procyclicality of financial systems in Asia*. Pp. 170–200, London: Palgrave Macmillan. https://doi.org/10.1057/9780230505759_8

Pattnaik, R.K., Bose, D., Bhattacharyya, I., and Chander, J. (2005). Public expenditure and emerging fiscal policy scenario in India. Paper presented at Public Finance Workshop, Bancad'Italia. Retrieved fromhttps://bit.ly/3sNs7E3.

Payne, J.L. (1991). Elections and government spending. *Public Choice*, 70(1), 71–82.

Peacock, A.T. and Wiseman, J. (1961). *The growth of public expenditure in the United Kingdom*. London: National Bureau of Economic Research.

Pestieau, P. (2009). Assessing the performance of the public sector. *Annals of Public and Cooperative Economics*, 80(1), 133–161.

Peters, A.C. (2010). Election induced fiscal and monetary cycles: Evidence from the Caribbean. *The Journal of Developing Areas*, 44(1), 287–302.

PILdAT (2010). Budget and budgetary process in the parliament of India. Background paper, Lahore: Pakistan Institute of Legislative Development and Transparency. Retrieved from https://bit.ly/2QkJyif.

Planning Commission (1951). *Reforms of Public Administration (Chapter 6), First Five-Year Plan 1951–56*, New Delhi: Government of India, Retrieved from https://bit.ly/2WTGTir on 27th September 2019

Potrafke, N. (2011). Does government ideology influence budget composition? Empirical evidence from OECD countries. *Economics of Governance*, 12(2), 101–134.

Premchand, A. (1966). *Control of public expenditure in India: A historical and analytical account of the administrative, audit and parliamentary processes*. Bombay: Allied Publishers.

——— (1983). *Government budgeting and expenditure controls: Theory and practice*. International Monetary Fund.

PRS (2010). *How many reports has PAC tabled since 1952*? Retrived from, https://prsindia.org/theprsblog/how-many-reports-has-pac-tabled-since-1952, on 30 September 2021.

PTI (2018). Lok Sabha approves Rs 11,698 cr additional expenditure. Economic Times, August 07, 2018. Retrieved from https://bit.ly/3d3vt1f, on April 8, 2021.

Raizen, S.A. and Rossi, P.H. (1981). *Program evaluation in education: When? how? to what ends?* Washington, DC: National Academy Press.

Ram, R. (1986). Government size and economic growth: A new framework and some evidence from cross-section and time-series data. *The American Economic Review*, 76(1), 191–203.

Rao, M.G. (2015). Political economy of government finance in India. *India Review*, 14(1), 58–72.

——— (2017). *Central transfers to states in India: Rewarding performance while ensuring equity, A report submitted to NITI Aayog*. New Delhi: National Institute of Public Finance and Policy (NIPFP). Retrieved from https://bit.ly/31SScGz.

Rao, M.G. and Sen, T.K. (1993). *Government expenditure in India level, growth and composition*. New Delhi: National Institute of Public Finance and Policy (NIPFP).

Rao, M.G. and Rajagopalan, D. (1990). *Public expenditure control in India*. New Delhi: NIPFP. Retrieved from https://bit.ly/3njhuHW.

RBI (2004). *Handbook of statistics on state government finances 2004*. Mumbai: Reserve Bank of India.

——— (2005). Handbook of Statistics on Indian Economy 2003–04, Mumbai & Real-time Handbook of Statistics on Indian Economy, Retrieved from https://bit.ly/3DS7Gwn

——— (2006). State finances: A study of budgets 2006–07, Mumbai: Reserve Bank of India.

——— (2010). Handbook of Statistics on Indian Economy 2008–09, Mumbai & Real-time Handbook of Statistics on Indian Economy, Retrieved from https://bit.ly/3DS7Gwn

——— (2015). *Handbook of statistics on state government finances 2010*. Mumbai: Reserve Bank of India.

——— (2020). Handbook of Statistics on Indian Economy 2019–20, Mumbai & Real-time Handbook of Statistics on Indian Economy, Retrieved from https://bit.ly/3DS7Gwn

Rossi, P.H. and Freeman, H.E. (1982). *Evaluation: A systematic approach*. Beverly Hills, CA: Sage Publications.

Schacter, M. (2005). A framework for evaluating institutions of accountability, in: A. Shah (ed). *Fiscal management: Public sector governance and accountability series*. Washington DC: The World Bank. https://doi.org/10.1596/978-0-8213-6142-9.

Schedler, A. (1999). Restraining the state: Conflicts and the agents of accountability, in: A. Schedler, L.J. Diamond, M.F. Plattner (eds). *The self-restraining state: power and accountability in new democracies*, pp. 330–350. London: Lynne Rienner.

Schick, A. (2001). *Reflections on the New Zealand model*. Retrieved from https://bit.ly/3sZ71nb, on April 8, 2021.

Schuknecht, L. (2000). Fiscal policy cycles and public expenditure in developing countries. *Public Choice*, 102(1/2), 115–130.

Scott, G., Ball, I., and Dale, T. (1997). New Zealand's public sector management reform: Implications for the United States. *Journal of Policy Analysis and Management*,16, 357–381.

Sen, K., and Vaidya, R.R. (1996). Political budget cycles in India. *Economic and Political Weekly*, 31(30), 2023–2027.

Sharma, R. (2019). *Democracy on the road: A 25-year-oldjourney through India*. New Delhi: Penguin Random House.

Shi, M. and Svensson, J. (2006). Political budget cycles: Do they differ across countries and why? *Journal of Public Economics*, 90(8–9), 1367–1389.

Shome, P. (1998). A Critical assessment of the public finances and a future agenda for reform, in: A.V. Desai (ed). *Economic Reforms: The Next Step*, Symposium Papers. New Delhi: Frank Bros and Co.

Shome, P., Sen, T.K., and Gopalakrishnan, S. (1996). Public expenditure policy and management in India: A consideration of the issues. Paper presented at Department of Expenditure, New Delhi: Ministry of Finance, Government of India.

Singh, C., Prasad, P.R., and Sharma, K.K. (2017). Should revenue and capital budgets be shown separately in the union budget? IIM Bangalore Research Paper, p.536.

Singh, N.K. (2009). *Not by reason alone: The politics of change.* New Delhi: Penguin Books India.

Srivastava, D.K., Rao, C.B., Chakraborty, P., and Rangamannar, T.S. (2003). *Budgetary subsidies in India: Subsidising social and economic services.* New Delhi: National Institute of Public Finance and Policy.

Srivastava, D.K., Sen, T.K., and Mukhopadhyay, H. (1997). *Government subsidies in India.* New Delhi: National Institute of Public Finance and Policy.

Srivastava, R.K. (2020). IMF backs India's 'very wise' COVID-19 lockdown move despite huge economic cost. Retrieved from https://bit.ly/39TcUKT, on April 8, 2021.

Tanzi, V. and Shome, P. (1993). A primer on tax evasion. *Staff Papers*, 40(4), 807–828.

Tanzi, V. and Zee, H.H. (1997). Fiscal policy and long-run growth. *Staff Papers*, 44(2), 179–209.

Tiwari, S. and Surya, S. (2019). *State of State finances.* New Delhi: PRS Legislative Research. Retrieved from https://bit.ly/39NiAGr, on April 8, 2021.

The Times of India (2020). Impact of Covid-19 significant on India's development, immediate priority is coordinated policy response: IMF. Retrieved from https://bit.ly/3fXHc3f, on April 8, 2021.

Toye, J. (1981). Public expenditure reforms in India and Malaysia. *Development and Change*, 12(1), 121–144. *https://doi.org/10.1111/j.1467-7660.1981.tb00091.x.*

Verma, S. and Arora, R. (2010). Does the Indian economy support Wagner s Law? An econometric analysis. *Eurasian Journal of Business and Economics*, 3(5), 77–91.

WHO (2003). How much should the countries spend on the health? Discussion paper No. 2, EIP/FER/DP.03.2, Geneva: World Health Organisation.

——— (2017). Controlling the spread of infectious diseases (chapter 10), in: *Advancing the right to health: The vital role of law*, pp. 151–164, Geneva: World Health Organisation. Retrieved from https://bit.ly/3nhrbqo.

World Bank (1997). *The state in a changing world.* Washington DC: The World Bank.

——— (1998). *Public expenditure management handbook.* Washington DC: The World Bank.

——— (2004). *Monitoring and evaluation: Some tools, methods and approaches.* Washington DC: The World Bank.

——— (2005). *Chile: Study of evaluation program—Impact evaluation and evaluations of government programs.* Washington, D.C.: The World Bank.

——— (2006). *Ukraine—Creating fiscal space for growth: A public finance review.* Report No. 36671-UA, p. 84, Washington DC: Poverty Reduction and Economic Management Unit, World Bank.

Zaltsman, A. (2006). *Experience with institutionalizing monitoring and evaluation systems in five Latin American countries: Argentina, Chile, Colombia, Costa Rica and Uruguay.* Independent Evaluation Group ECD working paper no. 16. Washington, D.C.: Independent Evaluation Group, The World Bank.

Index